Congratulations
on your new home Bob!
Here are a few ideas you
can spice up in your gourmet
Kitchen. Best wishes !!.

Laurie

# COMPLETE
# SEASONAL
## COOKBOOK

WILLIAMS-SONOMA

# COMPLETE
# SEASONAL
# COOKBOOK

GENERAL EDITOR

Chuck Williams

RECIPES

Joanne Weir

PHOTOGRAPHY

Penina

 Oxmoor HOUSE®

First published in the USA, 1997, by Time-Life Custom Publishing.

Originally published in 4 volumes titled *Spring, Summer, Autumn* and *Winter* (all copyright © 1997 Weldon Owen Inc.).

**OXMOOR HOUSE INC.**

Oxmoor House books are distributed by Sunset Books
80 Willow Road, Menlo Park, CA 94025
Phone: 650·321·3600  Fax: 650·324·1532

Vice-President/General Manager: Rich Smeby
Director of Special Sales: Gary Wright

Oxmoor House and Sunset Books are divisions of
Southern Progress Corporation

In collaboration with Williams-Sonoma Inc.
3250 Van Ness Avenue, San Francisco, CA 94109

**WILLIAMS–SONOMA**

Founder & Vice-Chairman: Chuck Williams
Book Buyer: Cecilia Michaelis

**PRODUCED BY WELDON OWEN INC.**

Chief Executive Officer: John Owen
President: Terry Newell
Chief Operating Officer: Larry Partington
Creative Director: Gaye Allen
Vice President, International Sales: Stuart Laurence
Sales Manager: Emily Jahn
Managing Editor: Lisa Atwood
Copy Editor: Sharon Silva
Consulting Editors: Norman Kolpas, Sarah Putman
Original Design: John Bull, The Book Design Company
Art Direction: Kari Ontko, India Ink
Production: Stephanie Sherman, Christine DePedro,
    Linda M. Bouchard, Kathryn Meehan, Chris Hemesath
Proofreader: Sharilyn Hovind
Indexer: Ken DellaPenta
Food Photographer: Penina
Food and Prop Stylist: Pouké
Illustrations: Thorina Rose
Location Prop Stylist: Leigh Noë
Front Cover Photographer: Daniel Clark
Front Cover Food Stylist: George Dolese
Front Cover Prop Stylist: Amy Denebeim

The Williams-Sonoma Complete Cookbook Series
conceived and produced by Weldon Owen Inc.
814 Montgomery Street, San Francisco, CA  94133

First printed in 1999
10 9 8 7 6 5 4 3

Library of Congress Cataloging-in-Publication Data is available.
ISBN 0-8487-2593-X

Separations by Colourscan Overseas Co. Pte. Ltd.
Printed in China by Leefung-Asco Printers Ltd.

**A Note on Weights and Measures**

*All recipes include customary U.S., U.K. and metric measurements.*
*Conversions are based on a standard developed for these books and*
*have been rounded off. Actual weights may vary.*

# CONTENTS

# Autumn

# Winter

# INTRODUCTION

In recent years, no trend has captured the imagination of home cooks more powerfully than cooking with the seasons. And with good reason. Seasonal ingredients are every cook's wisest choice.

❧ Bought at their natural peak, in-season vegetables and fruits have the finest taste and texture. As a result, they require only simple cooking to bring them to the table at their best, an advantage for health-conscious and busy cooks alike. Seasonal ingredients are also often the most economical choices in the market, as they appear in greater abundance than imported or greenhouse products. And the profusion of farmers' markets in both big cities and small towns, as well as the widespread improvement of produce departments in food stores everywhere, makes a greater variety of fresh vegetables and fruits available to home cooks than ever before. Not surprisingly, home gardeners are also being inspired to grow and cook their own seasonal favorites. The *Complete Seasons Cookbook* celebrates these trends with a selection of over 200 recipes inspired by seasonal produce and other seasonal items such as seafood, poultry and dried legumes. On these introductory pages, you'll find comprehensive overviews of how to select the best each season has to offer. The recipes follow, divided into chapters by season and, within each chapter, by courses. Concluding the book are full-color visual glossaries of seasonal ingredients.

❧ All these elements share a common goal: To inspire you to cook your everyday meals with the seasons.

## SPRING

Spring arrives in a wash of green. Leafy vegetables, tender shoots and slender stalks fill farmers' market stalls, grocer's aisles and garden plots. Shiny snap peas rest in mounds alongside prickly artichoke buds and pale green fennel bulbs.

❧ Bright orange citrus fruits, deep red strawberries and yellow-gold papayas and mangoes are piled alongside.

### Selecting Spring Ingredients

SPRING VEGETABLES.    Greens flourish in springtime's cool, damp earth and gentle sunlight. As a result, a wide range of greens, in ever-growing diversity, is available throughout the season. Choose lettuces and cabbages that appear crisp and bright, with no signs of wilting or browning. Those that form heads should be densely packed and feel heavy. Kale, a holdover into early spring from late autumn and winter, and Swiss chard, which first appears in late spring and lasts into early autumn, should have smooth, unblemished stalks and crisp leaves.

❧ Also at their best when harvested young are bitter greens and chicories such as sorrel, available midspring through summer; frisée; dandelion greens; arugula (rocket); and Belgian endive (chicory/witloof), the latter a holdover from autumn and winter. Look for slender, tightly closed, nearly white endive; small sorrel and arugula leaves; and dandelion leaves no longer

than a pencil. Broccoli rabe, a newly appreciated green that is a close botanical kin of the turnip, should have fleshy stalks, compact florets and only a few flowers.

❧ Bins of freshly cut tender shoots and stalks are another icon of spring. Asparagus, which first appears in late winter and lasts into summer's early weeks, is at its absolute peak now. Look for straight, sturdy stalks evenly colored from furled tip to cut end. Artichokes, which enjoy a second, smaller harvest in autumn, are at their best in early spring. The prickly leaves of these edible buds should look fresh and snugly compact. The cut bases of both asparagus and artichokes should always appear smooth and unwithered.

❧ Of the edible pea pods, sold year-round but at their crispest and sweetest now, seek out bright green snow peas (mangetouts) and sugar snap peas that feel firm. Fava (broad) beans and English peas, which also fill springtime produce stands, should be plump and flexible but not soft.

❧ Immature bulbs, such as green onions and baby leeks, are sweetest and tenderest during spring's mild days. The best of these have pure white, moist-looking heads and crisp green leaves. When selecting dried onions, seek out those with dry, papery skins and no signs of sprouting. The best sweet varieties, such as Vidalias, Mauis and Walla Wallas, are all at their peak now.

❧ Springtime's roots and tubers also stay sweet and mellow in the season's gentle sunshine. Look for radishes, harvested into the summer months, that are smooth and bright. Seek out new potatoes, a seasonal specialty, with thin, fragile skins, and beets, crowned with fresh-looking green tops,

Immature heads of spring's green garlic are prized for their sweet, mild flavor.

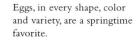

Lettuce grows well in this season's mild weather and damp soil.

Eggs, in every shape, color and variety, are a springtime favorite.

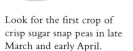

Look for the first crop of crisp sugar snap peas in late March and early April.

the latter reaching markets in late winter and lasting into early autumn.

❧ The finest seasonal mushrooms—button, oyster, morel, shiitake—should be firm, plump, well formed and neither moist nor dried out. Smell them: they should offer a clean, fresh aroma.

SPRING FRUITS.   Only a limited variety of fresh fruits are available now. Look primarily for citruses, which bridge winter and spring, and for tropicals shipped in from sunnier climes.

❧ Select citrus fruits that have shiny skins and feel heavy for their size, a sign of juiciness. Blood oranges and Valencias are especially good in spring. Tropical fruits—pineapples, mangoes, papayas—give off a strong, sweet perfume when ripe. You can test a pineapple's readiness by gently tugging at a central leaf, which should pull free easily. Ripe mangoes and papayas, both at peak of season, will yield to gentle thumb pressure; and passion fruits, reliable holdovers from winter, will be ready to eat when deeply wrinkled, maybe even with a trace of mold on their purplish brown skins. Like green bananas, which are at their peak in winter and spring, they ripen when stored at room temperature.

❧ Strawberries and fraises des bois are the only two berries available now; the former are at their peak, although they can be found in most locales from winter into midsummer. Seek out deeply and evenly colored, plump fruits with leafy stems. Fraises des bois, small intensely flavored wild strawberries, are a particular treat and should be scooped up whenever they are seen in the market

When the husks and silks are pulled back from fresh corn cobs, the kernels beneath should appear smooth and plump.

## SUMMER

In summertime, nature bestows a bounty of diverse and flavorful ingredients. The season's colorful wealth shows in bell peppers (capsicums) shading from green to yellow to crimson, vine-ripened tomatoes of various hues, slender green and purple beans and sunny yellow squashes. Bushel baskets overflow with tree fruits and jewellike berries beckon. Tough melon rinds conceal promises of sweet refreshment. Everywhere, fresh herbs scent the air.

### Selecting Summer Ingredients

SUMMER VEGETABLES.   Many of the year's most flavorful vegetables ripen in summer, the most characteristic being vegetable fruits and soft-skinned summer squashes. When choosing vegetable fruits such as bell peppers, chilies, tomatoes, cucumbers or eggplants (aubergines), look for those that feel firm and have bright, glossy skins. The same applies to the many varieties of summer squash, of which smaller specimens have the best flavor and texture. Perfectly ripe avocados yield to gentle finger pressure, although still-hard ones ripen easily at room temperature. The outstanding Hass variety is at its best in these warm months.

❧ Look for crisp, bright heads of red-leaf lettuce and frisée in the early days of the season. Various snap beans should also be crisp, cleanly breaking in half when bent. The best fresh shell beans fill barely plump, flexible, firm pods.

❧ Garlic, shallots and most other onion varieties are in peak season now and will last

Bell peppers, like tomatoes, range in color from deep green to yellow to orange to crimson red.

Summer squashes are characterized by their thin, edible skins and seeds.

well into spring. Look for firm, dry-skinned, blemish-free specimens. Ginger, also at its best now, should be firm and free of moisture or wrinkles. Potatoes, as the peak autumn harvest swiftly approaches, should feel heavy, look firm and be free of sprouting eyes.

SUMMER FRUITS.   The best summer fruits brim with juice. Melons, now in their prime, although available from spring into autumn, should feel heavy for their size. Ripe specimens of smaller varieties yield slightly to thumb pressure and reveal a hint of sweet, musky aroma. When choosing watermelons, seek out firm, evenly colored, well-shaped specimens with blemish-free, waxy rinds.

❧ Berries of all kinds are at their height now, although strawberries begin to wane as summer progresses. Bright, deep, clear colors and sweet aromas will tip you off to the tastiest of the lot. Be careful when buying juicy-ripe berries packed in containers. Check the bottoms for signs of leakage, an indication that crushed or moldy specimens might be buried within.

❧ Tree fruits abound the summer long, but be on the lookout for fleeting cherries, harvested only from midspring to midsummer. All tree fruits should feel heavy for their size, and ripe ones will yield slightly to finger pressure. Most specimens bought firm will ripen at room temperature. Good plums often show a harmless white bloom on their shiny skins. Mature peaches, nectarines, apricots and figs give off sweet perfumes hinting at their flavor. And in late summer when figs are at their peak, don't turn away from those with cracked skins, as they are often the sweetest.

Ripe summer peaches should feel tender to the touch and smell sweet.

SUMMER SEASONINGS. The scent of fresh-picked herbs is summer's kitchen perfume. Nearly every variety, especially the hardier ones, are at their best now. Choose herbs with bright leaves free of wilting, blemishes or discoloration.

❧ A wide range of edible flowers, with roses, pansies and lavender among the most popular, also flourish in summertime. Use caution when selecting them. Those from florists have usually been chemically treated and are potentially harmful. For safety's sake, buy flowers only from a specialty grower that can attest to growing conditions free of pesticides or other harmful additives. Better still, grow them yourself.

## AUTUMN

At this time of year, garden plots and market stalls overflow with a harvest that was first coaxed to life by the summer sun. Hard-shelled squashes delight with their harlequin array of shapes, sizes and colors. Boughs hang heavy with apples and pears. Beneath fallen leaves, wild mushrooms push upward. The cool, sheltering ground transforms the starch of roots, tubers and onions to a sublime sweetness. Brussels sprouts and cabbages are ready to be cut from sturdy stalks.

### Selecting Autumn Ingredients

AUTUMN VEGETABLES. Autumn brings a wonderfully diverse harvest whose very variety calls for discerning senses. When selecting hard-shelled winter squashes (inaccurately named, since they first come to

market in early autumn), opt for those that feel heavy and have good overall color; reject any with cracks or soft spots. Tiny brown dots on pumpkins indicate sweetness. Mushrooms, among which cepes and chanterelles are particular autumn specialties, should look firm and plump, feel slightly spongy and neither dry nor overly moist, and smell fresh, clean and earthy.

❧ When choosing parsnips and rutabagas (swedes), both especially sweet now, opt for smaller ones, which have a finer texture and flavor. Select those that feel firm and heavy and are blemish free. The same is true for potatoes and sweet potatoes. With potatoes, also remember to pass over those with any green patches.

❧ Members of the chicory family in season now, specifically escarole (Batavian endive), Belgian endive and frisée, will have the best flavor and texture if harvested young. In addition, their lighter-colored, more central leaves will be milder and more tender. Cabbages should be heavy for their size and look crisp and fresh, and the red variety should show no hint of black along the edges of its leaves. The same general rules apply to Brussels sprouts. The heads of broccoli, at seasonal peak from early to midautumn, and cauliflower, at its best throughout the cool months, should be compact and their stalks uniformly firm.

❧ Leeks and bulb fennel, both of which appear abundantly at the season's start and continue through winter into spring, should have crisp, white bulb ends and healthy green leaves.

❧ Although vegetable fruits primarily belong to summer, some flourish into autumn. The best eggplants and red bell peppers are firm, bright, glossy and blemish free. Most garden herbs also grow into autumn, although more delicate varieties, such as basil and cilantro (fresh coriander), begin to wane as cold weather approaches.

AUTUMN FRUITS. Hardier fruits do best as autumn progresses from warmer to colder weather. Pears, for which the harvest begins in mid- to late summer and continues into spring, are generally picked and sold still unripe and very firm, to be ripened at room temperature until they give to gentle pressure. Look for apples, which peak from late summer to late autumn, that are firm and free of bruises. The same attributes also indicate good quinces, which first show up in summer, but are better suited to autumn's heartier dishes. Figs, whose harvest also extends into autumn, will have slightly cracked skins at their sweet, juicy best, but must be eaten soon after purchase. Size and colorful skins are good signs for juicy pomegranates, most plentiful now. Smooth skins, bright color and intact green caps indicate good persimmons, another signature autumn fruit. Grapes of all varieties, bountiful through most of autumn, should appear shiny and plump.

Winter squashes have hard protective shells that make them ideal for storing into the coming season.

Ripe persimmons still hang on the tree long after the leaves have fallen.

Like most autumn fruit, underripe pears reach maturity in a few days at room temperature.

Autumn's abundant and varied nut crops lend rich flavor and texture to seasonal dishes.

## WINTER

Although a season of cold and barren landscapes, winter nonetheless produces a generous harvest. Robust greens such as kale, escarole (Batavian endive) and other bitter chicories thrive in the waning sunlight. In the cold ground, roots and tubers grow plump and sweet. Citrus crops from milder climes bring bright color and zesty flavor to even the grayest days.

### Selecting Winter Ingredients

WINTER VEGETABLES.    The best winter vegetables generally fall into two categories: those that thrive in adverse climates and the good keepers that have been stored in the autumn pantry. When selecting hard-shelled squashes, particularly abundant now, choose heavy ones with good color, avoiding any with signs of cracking or decay.

Many of the more robust greens continue to thrive in the cold months. As you would when buying them in other seasons, choose watercress, frisée, kale, escarole and Belgian endive with an eye for younger, more tender specimens. Brussels sprouts, whose harvest began in late summer and continues into midwinter, should have solid, compact heads that look crisp and fresh. Many bulbs and most roots and tubers—fennel, leeks, parsnips, Jerusalem artichokes, potatoes, sweet potatoes, yams—are available throughout the colder months. Apply the same criteria in selecting them that was outlined for buying these earth-sheltered vegetables in autumn. Do the same for mushrooms.

Dried beans, a winter pantry staple, may be bought in bulk and stored for months at room temperature in airtight containers. Those that have not been kept for too long cook more quickly and have a finer texture and flavor. Purchase them from a shop with a high turnover, choosing bean varieties with bright, shiny skins free of wrinkles or other signs of improper handling.

WINTER FRUITS.    Many of winter's fruits—apples, pears, quinces—are hardy crops that endure cold storage after their autumn harvest. Still other autumn fruits, particularly pomegranates and persimmons, have harvests that last into winter's early days. Winter's citrus crops, by contrast, are a harbinger of spring, with nearly all varieties available now and most grapefruits, tangerines and sweet navel oranges at their absolute best. Citrus fruits should feel heavy for their size, indicating juiciness.

Kiwifruits from California are finest from early autumn right through winter and into early spring, when the New Zealand harvest takes over. Hard ones will ripen at room temperature and, when ripe, will give slightly to fingertip pressure. Autumn's cranberries will last well into the winter months. They should feel firm and have shiny, bright skins.

Even winter's dried fruits have varying degrees of freshness. Look for specimens that are plump and have good color, signs that they were recently dried and are moister and more flavorful.

Crisp, green turnip tops are delicious cooked like kale as a robust winter green.

The tangelo, also called Minneola, is a hybrid of the tangerine and the pomelo or grapefruit.

Brussels sprouts thrive in mild climates throughout the damp winter season.

The pale inner leaves from a head of escarole are less bitter and more tender than the outer ones.

# Spring

# $\mathcal{S}$pring Openers

First courses for springtime meals often feature tender young produce, most notably the asparagus and artichokes that fill the season's bushel baskets with their bold shapes and vivid greens. Simple simmering or steaming and a touch of imaginative seasonings suffice to ready these heralds of spring for use in such starters as Artichoke and Lemon Fritters (at right), Warm Asparagus with Eggs Mimosa (page 17) or Risotto with Artichokes (page 22). The results taste as fresh as the first clear day of the season.

Not all spring openers need to dwell on the delicacy of the ingredients available now, however. Green Onion, Thyme and Goat Cheese Tart (page 21), which combines immature garlic and onions with a rich and tangy filling, illustrates the presence of the season's more robust tastes. So, too, does Sweet Vidalia Onion Rings (page 25), a wonderful dish that turns this rare harvest of late spring into a hearty appetizer.

## ARTICHOKE AND LEMON FRITTERS

SERVES 6

*If you can find Meyer lemons, use them in this recipe; they add a more complex, delicate perfume and less acidity than the more common Lisbon and Eureka varieties.*

1 cup (5 oz/155 g) plus 2 tablespoons
    all-purpose (plain) flour
½ teaspoon salt, plus salt as needed
1½ teaspoons grated lemon zest
2 eggs, separated
3 tablespoons olive oil
juice of 1 lemon
¾ cup (6 fl oz/180 ml) beer, at room
    temperature
6 large artichokes
¼ cup (2 fl oz/60 ml) water
freshly ground pepper
corn oil or peanut oil for deep-frying
lemon wedges
fresh flat-leaf (Italian) parsley leaves

Sift together the flour, the ½ teaspoon salt and the lemon zest into a bowl. Make a well in the center. Add the egg yolks to the well, beat until blended and then add 2 tablespoons of the olive oil, 1 tablespoon of the lemon juice and the beer. Using a whisk, mix well. Let rest for 1 hour at room temperature.

❧ Meanwhile, have ready a large bowl of water to which you have added the remaining lemon juice. Cut off the top half of each artichoke and remove the tough outer leaves down to the pale green leaves. Cut off the base of the stem and peel away its dark outer layer. Cut the artichokes in half lengthwise. Scoop out the prickly chokes, then cut lengthwise into thin slices. As each is cut, drop into the lemon water.

❧ In a frying pan over medium heat, warm the remaining 1 tablespoon olive oil. Drain the artichokes and add them to the pan along with the ¼ cup (2 fl oz/60 ml) water and a large pinch each of salt and pepper. Cover and cook over medium heat until the liquid evaporates, about 15 minutes. Remove from the heat and let cool.

❧ In a deep, heavy sauté pan, pour in corn or peanut oil to a depth of 2 inches (5 cm) and heat to 375°F (190°C) on a deep-frying thermometer. Meanwhile, in a bowl, using an electric mixer on high speed, beat the egg whites until stiff peaks form. Using a rubber spatula, fold the egg whites and artichokes into the batter.

❧ Working in batches, drop the batter by heaping tablespoonfuls into the hot oil. Fry, turning often, until golden brown, about 2 minutes. Using a slotted spoon, transfer to a paper towel-lined plate and keep warm until all are cooked.

❧ Arrange on a warmed platter with lemon wedges and parsley.

## WARM ASPARAGUS WITH EGGS MIMOSA

SERVES 6

*This signature spring dish works equally well as a simple first course or as a side dish. Pencil-thin asparagus can be used in place of larger spears, in which case you can omit their peeling. Braised baby leeks can also replace the asparagus. Serve with slices of toasted country-style bread brushed with olive oil and garnish each serving with a few Niçoise olives, if you like.*

2 eggs
1 tablespoon Champagne vinegar
1 shallot, minced
3 tablespoons extra-virgin olive oil
salt and freshly ground pepper
2¼ lb (1.1 kg) large asparagus spears

Have ready a bowl of ice water. Bring a small saucepan three-fourths full of water to a boil. Reduce the heat to medium and add the eggs, being careful not to crack them. Simmer for 10 minutes until hard-cooked. Using a slotted spoon, transfer the eggs to the ice water and let cool for 30 minutes.

❧ In a small bowl, whisk together the vinegar, shallot, olive oil and salt and pepper to taste. Set the vinaigrette aside.

❧ Remove the eggs from the water and peel them. Press them through a coarse-mesh sieve into a bowl. Set aside.

❧ Cut or snap off the tough stem ends from the asparagus spears and discard. Using a vegetable peeler, peel the bottom 3 inches (7.5 cm) of each asparagus spear to remove the tough outer skin. Bring a large sauté pan filled with salted water to a boil. Add the asparagus, reduce the heat to medium and cook just until tender, 4–6 minutes.

❧ Using tongs, transfer the asparagus to a double thickness of paper towels

to drain briefly, then arrange the spears on a warmed platter or individual plates. Drizzle the vinaigrette over the warm asparagus, distributing it evenly. Sprinkle the eggs over the center of the asparagus spears and serve immediately.

## SPICY DEVILED EGGS

SERVES 6

*Eggs are a wonderfully versatile and inexpensive ingredient. Employed in moderation, they are also nutritious, being excellent sources of protein. Chicken, goose, duck and quail eggs, as well as the pastel-colored Araucana chicken eggs, can bring rich flavor and a fanciful presentation to the Easter brunch table.*

6 eggs
¼ red bell pepper, seeded and deribbed
2 tablespoons mayonnaise
2 tablespoons plain nonfat yogurt
2 teaspoons Dijon mustard
1 clove garlic, minced
1 teaspoon fresh lemon juice
¼ teaspoon cayenne pepper
¼ teaspoon sweet paprika
2 green (spring) onions, minced
very small pinch of saffron threads
2 teaspoons boiling water
salt and freshly ground pepper
fresh chives, finely snipped or cut into
    1-inch (2.5-cm) lengths

Have ready a bowl of ice water. Fill a large saucepan three-fourths full with water and bring to a boil over high heat. Reduce the heat to medium, add the eggs, being careful not to crack them, and simmer for 10 minutes until hard-cooked. Using a slotted spoon, transfer the eggs to the ice water and let cool for 30 minutes.

❧ Meanwhile, preheat a broiler (griller). Place the pepper, cut side down, on a baking sheet. Place in the broiler about 4 inches (10 cm) from the heat source and broil (grill) until charred and blistered. Remove from the broiler, cover loosely with aluminum foil and let cool for 10 minutes, then peel and finely dice.

❧ In a bowl, combine the mayonnaise, yogurt, mustard, garlic, lemon juice, cayenne, paprika, green onions and diced bell pepper. Stir to mix well. Place the saffron in a small bowl and pour the boiling water over it to moisten fully. Let stand for 1 minute, then add the saffron mixture to the mayonnaise mixture, mixing well. Season to taste with salt and pepper.

❧ Remove the eggs from the water and peel them. Cut each egg in half lengthwise. Carefully scoop out the yolks into a bowl; reserve the whites. Using a fork, mash the yolks until smooth. Add the yolks to the mayonnaise mixture and stir to mix well.

❧ Spoon the mayonnaise-yolk mixture into the hollows of the egg white halves, dividing it evenly. Garnish with the chives and serve at once.

## SALMON GRAVLAX WITH PICKLED RED ONIONS AND MUSTARD CREAM

SERVES 6

*Scandinavians preserve salmon, caught during their spring migration, in a method that predates refrigeration. In the centuries-old method, the fish is coated with a cure of salt, sugar and dill to make gravlax, from gravad lax—"buried salmon."*

FOR THE SALMON:

1¼ lb (625 g) center-cut salmon fillet
    with skin intact
½ cup (¾ oz/20 g) chopped fresh dill
½ cup (¾ oz/20 g) chopped fresh chives
2 tablespoons kosher salt
1½ tablespoons sugar
2 teaspoons crushed peppercorns

FOR THE GARNISHES:

2 cups (1 lb/500 g) plain yogurt
1 red (Spanish) onion, thinly sliced
salt
½ cup (4 fl oz/125 ml) red wine
    vinegar
2 tablespoons Dijon mustard
2 tablespoons fresh lemon juice
freshly ground pepper
2 tablespoons drained capers
lemon wedges
fresh dill sprigs, optional

To prepare the salmon, run your fingers along the fillet to check for errant bones and remove any you find. Cut the fillet into 2 equal pieces. Place 1 piece, skin side down, in a glass dish. In a small bowl, stir together the dill, chives, salt, sugar and peppercorns. Spread the mixture on top of the fish. Top with the second piece of fish, skin side up. Cover first with plastic wrap and then with aluminum foil. Weight the fish with a flat 5-lb (2.5-kg) weight such as a brick. Refrigerate for 48–72 hours, turning the entire salmon and herb stack and basting every 24 hours with the juices that have accumulated in the dish.

❧ Prepare the garnishes 1 day before serving: Line a fine-mesh sieve with cheesecloth (muslin) and place over a bowl. Spoon the yogurt into the sieve and cover with plastic wrap. Place in the refrigerator and let drain for 24 hours.

❧ Place the onion slices in a bowl and sprinkle liberally with salt. In a small saucepan, bring the vinegar almost to a boil, pour over the onion slices and let cool. Transfer to a sieve and rinse under running water. Drain well and pat dry with paper towels. Use immediately, or cover and refrigerate for up to 1 day.

❧ Just before serving, in a small bowl, combine the drained yogurt, the mustard and lemon juice and stir to mix well. Season to taste with salt and pepper.

❧ To serve, turn the salmon flesh side up and scrape off the herb mixture. Thinly slice on the diagonal and arrange on a platter. Garnish with the onions, capers, lemon wedges and dill sprigs, if using. Pass the mustard sauce at the table.

*For lo, the winter is past,
the rain is over and gone;
The flowers appear on the earth,
the time of singing has come
— Song of Solomon*

# FETTUCCINE WITH CILANTRO, MINT AND CASHEW PESTO

SERVES 6

*A refreshing seasonal variation on the traditional basil–pine nut pesto, this sauce is also good with other fresh or dried pasta ribbons or strands. Mint is among the first herbs to push up in early spring. Fresh cilantro, also known as fresh coriander or Chinese parsley, is abundant year-round, ready to add its own pungent flavor to a wide variety of savory dishes.*

⅓ cup (2 oz/60 g) cashews
1 small fresh jalapeño chili pepper, seeded and minced
2 cloves garlic, minced
1 tablespoon peeled and grated fresh ginger
½ teaspoon ground coriander
⅓ cup (3 fl oz/80 ml) peanut oil
3 tablespoons olive oil
2 cups (2 oz/60 g) lightly packed fresh cilantro (fresh coriander) leaves
⅓ cup (⅓ oz/10 g) lightly packed fresh mint leaves
⅓ cup (⅓ oz/10 g) lightly packed fresh flat-leaf (Italian) parsley leaves
⅓ cup (⅓ oz/10 g) lightly packed fresh basil leaves
1½ tablespoons fresh lime juice
salt and freshly ground pepper
1 lb (500 g) dried semolina fettuccine
fresh herb sprigs

Preheat an oven to 350°F (180°C). Spread the cashews on a baking sheet and place in the oven until toasted and fragrant, 5–7 minutes. Remove from the oven and let cool.

❧ Bring a large pot three-fourths full of salted water to a rolling boil.

❧ Meanwhile, place the cashews in a food processor fitted with the metal blade and process until they form a rough paste. Add the jalapeño, garlic, ginger and coriander and pulse several times until the mixture is again a rough paste. Combine the peanut and olive oils in a small bowl. Add the cilantro, mint, parsley and basil leaves and half of the mixed oils to the food processor and process to make a rough paste once again. Add the lime juice and the remaining oil mixture and process until smooth. Season to taste with salt and pepper and set aside at room temperature.

❧ Add the pasta to the pot of boiling water, stir well and cook until al dente (tender but firm to the bite), 10–12 minutes or according to the package directions. Drain and transfer to a warmed platter. Pour the sauce over the pasta and toss well. Garnish with herb sprigs and serve immediately.

# GREEN ONION, THYME AND GOAT CHEESE TART

SERVES 6–8

*You can make this tart with sautéed leeks in place of the green onions: Use the white portions and about 1 inch (2.5 cm) of the green parts of 6 leeks. Cut into ½-inch (12-mm) dice and place in a saucepan. Add 2 cups (16 fl oz/500 ml) water and cook over medium heat until very soft, about 20 minutes.*

1 prebaked 9-inch (23-cm) short-crust tart shell (recipe on page 62)

### FOR THE FILLING:
1 tablespoon unsalted butter
24 green (spring) onions, cut into ½-inch (12-mm) lengths
2 heads green garlic or 2 cloves regular garlic, coarsely chopped (optional)
¼ cup (2 fl oz/60 ml) chicken stock or water
¼ lb (125 g) fresh goat cheese
½ cup (4 fl oz/125 ml) sour cream
2 eggs
½ teaspoon chopped fresh thyme, plus thyme sprigs for garnish
salt and freshly ground pepper

Prepare the tart shell, omitting the sugar, and bake until lightly golden as directed.

❧ While the tart shell is baking, make the filling: In a large frying pan over medium-high heat, melt the butter. Add the green onions, garlic (if using) and the stock or water and stir well. Reduce the heat to low, cover and simmer until the green onions are soft, about 15 minutes.

❧ Remove the pastry shell from the oven and set aside. Position the rack in the upper part of the oven. Leave the oven set at 375°F (190°C).

❧ In a bowl, mash together the goat cheese and sour cream with a fork until soft and well mixed. Add the eggs and chopped thyme and mix well.

❧ Uncover the green onions and raise the heat to high. Cook until the liquid has evaporated, about 3 minutes. Stir the green onions into the cheese mixture, then season to taste with salt and pepper. Pour the cheese mixture into the prebaked pastry shell.

❧ Bake on the top rack of the oven until a skewer inserted into the center of the tart comes out clean, 25–35 minutes. Remove from the oven and garnish with thyme sprigs. Cut into wedges and serve warm or at room temperature.

## RISOTTO WITH ARTICHOKES

SERVES 6

¼ cup (1¼ oz/37 g) hazelnuts (filberts)
3 tablespoons fresh lemon juice
4 large or 20 baby artichokes
2 tablespoons extra-virgin olive oil
1 very small yellow onion, diced
2 cloves garlic, minced
2½ cups (20 fl oz/625 ml) water
salt and freshly ground pepper
3 cups (24 fl oz/750 ml) chicken stock
1½ cups (10½ oz/330 g) Italian
    Arborio rice
½ cup (2 oz/60 g) freshly grated
    Parmesan cheese
2 tablespoons chopped fresh flat-leaf
    (Italian) parsley
lemon wedges

Preheat an oven to 350°F (180°C). Spread the hazelnuts on a baking sheet and toast until fragrant and the skins have loosened, 5–7 minutes. While still warm, place in a kitchen towel. Rub the towel vigorously to remove the skins; do not worry if small bits remain. Chop coarsely and set aside.

❧ Have ready a large bowl of water to which you have added 2 tablespoons of the lemon juice. Cut off the top half of each artichoke and remove the tough outer leaves down to the pale green leaves. Cut off the base of the stem and peel away its dark green outer layer. If using large artichokes, cut in half lengthwise and scoop out the prickly chokes. Cut the artichokes, large or small, lengthwise into thin slices. As each artichoke is cut, drop into the bowl of lemon water.

❧ In a frying pan over medium heat, warm 1 tablespoon of the oil. Add the onion and sauté until soft, about 7 minutes. Add the garlic and sauté for 1 minute longer. Drain the artichokes; add to the pan along with ½ cup (4 fl oz/125 ml) of the water and a pinch each of salt and pepper. Cover and cook until the liquid evaporates and the artichokes are nearly tender, about 15 minutes.

❧ Meanwhile, combine the stock and the remaining 2 cups (16 fl oz/500 ml) water in a saucepan and bring to a gentle simmer over medium-low heat.

❧ Uncover the artichokes, add the remaining 1 tablespoon olive oil and the rice and stir constantly until the edges are translucent, about 2 minutes. Add a ladleful of the simmering stock-water mixture and continue to stir constantly over medium heat. When the liquid is almost absorbed, add another ladleful. Stir steadily to keep the rice from sticking and continue to add more liquid, a ladleful at a time, as soon as each previous ladleful is almost absorbed. The risotto is done when the rice is tender but firm, 20–25 minutes total. If you run out of stock before the rice is tender, use hot water.

❧ Remove the rice from the heat. Stir in a ladleful of the stock-water mixture (or hot water), the Parmesan, hazelnuts, parsley and the remaining 1 tablespoon lemon juice. Transfer to a warmed serving dish and serve with lemon wedges.

## ASPARAGUS–PARMESAN CHEESE PUFFS

MAKES 36 PUFFS; SERVES 6

*Asparagus season lasts from late winter through spring and into early summer.*

¼ lb (125 g) asparagus spears
¾ cup (6 fl oz/180 ml) milk
5 tablespoons (2½ oz/75 g) unsalted butter, cut into pieces
¾ cup (4 oz/125 g) all-purpose (plain) flour
½ teaspoon salt
¼ teaspoon cayenne pepper
3 eggs, at room temperature
¾ cup (3 oz/90 g) freshly grated Parmesan cheese
½ cup (2 oz/60 g) shredded Gruyère cheese

Cut or snap off the tough stem ends from the asparagus spears and discard. Cut the spears crosswise on the diagonal into ¼-inch (6-mm) pieces. Bring a sauté pan three-fourths full of salted water to a boil. Add the asparagus and simmer just until tender, about 1 minute. Drain immediately; set aside.

❧ In a heavy saucepan, combine the milk and butter and bring to a boil over medium-high heat. Meanwhile, sift together the flour, salt and cayenne pepper into a small bowl. As soon as the milk reaches a boil and the butter has melted, remove from the heat and add the flour mixture all at once. Using a wooden spoon, beat vigorously until the mixture thickens and pulls away from the sides of the pan, about 1 minute. Transfer to a bowl. Add the eggs, one at a time, beating well after each addition. Let cool for 10 minutes.

❧ Preheat an oven to 400°F (200°C). Line 2 baking sheets with parchment paper and lightly butter the paper.

❧ Add the asparagus, Parmesan and Gruyère to the cooled dough and stir to mix well. Using a teaspoon, scoop up rounded spoonfuls of the dough and place on the baking sheets, spacing them about 1 inch (2.5 cm) apart.

❧ Bake until golden brown, 20–25 minutes. Remove from the oven and, using a spatula, transfer the puffs to a warmed serving dish. Serve at once.

## SWEET VIDALIA ONION RINGS WITH CHILI CATSUP

SERVES 6

*Vidalia onions hail from Vidalia, Georgia, where perfect conditions exist for their cultivation. These large yellow onions, most widely available in late spring, are sweet and juicy. If you can't find them, substitute Maui onions (from Hawaii) or Walla Wallas (from Washington), or use any other sweet onions. Offer these spicy rings as an appetizer or a side dish.*

FOR THE ONION RINGS:

2 cups (10 oz/315 g) all-purpose (plain) flour
1 teaspoon baking powder
2 cups (16 fl oz/500 ml) beer, at room temperature
1 teaspoon salt, plus salt to taste
1 teaspoon freshly ground pepper
4 egg whites, at room temperature
2½ cups (10 oz/315 g) fine dried bread crumbs
peanut oil for deep-frying
3 extra-large Vidalia onions, cut crosswise into slices ¾ inch (2 cm) thick and separated into rings

FOR THE CHILI CATSUP:

1 cup (8 fl oz/250 ml) catsup
½ teaspoon cayenne pepper
1 fresh jalapeño chili pepper, seeded and minced

To make the onion rings, in a large bowl, combine the flour, baking powder, beer, ½ teaspoon of the salt and ½ teaspoon of the pepper. Mix well. Cover with plastic wrap and let rest at room temperature for 30 minutes.

❧ In a bowl, using an electric mixer on high speed, beat the egg whites until soft peaks form. Using a rubber spatula, fold the whites into the batter. In another bowl, combine the bread crumbs and the remaining ½ teaspoon each salt and pepper. Stir to mix well.

❧ In a deep, heavy sauté pan or saucepan, pour in peanut oil to a depth of 2 inches (5 cm) and heat to 375°F (190°C) on a deep-frying thermometer, or until a little batter dropped into the oil sizzles immediately upon contact.

❧ Dip the onion rings, a few at a time, into the batter, shaking off any excess. Next, dip the rings into the bread crumbs, coating them evenly and shaking off any excess. Place the breaded onion rings in single layers on a baking sheet, separating the layers with waxed or parchment paper.

❧ To make the chili catsup, in a small bowl, whisk together the catsup, cayenne pepper and jalapeño pepper. Set aside.

❧ When the oil is ready, working in batches, slip the rings into the hot oil, being careful not to crowd the pan. Fry until golden brown and crisp, 1–2 minutes. Using a slotted spoon or tongs, transfer to paper towels to drain.

❧ Arrange the hot onion rings on a platter and sprinkle with salt. Place the chili catsup alongside. Serve at once.

# Spring Soups & Salads

It is no coincidence that shades of bright green predominate in the soups and salads of spring. The season's tempting young shoots, stalks, pods and leaves deliver fresh, pure flavors to a variety of such dishes. Tiny young peas, for example, are simply puréed to make Fresh Pea Soup with Lemon Crème Fraîche (page 35), while snowy white cheese and crunchy brown nuts highlight the emerald color, elegant contours and refreshingly bitter taste of wild greens in Dandelion Greens, Goat Cheese and Walnut Salad (at right).

Vegetables also share the seasonal spotlight with bright-flavored citruses and tropical fruits in such recipes as Watercress, Papaya and Grapefruit Salad (page 35) and Belgian Endive, Arugula and Blood Orange Salad (page 29). And fresh shellfish from the still-icy waters of spring's early weeks star against a subtly composed backdrop in Celery, Leek and Oyster Bisque (page 30).

## FAVA BEAN AND FARFALLE SOUP

SERVES 6

2½ lb (1.25 kg) fava (broad) beans in the pod, shelled
9 cups (2¼ qt/2.25 l) chicken stock
6 oz (185 g) dried farfalle pasta
1 tablespoon fresh lemon juice
salt and freshly ground pepper
½ cup (2 oz/60 g) freshly grated Parmesan cheese

Bring a pot three-fourths full of water to a boil. Add the fava beans and blanch for 20 seconds. Drain and let cool. Split open the skin of each bean along its edge and slip the bean from the skin. Discard the skins.

❧ In a large pot, bring the chicken stock to a boil. Add the farfalle and cook until al dente (tender but firm to the bite), 10–12 minutes or according to the package directions. Add the fava beans and lemon juice. Season to taste with salt and pepper.

❧ Ladle the soup into warmed bowls and serve immediately. Pass the Parmesan cheese at the table.

## DANDELION GREENS, GOAT CHEESE AND WALNUT SALAD

SERVES 4–6

*The time to pick dandelion greens is in the early spring, when they are still tender shoots less than 5 inches (13 cm) high. The older and taller the leaves, the more bitter the flavor. If dandelion greens cannot be found, arugula (rocket) or mixed salad leaves may replace them in this recipe. Crumbled crisp bacon and garlic croutons make nice additions.*

½ cup (2 oz/60 g) walnuts
2 tablespoons red wine vinegar
3 tablespoons extra-virgin olive oil
1 teaspoon walnut or hazelnut oil
salt and freshly ground pepper
2 bunches young, tender dandelion greens, tough stems removed
¼ lb (125 g) fresh goat cheese, crumbled

Preheat an oven to 350°F (180°C). Spread the walnuts on a baking sheet and toast in the oven until lightly browned and fragrant, 5–7 minutes. Remove from the oven, let cool and chop coarsely.

❧ To make the dressing, in a small bowl, whisk together the vinegar, olive oil, walnut or hazelnut oil and salt and pepper to taste. Set aside.

❧ Rinse the dandelion greens and dry thoroughly. Place in a serving bowl.

❧ To serve, add the walnuts to the dandelion greens and toss to combine. Drizzle with the dressing and toss again to coat the ingredients evenly. Sprinkle with the goat cheese and serve immediately.

# SORREL SOUP

SERVES 6

*Sorrel thrives in the coolness of early spring, when its young leaves have their most delicate taste and tender texture. The plant's sharp, acidic flavor becomes mellow in this creamy soup. Croutons add yet another flavor dimension. To make them, tear day-old bread into small pieces, drizzle with butter and bake at 400°F (200°C) until crisp.*

2 tablespoons unsalted butter
2 yellow onions, chopped
9 oz (280 g) young, tender sorrel leaves, stems removed
1¼ lb (625 g) red new potatoes, peeled and thinly sliced
2 cups (16 fl oz/500 ml) chicken or vegetable stock
4 cups (32 fl oz/1 l) water
½ cup (4 fl oz/125 ml) heavy (double) cream
salt and freshly ground pepper

In a soup pot over medium heat, melt the butter. Add the onions and sauté, stirring, until soft, about 10 minutes. Add the sorrel and cook, stirring, until wilted, about 2 minutes. Raise the heat to high, add the potatoes, stock and water and bring to a boil. Reduce the heat to medium-low, cover and simmer until the potatoes are soft, 15–20 minutes. Remove from the heat and let cool slightly.

❧ Using a blender and working in batches, purée the soup on high speed until smooth, 3–4 minutes for each batch. Strain the purée through a fine-mesh sieve into a clean saucepan. Stir in the cream, mixing well. Season to taste with salt and pepper.

❧ To serve, place the soup over medium heat and reheat to serving temperature. Ladle the soup into warmed bowls and serve immediately.

# BELGIAN ENDIVE, ARUGULA AND BLOOD ORANGE SALAD

SERVES 4–6

*Arugula, which grows best in the cooler temperatures of spring and autumn, has a flavor that brings to mind pepper, mustard and horseradish. It is an excellent component of salads that contrast its tangy character with sweet ingredients such as blood oranges and rich components such as walnut oil. Garnish each serving with a sprinkling of blood orange zest, if you like.*

½ cup (2 oz/60 g) pecan halves
4 heads Belgian endive (chicory/witloof)
1 large bunch arugula (rocket), tough stems removed
3 blood oranges
1 teaspoon walnut or hazelnut oil
2 tablespoons extra-virgin olive oil
1 tablespoon sherry vinegar or Champagne vinegar
salt and freshly ground pepper

Preheat an oven to 350°F (180°C). Spread the pecans on a baking sheet and place in the oven until toasted and fragrant, 5–7 minutes. Let cool.

❧ Trim off 1 inch (2.5 cm) from the stem end of each endive and separate the leaves into individual spears. Rinse the endive and arugula leaves and dry thoroughly. Place them in a large bowl, cover with a damp towel and refrigerate until serving, or for up to 3 hours.

❧ Grate enough zest from 1 orange to measure ½ teaspoon; set aside. Using a

sharp knife, cut a thick slice off the top and bottom of each orange to reveal the flesh. Then, standing each orange upright on a cutting surface, cut off the peel and white membrane in thick, wide strips. Working with 1 orange at a time, hold the orange over a bowl and cut along either side of each segment between the membrane and flesh to free the segments from the membrane. As the segments are freed, let them drop into the bowl. When all are removed, squeeze the membrane to release as much juice as possible into the bowl. Using a slotted spoon, transfer the orange segments to a serving bowl and remove any seeds. Set aside. (You should have about 2 tablespoons juice remaining in the bowl.)

❧ To the bowl containing the orange juice, add the walnut or hazelnut oil, olive oil, sherry or Champagne vinegar, and reserved orange zest. Whisk together, then season to taste with salt and pepper.

❧ To serve, add the endives and arugula to the orange segments. Drizzle with the dressing and scatter on the pecans. Toss well and serve.

## CELERY, LEEK AND OYSTER BISQUE

SERVES 6

*Oysters are best when harvested in cool weather—in months that include an r—so look for them in March and April.*

18 small oysters in the shell or bottled shucked oysters
2 tablespoons unsalted butter
1 yellow onion, coarsely chopped
5 large leeks, including 2 inches (5 cm) of green, coarsely chopped and carefully rinsed
5 celery stalks, coarsely chopped
3 bottles (8 fl oz/250 ml each) clam juice
3 cups (24 fl oz/750 ml) water
½ cup (4 fl oz/125 ml) heavy (double) cream
1–2 teaspoons fresh lemon juice
salt and freshly ground pepper

If using oysters in the shell, shuck them, reserving their liquor; see page 299 for directions. Cover and refrigerate the oysters, then strain the liquor and set aside. If using bottled oysters, strain the oysters from the liquor, then set the liquor aside and refrigerate the oysters.

In a soup pot over medium-low heat, melt the butter. Add the onion, leeks and celery and sauté, stirring occasionally, until the vegetables are soft, about 20 minutes. Add the clam juice, water and reserved oyster liquor. Raise the heat to high and bring to a boil. Reduce the heat to medium and simmer, uncovered, until the vegetables are very soft, about 30 minutes. Remove from the heat and let cool slightly.

Using a blender and working in batches, purée the soup on high speed until smooth, 3–4 minutes for each batch. Strain the purée through a fine-mesh sieve into a clean saucepan.

Place the pan over medium heat. Add the reserved oysters, cream and lemon juice and bring to a gentle simmer. Simmer, uncovered, until the oysters are slightly firm to the touch and their edges curl slightly, 1–2 minutes. Season to taste with salt and pepper.

Ladle the soup into warmed bowls and serve immediately.

## WARM PANCETTA-WRAPPED ENDIVE SALAD

SERVES 6

*Belgian endives, prized for their refreshing crispness and sharp flavor, would be overwhelmingly bitter were it not for the labor-intensive cultivation method of blanching, in which the heads are grown covered with sand in total darkness to yield plump, pale, mild-tasting shoots.*

18 paper-thin slices pancetta, 6 oz (185 g) total weight
9 heads Belgian endive (chicory/witloof), 1½–2 lb (750 g–1 kg)
5 tablespoons (2 fl oz/60 ml) fresh lemon juice
5 tablespoons (2 fl oz/60 ml) extra-virgin olive oil
salt and freshly ground pepper
1 clove garlic, minced
1 head frisée lettuce, leaves separated and carefully rinsed
lemon wedges

Uncurl each pancetta slice so that it forms a long strip, and cut each piece crosswise to form 2 equal pieces. Trim the stem end of each endive, being careful not to separate the leaves, and cut lengthwise into quarters.

Position a rack in the upper part of an oven and preheat to 400°F (200°C).

Bring a large pot three-fourths full of salted water to a boil. Add 3 tablespoons of the lemon juice and the endive quarters and cook for 1 minute. Using a slotted spoon, transfer the endive quarters to paper towels to drain, then place in a bowl and drizzle with 1 tablespoon of the olive oil. Toss well and season to taste with pepper.

Working with 1 endive quarter at a time, wrap a piece of pancetta around it. Arrange the wrapped endives in a single layer in a baking dish, allowing ample space between them. Bake until the endives are tender when pierced with a knife and the pancetta begins to crisp on the edges, about 15 minutes.

Meanwhile, in a large bowl, whisk together the remaining 2 tablespoons lemon juice and 4 tablespoons olive oil and the garlic. Season to taste with salt and pepper. Add the frisée. Toss lightly.

To serve, arrange the frisée on warmed individual plates. Place the endive atop the frisée. Drizzle the endive with any remaining vinaigrette. Serve warm, garnished with lemon wedges.

## SUGAR SNAP PEA AND MINT SALAD

SERVES 4–6

*Fresh peas and mint are natural partners and are often paired in hot side dishes and soups. This version of the classic combination, featuring spring's sugar snap peas rather than the more traditional garden peas, appeals to the season's celebration of fresh, light flavors. Thin strips of prosciutto can be added for a more robust taste. Serve this versatile salad to open a meal or to accompany a main course of grilled lamb.*

1½ lb (750 g) sugar snap peas, ends
    trimmed
1 tablespoon Champagne vinegar
1 small shallot, minced
3 tablespoons extra-virgin olive oil
salt and freshly ground pepper
¼ cup (¼ oz/7 g) fresh mint leaves,
    cut into thin strips, plus mint sprigs
    for garnish

Have ready a bowl of ice water. Bring a large saucepan three-fourths full of salted water to a boil. Add the sugar snap peas and simmer until bright green and almost tender, 1½–2 minutes. Drain immediately and transfer to the ice water to halt the cooking. Let stand for 5 minutes, then drain and set aside.

To make the dressing, in a small bowl, whisk together the vinegar, shallot, olive oil and salt and pepper to taste.

To serve, place the sugar snap peas and mint strips in a bowl and drizzle with the dressing. Toss to coat evenly. Transfer to a serving bowl and garnish with mint sprigs. Serve immediately, arranging the salad attractively on each plate, if desired.

# MATZO BALL SOUP

SERVES 6

*Passover, the most widely observed Jewish holiday, commemorates the exodus of Jews from Egypt. It falls on the first full moon of early spring, and the first evening is celebrated with a Seder, a ceremonial meal at which chicken soup with matzo balls is traditionally served. Seltzer water or chicken stock is used to bind the dumplings, with the seltzer yielding a lighter result.*

4 eggs

3 tablespoons vegetable oil

1 cup (5 oz/155 g) matzo meal

2 tablespoons chopped fresh flat-leaf (Italian) parsley

¼ cup (⅓ oz/10 g) chopped fresh cilantro (fresh coriander)

½ teaspoon kosher salt

⅛ teaspoon freshly ground pepper

2–4 tablespoons seltzer water or club soda

6 cups (48 fl oz/1.5 l) chicken stock

8 slices fresh ginger, each about ¼ inch (6 mm) thick

1 leek, including 1 inch (2.5 cm) of green, cut into ½-inch (12-mm) dice and carefully rinsed

2 tablespoons finely snipped fresh chives or garlic chives

In a bowl, whisk together the eggs and vegetable oil. Stir in the matzo meal, parsley, cilantro, salt and pepper. Add 2 tablespoons seltzer or soda water and stir to form a slightly sticky mixture. If it is too dry, add 1–2 additional tablespoons seltzer or soda water. Cover the bowl with plastic wrap and refrigerate until cold, about 2 hours.

❧ Bring a large soup pot three-fourths full of salted water to a boil, then reduce the heat to a simmer. Form the matzo mixture into balls 1 inch (2.5 cm) in diameter. You should have 12 balls in all. Drop the balls into the simmering water and cook, uncovered, until they rise to the top and are cooked all the way through, 30–40 minutes. To see if they are ready, cut into one; the color and texture should be consistent throughout. Using a slotted spoon, transfer the matzo balls to a baking sheet. Set aside.

❧ In a saucepan over medium-high heat, combine the chicken stock and ginger and bring to a simmer. Reduce the heat to medium-low, add the leek and simmer, uncovered, until tender, about 10 minutes. Discard the ginger.

❧ Add the matzo balls to the simmering stock and reheat for 3 minutes. Ladle the soup into warmed bowls, placing 2 matzo balls in each bowl. Garnish with the chives or garlic chives and serve immediately.

## WATERCRESS, PAPAYA AND GRAPEFRUIT SALAD

SERVES 4–6

*All three ingredients featured here flourish during spring, but watercress in particular loves the cool, moist ground that only this season brings.*

2 grapefruits, white, yellow or pink
1 papaya, about 1 lb (500 g)
2 tablespoons fresh grapefruit juice
1½ tablespoons white wine vinegar
2 tablespoons extra-virgin olive oil
salt and freshly ground pepper
1 bunch watercress, tough stems
   removed and carefully rinsed

Into a small bowl, grate enough zest from 1 grapefruit to measure 1 teaspoon. Set aside.

❧ Using a sharp knife, cut a thick slice off the top and bottom of each grapefruit to reveal the flesh. Then, standing each grapefruit upright on a cutting surface, cut off the peel and white membrane in thick, wide strips. Cut the grapefruit crosswise into slices ¼ inch (6 mm) thick. Cut each slice into quarters and place in a bowl. Set aside.

❧ Peel the papaya and cut in half through the stem end. Scoop out the seeds and discard. Cut crosswise into slices ¼ inch (6 mm) thick. Place in the bowl with the grapefruit slices.

❧ To the bowl containing the grapefruit zest, add the grapefruit juice, vinegar and olive oil to make a dressing. Whisk together, then season to taste with salt and pepper.

❧ To serve, place the watercress in a serving bowl and drizzle with the dressing. Top with the grapefruit and papaya slices. Toss lightly and serve immediately.

## FRESH PEA SOUP WITH LEMON CRÈME FRAÎCHE

SERVES 4–6

*It is essential to use very fresh, tiny, young spring peas for this soup, as the larger ones are starchy. Cooling the soup in an ice-water bath will ensure that it keeps its bright green color. This soup can also be served cold: chill for 1–2 hours, adjust the seasonings and ladle into chilled bowls.*

**FOR THE PEA SOUP:**
4½ lb (2.25 kg) fresh garden peas
1 tablespoon unsalted butter
10 green (spring) onions, thinly sliced
2½ cups (20 fl oz/625 ml) chicken
   stock
2 cups (16 fl oz/500 ml) water
½ cup (4 fl oz/125 ml) heavy (double)
   cream
salt and freshly ground pepper

**FOR THE LEMON CRÈME FRAÎCHE:**
½ cup (4 fl oz/125 ml) crème fraîche
1–2 tablespoons milk
½ teaspoon grated lemon zest
1½ teaspoons fresh lemon juice
salt and freshly ground pepper

fresh lemon zest, optional
fresh chive blossoms, optional

To make the pea soup, shell the peas, reserving 8 of the pods. You should have about 5½ cups (1¾ lb/875 g) peas. Set the peas and pods aside.

❧ Have ready a large bowl of ice water in which a soup pot can be nested. In the soup pot over medium heat, melt the butter. Add the green onions and cook, stirring occasionally, until soft,

about 5 minutes. Increase the heat to medium-high and add the peas, the reserved pods, chicken stock and water. Bring to a boil, reduce the heat to medium-low and simmer until the peas and pods are tender, about 5 minutes. Remove from the heat and nest the pot in the bowl of ice water. Stir occasionally until cool, about 20 minutes.

❧ Using a blender and working in batches, purée the cooled pea mixture on high speed until smooth, 2–3 minutes for each batch. Strain through a fine-mesh sieve into a clean saucepan. Stir in the cream. Season to taste with salt and pepper.

❧ To make the lemon crème fraîche, in a bowl, whisk together the crème fraîche and enough of the milk to make a barely fluid mixture. Add the zest and lemon juice and season to taste with salt and pepper.

❧ To serve, place the soup over medium heat and reheat to serving temperature. Ladle into warmed bowls and drizzle with the lemon crème fraîche. Garnish with lemon zest and chive blossoms, if desired, and serve hot.

## FENNEL, RADISH AND PARSLEY SALAD

SERVES 6

*Radish, with its pungent bite, and fresh-tasting parsley find a perfect companion in fennel, with its hint of licorice flavor. Fennel's name comes from the Latin for "little hay," probably describing its feathery green foliage.*

2 fennel bulbs
1 small bunch fresh flat-leaf (Italian)
    parsley, stems removed and leaves
    minced, plus parsley sprigs for garnish
12 radishes, trimmed and cut into
    paper-thin slices
3 tablespoons extra-virgin olive oil
2 tablespoons fresh lemon juice
1 clove garlic, minced
salt and freshly ground pepper
lemon wedges

Cut off the feathery tops and stems from the fennel bulbs and discard. Trim away any yellowed or bruised outer leaves and then cut each bulb in half through the stem end. Cut out the tough core portion and place the halves, cut side down, on a work surface. Using a sharp knife, cut the fennel crosswise into paper-thin slices. Place the slices in a bowl. Add the parsley and radishes and toss well to mix. Set aside.

❧ To make the dressing, in a small bowl, whisk together the olive oil, lemon juice, garlic and salt and pepper to taste.

❧ To serve, drizzle the dressing over the salad and toss to coat the ingredients evenly. Transfer to a serving bowl, garnish with lemon wedges and parsley sprigs and serve immediately.

## GREEN GARLIC AND NEW POTATO SOUP

SERVES 6

*Green garlic is simply immature garlic—the bulb before it forms its characteristic cloves and the papery sheaths that enclose them. Milder in flavor than its adult counterpart, it resembles a baby leek or green (spring) onion with its long green tops and pale green or white bulb sometimes streaked with pink. Look for it at specialty markets in early spring, or substitute 1 clove of mature garlic for every head of green garlic.*

**FOR THE SOUP:**

1 tablespoon unsalted butter
20 heads green garlic, about 6 oz
    (185 g) total weight and ½–1 inch
    (12 mm–2.5 cm) in diameter
    at root end
8 cups (64 fl oz/2 l) chicken stock
1½ lb (750 g) red new potatoes, peeled
    and quartered
¼ cup (2 fl oz/60 ml) heavy (double)
    cream
2 tablespoons white wine vinegar
salt and freshly ground pepper

**FOR THE GARNISH:**

1½ tablespoons extra-virgin olive oil
3 heads green garlic, ½–1 inch (12
    mm–2.5 cm) in diameter at root end,
    bulbs minced
2 tablespoons chopped fresh flat-leaf
    (Italian) parsley
salt and freshly ground pepper

To make the soup, in a soup pot over low heat, melt the butter. Coarsely chop the garlic bulbs and add them to the pot along with ½ cup (4 fl oz/125 ml) of the chicken stock. Cover and cook until tender, about 20 minutes. Add the potatoes and the remaining 7½ cups (60 fl oz/1.75 l) chicken stock and raise the heat to medium-high. Simmer, covered, until the potatoes are soft, about 20 minutes. Remove from the heat and let cool slightly.

❧ Using a blender and working in batches, purée the soup on high speed until smooth, 3–4 minutes for each batch. Strain the purée through a fine-mesh sieve into a clean saucepan. Stir in the cream and vinegar, mixing well. Season to taste with salt and pepper.

❧ To make the garnish, in a small saucepan over low heat, warm the olive oil. Add the minced green garlic and sauté, stirring constantly, until soft, about 2 minutes. Do not let the garlic turn golden. Remove from the heat and let cool for 10 minutes. Stir in the parsley, mixing well, and season to taste with salt and pepper.

❧ Just before the garnish is ready, place the soup over medium heat and reheat to serving temperature. Ladle into warmed bowls and distribute the garnish evenly among the bowls, drizzling it over the tops. Serve immediately.

# Spring Main Courses
❧

The season's main dishes are determined by both the product that fills the markets and the meat, poultry and seafood that are now at their best and most abundant. All kinds of salmon, for example, come into season, making possible such creations as Peppered Salmon with Snow Peas and Ginger (page 40). Young poultry features in flavorful dishes like Roasted Cornish Hens with Rhubarb Chutney (page 48) and Asian Chicken in Ginger-Lemongrass Broth (page 43). A wealth of modestly priced pork ensures that Pork Chops with Morels and Thyme (page 47) is a relative bargain, despite the high prices that may be paid for the precious wild mushrooms that accompany the meat.

Lamb, of course, is the signature main-course ingredient of spring. At its sweet, tender and succulent best, spring lamb is shown off not only in the recipe that shares this page, but also in Roast Leg of Lamb with Mint Sauce (page 51), both ideal centerpieces for any seasonal celebration.

## RACK OF SPRING LAMB WITH ROASTED GARLIC
SERVES 6

*For this recipe, you (or your butcher) must first "french" the racks: Trim off 2 inches (5 cm) of fat and membrane between the ribs to expose the tips of the bones, then cut through the backbone between the ribs to make carving easier. Fresh spring vegetables, such as asparagus, baby carrots and new potatoes, make a delicious accompaniment.*

2 heads garlic
2½ tablespoons olive oil
¼ cup (2 fl oz/60 ml) water
3 tablespoons whole-grain mustard
2 tablespoons fresh lemon juice
½ teaspoon salt, plus salt to taste
½ teaspoon freshly ground pepper, plus pepper to taste
1½ cups (3 oz/90 g) fresh white bread crumbs
3 racks of lamb, about 1½ lb (750 g) each, trimmed of excess fat
2 tablespoons unsalted butter, melted

Preheat an oven to 400°F (200°C). Discard the excess papery sheath from the garlic heads and place in a small baking dish. Drizzle with ½ tablespoon of the olive oil and the water. Cover with aluminum foil and bake until soft, about 45 minutes. Let cool slightly. Leave the oven set at 400°F (200°C).
❧ Separate the garlic cloves and squeeze the pulp from the skins into a small bowl; discard the skins. Whisk in the remaining 2 tablespoons olive oil, the mustard, lemon juice and ½ teaspoon each salt and pepper. In another bowl, season the bread crumbs with salt and pepper to taste.
❧ Lay the racks of lamb in a roasting pan side by side and fat side up. Roast for 10 minutes. Remove from the oven and immediately rub the garlic mixture over the fat side of each rack. Then spread the bread crumb mixture over the garlic mixture. Drizzle with the melted butter and return the lamb to the oven. Continue to roast until the crumbs are lightly golden and an instant-read thermometer inserted into the thickest portion of a rack away from the bone registers 130°–135°F (54°–57°C) for medium-rare, or the meat is pink when cut into with a sharp knife, about 25 minutes longer. Remove from the oven, cover with aluminum foil and let rest for 10 minutes.
❧ Preheat a broiler (griller). Uncover and place the roasting pan under the broiler about 5–6 inches (13–15 cm) from the heat source. Broil (grill) the lamb racks until the crumbs are deep golden brown, 30–60 seconds.
❧ To serve, place the racks on a cutting board and slice between the ribs. Arrange 2 or 3 ribs on each warmed individual plate.

## PEPPERED SALMON WITH SNOW PEAS AND GINGER

SERVES 6

*Snow peas are available year-round, but they are at their most tender and sweet in the spring. The entire legume is edible, which accounts for the French name* mangetout, *meaning "eat it all." These are not to be confused with sugar snap peas, the crisp chubby pods filled with immature peas available at the same time of year. For this recipe, either variety can be used.*

1 lb (500 g) snow peas (mangetouts)
    or sugar snap peas, ends trimmed
1 tablespoon finely ground Sichuan
    peppercorns, optional
6 salmon fillets, each 5–6 oz
    (155–185 g), skinned
2 teaspoons corn oil
1 teaspoon Asian sesame oil
salt
freshly ground black pepper, if not
    using Sichuan peppercorns
6 green (spring) onions, thinly sliced
2 teaspoons peeled and grated fresh
    ginger
⅓ cup (3 fl oz/80 ml) dry sherry
3 tablespoons soy sauce
3 tablespoons unseasoned rice vinegar

Bring a large pot three-fourths full of salted water to a boil. Add the peas and simmer until bright green, about 1 minute. Drain and set aside.

❧ If using the ground Sichuan pepper, sprinkle it on both sides of each salmon fillet, distributing it evenly.

❧ In a wide, nonstick frying pan large enough to hold the salmon in a single layer without crowding, warm the corn oil and sesame oil over medium-high heat. Add the salmon fillets and cook until lightly golden on one side, about 4 minutes. Turn, season with salt

and, if the Sichuan pepper has been omitted, with black pepper as well. Continue to cook until lightly golden on the second side and opaque throughout when pierced with a knife, about 4 minutes longer. Transfer the salmon to a warmed platter or individual plates and cover loosely with aluminum foil to keep warm.

❧ Place the same pan over medium-high heat. When it is hot, add the peas, green onions and ginger and toss and stir constantly until the green onions soften, about 1 minute. Add the sherry, soy sauce and vinegar and bring to a boil. Boil until the liquid reduces by one-fourth, 20–30 seconds.

❧ Remove from the heat and pour the vegetables and sauce over and around the salmon. Serve immediately.

# SOUFFLÉED SHELLFISH OMELET

SERVES 4–6

*Elegant, yet not too complicated, this recipe is ideal for a springtime brunch. Shrimp and bay scallops are at their peak at this time of year; you can also add steamed asparagus, raw baby spinach leaves or blanched sugar snap peas to the omelet, or simply serve them alongside. Accompany with chilled glasses of Champagne topped off with a splash of blood-orange juice.*

½ cup (4 fl oz/125 ml) bottled clam
   juice or water
6 oz (185 g) medium shrimp (prawns),
   peeled and deveined
6 oz (185 g) bay scallops
1 teaspoon saffron threads
6 eggs, separated
¼ cup (1½ oz/45 g) all-purpose (plain)
   flour
6 oz (185 g) fresh-cooked crab meat
salt and freshly ground pepper
1 tablespoon unsalted butter

In a frying pan over medium heat, bring the clam juice or water to a boil. Add the shrimp and scallops, reduce the heat to low, cover and simmer for 1 minute. Uncover, stir lightly, re-cover and cook until the shrimp curl and the shrimp and scallops are firm to the touch, about 1 minute longer. Using a slotted spoon, transfer the shrimp and scallops to a bowl and let cool. Meanwhile, raise the heat to high and boil until the cooking liquid reduces by half, 20–30 seconds. Place the saffron in a small bowl and pour the reduced cooking liquid over it. Set aside.

❧ Preheat an oven to 375°F (190°C).

❧ In a large bowl, whisk the egg yolks with the flour until smooth. Add the saffron mixture and whisk well. Stir in the shrimp and scallop mixture and the crab until blended. Season to taste with salt and pepper.

❧ In another bowl, using an electric mixer, beat the egg whites until stiff peaks form. Using a spatula, stir one-fourth of the whites into the shellfish mixture to lighten it, then gently fold in the remaining whites just until no white drifts remain. Do not overmix.

❧ Melt the butter in a 10-inch (25-cm) nonstick ovenproof frying pan over medium heat. Tilt the pan to coat the bottom and sides with the butter. Pour the mixture into the pan, spreading it evenly.

❧ Bake until puffed and golden and the center is almost set when the pan is gently shaken, 30–35 minutes. Remove from the oven and serve immediately, spooning the omelet directly from the pan onto individual serving plates.

# ASIAN CHICKEN IN GINGER-LEMONGRASS BROTH

SERVES 6

*Daikon comes from the Japanese words* dai, *meaning "large," and* kon, *or "roots." It looks like a gigantic white icicle, and although it is a member of the turnip family, the flavor is more akin to radish. Here it is paired with other spring ingredients—snow peas, green onions, lemongrass—in a light Asian stew.*

**FOR THE BROTH:**

1 chicken, 3½ lb (1.75 kg), cut into 6 pieces, then skinned
3 qt (3 l) water
1 piece fresh ginger, 2 inches (5 cm) long, cut crosswise into 8 slices
2 lemongrass stalks, ends trimmed, then cut into 1-inch (2.5-cm) lengths
1 carrot, peeled and coarsely chopped
1 yellow onion, coarsely chopped

2 carrots, peeled and cut in half lengthwise, then cut on the diagonal into thin slices
½ daikon, peeled and cut in half lengthwise, then cut on the diagonal into thin slices
¾ lb (375 g) snow peas (mangetouts), ends trimmed, then cut on the diagonal into ½-inch (12-mm) pieces
3 green (spring) onions, cut on the diagonal into thin slices
salt and freshly ground pepper

To make the broth, in a large soup pot, combine the chicken pieces, water, ginger, lemongrass, carrot and onion. Place over high heat and bring to a boil, using a skimmer to skim off any foam that forms on the surface. Reduce the heat to low and simmer very gently, skimming as needed, until the chicken falls from the bones, 50–60 minutes. Remove from the heat and let cool for 1 hour. Using a large spoon, skim off any fat from the top and discard.

❧ Strain the broth through a fine-mesh sieve into a clean saucepan. Remove the pieces of chicken from the sieve and remove the meat from the bones. Tear the meat into 1-inch (2.5-cm) pieces and return them to the broth. Discard the remaining contents of the sieve.

❧ Place the broth over medium heat and bring to a gentle simmer. Add the carrot and daikon slices and simmer until the vegetables are tender, about 7 minutes. Add the snow peas and green onions and continue to simmer until tender, about 2 minutes longer. Season to taste with salt and pepper.

❧ Ladle into warmed bowls and serve hot.

## SPINACH AND BACON SOUFFLÉ

SERVES 4

*Although spinach is sold in markets year-round, its prime season is early spring. It is when you are most likely to find baby leaves, which some growers market already washed and bagged.*

1 teaspoon olive oil
3 slices bacon, about 3 oz (90 g), cut
    into ½-inch (12-mm) squares
⅓ cup (1½ oz/45 g) freshly grated
    Parmesan cheese
2 tablespoons unsalted butter
1 yellow onion, diced
6 tablespoons (2 oz/60 g) all-purpose
    (plain) flour
2 cups (16 fl oz/500 ml) milk
5 egg yolks
salt and freshly ground pepper
6 egg whites, at room temperature
1½ cups (6 oz/185 g) lightly packed
    shredded Gruyère cheese
2 cups (2 oz/60 g) lightly packed baby
    spinach leaves or tender larger leaves,
    torn into pieces, carefully rinsed
    and dried

In a frying pan over medium heat, warm the olive oil. Add the bacon and cook, stirring occasionally, until lightly golden and crisp and all the fat is rendered, 6–8 minutes. Using a slotted spoon, transfer to paper towels to drain.

Meanwhile, preheat an oven to 450°F (230°C). Butter a 2-qt (2-l) soufflé dish and dust with half of the Parmesan cheese. Measure out a sheet of aluminum foil long enough to encircle the soufflé dish with an extra 2 inches (5 cm) left over and fold it in half lengthwise. Butter one side of the foil. Wrap it, butter side in, around the soufflé dish, positioning it so that it stands 2 inches (5 cm) above the rim of the dish. Secure the foil in place with kitchen string.

In a saucepan over medium-low heat, melt the 2 tablespoons butter. Add the onion and sauté, stirring occasionally, until soft, about 10 minutes. Stir in the flour and cook, stirring constantly, for 2 minutes, allowing the mixture to bubble. Meanwhile, pour the milk into a saucepan over medium heat and bring it to just below a boil. Remove the onions from the heat and gradually whisk in the hot milk. Return to medium-low heat and cook, stirring constantly with a wooden spoon, until thick and smooth, 2–3 minutes. Transfer to a large bowl and stir in the bacon. Add the egg yolks, one at a time, stirring well after each addition. Season with salt and pepper and set aside.

In a bowl, beat the egg whites until stiff peaks form. Using a spatula, fold half of the whites into the yolk mixture to lighten it. Top with the Gruyère, the remaining whites and the spinach and fold in just until no white drifts remain. Do not overmix. Pour into the prepared soufflé dish. Sprinkle the remaining Parmesan evenly over the top.

Bake until the top is golden and the center no longer quivers when the dish is shaken, 35–45 minutes. Remove the foil and serve immediately.

*The awakened heart can sense spring in the air when there is no visible suggestion in calendar or frosted earth…*
—*Hannah Rion*

# PORK CHOPS WITH MORELS AND THYME

SERVES 6

*Morels signify spring for mushroom lovers. Thin fleshed, spongy and brown, these wild mushrooms have a delicate, earthy, nutty flavor. To clean their honeycombed ridges, whisk with a soft-bristled mushroom brush; do not rinse them, as they readily absorb water. If fresh morels are not available, substitute any other flavorful, fresh wild or cultivated mushrooms. Accompany with wilted spring greens (recipe on page 58), if you like.*

½ cup (4 fl oz/125 ml) boiling water
¼ oz (7 g) dried morel mushrooms
    or other dried wild mushrooms
2 teaspoons vegetable oil
6 center-cut pork chops, each about
    6 oz (185 g) and 1 inch (2.5 cm)
    thick, trimmed of excess fat
salt and freshly ground pepper
2 teaspoons unsalted butter
½ lb (250 g) fresh morel or other
    fresh wild or cultivated mushrooms,
    trimmed and brushed clean
    (see note)
1½ cups (12 fl oz/375 ml) chicken
    stock
1 teaspoon chopped fresh thyme, plus
    thyme sprigs for garnish

In a small bowl, combine the boiling water and the dried morels. Let cool to room temperature, about 20 minutes. Line a sieve with cheesecloth (muslin) and place over a bowl. Drain the mushrooms in the sieve, then chop them. Reserve the chopped mushrooms and the mushroom liquid separately.

❧ In a frying pan large enough to hold the chops in a single layer without crowding, warm the vegetable oil over medium heat. Add the pork chops and cook, uncovered, for 5 minutes. Turn the chops over and season to taste with salt and pepper. Reduce the heat to medium-low and continue to cook uncovered, turning occasionally, until golden and firm to the touch, 8–9 minutes longer. Transfer the chops to a warmed platter and cover with aluminum foil to keep warm.

❧ In the same pan over medium-high heat, melt the butter. Add the fresh and dried morels (or other mushrooms) and sauté, stirring often, until the fresh mushrooms are soft, 3–4 minutes. Transfer the mushrooms to the platter holding the pork to keep warm. Raise the heat to high and add the chicken stock, chopped thyme and reserved mushroom liquid. Cook until reduced by half, 3–4 minutes.

❧ To serve, transfer the chops to warmed individual plates. Divide the sauce and mushrooms evenly among the chops, spooning them over the top. Garnish with thyme sprigs and serve immediately.

*Mushrooms in good condition should feel firm and dry to the touch. Since they can become soggy easily, keep them in a basket, brown paper bag or other container which allows air to circulate freely, and store them in the refrigerator.*

## BAKED HAM WITH GINGER-RUM GLAZE

SERVES 8

*There is no better centerpiece for the Easter table than an old-fashioned country ham punctuated with cloves and glazed to a rich mahogany brown. The mix of sweet and salty flavors is particularly pleasing. Always seek out the best-quality ham you can find, asking at the butcher shop or delicatessen for one that has been dry-cured with salt and sugar and lightly smoked.*

½ partially boned country-style cured ham such as a Virginia ham, 6–7 lb (3–3.5 kg)
30 whole cloves
¼ cup (2 fl oz/60 ml) fresh orange juice
3 tablespoons maple syrup
3 tablespoons firmly packed brown sugar
¼ cup (1½ oz/45 g) preserved ginger in syrup or crystallized ginger
¼ cup (2 fl oz/60 ml) light or dark rum

Rinse the ham well in several changes of cold water. Place in a large bowl, add water to cover and refrigerate overnight.

❧ Remove the ham from the water and discard the water. Pat dry with paper towels. Using a sharp knife, remove the skin and slice off enough fat so that a layer only ⅓ inch (9 mm) thick remains. Score the ham fat with crisscrosses to form a diamond pattern. Stick a clove in the center of each diamond.

❧ Preheat an oven to 325°F (165°C). In a small saucepan over high heat, combine the orange juice, maple syrup, brown sugar and ginger and stir until the sugar dissolves, about 1 minute. Add the rum and transfer the mixture to a blender. Blend on high speed to form a smooth glaze. Brush the surface of the ham with some of the glaze and place the ham on a rack in a roasting pan.

❧ Place the pan in the oven and bake, basting every 30 minutes with some of the remaining glaze, until the ham is golden brown and a thick glaze has formed on the surface, 2–2½ hours. Remove from the oven, cover with aluminum foil and let rest for 15 minutes before carving.

❧ To serve, cut the ham into slices and arrange on a warmed platter or individual plates. Serve at once.

## ROASTED CORNISH HENS WITH RHUBARB CHUTNEY

SERVES 6

*Each of these flavorful 1-pound (500-g) hens, also known as Rock Cornish game hens, provides a perfect serving for one. Rhubarb, available from late winter to early summer, provides a wonderfully tangy sauce; take care to discard any leaves from the stalks, as they are toxic.*

FOR THE RHUBARB CHUTNEY:
¾ cup (6 fl oz/180 ml) red wine vinegar
⅛ teaspoon ground cloves
¼ teaspoon ground ginger
½ cup (4 oz/125 g) sugar
½ cup (3 oz/90 g) golden raisins (sultanas)
1¼ lb (625 g) rhubarb, trimmed and cut into 1-inch (2.5-cm) pieces
½ cup (4 fl oz/125 ml) boiling water

FOR THE CORNISH HENS:
6 Cornish hens, about 1 lb (500 g) each, halved
salt and freshly ground pepper
1½ tablespoons unsalted butter, melted

To make the chutney, in a saucepan, combine the vinegar, cloves, ginger, sugar and raisins. Bring to a boil, reduce the heat to medium-low and simmer, uncovered, until the raisins soften, about 5 minutes. Add the rhubarb and boiling water. Continue to cook, stirring occasionally, until the rhubarb is soft, about 20 minutes. If any liquid still remains, simmer over high heat until it almost evaporates. Transfer the chutney to a bowl and let cool.

❧ To prepare the hens, preheat an oven to 500°F (260°C). Rinse the hen halves well, then pat dry with paper towels. Sprinkle with salt and pepper and place, skin side up, in a single layer in a roasting pan. Brush lightly with some of the melted butter. Roast, basting with the remaining butter and the pan juices after about 12 minutes, until golden and the juices run clear when a thigh is pierced, about 25 minutes total. Remove from the oven, cover and let rest for 10 minutes before serving.

❧ To serve, place 2 hen halves on each warmed individual plate. Spoon the chutney on the side.

## ROAST LEG OF SPRING LAMB WITH MINT SAUCE

SERVES 6–8

*Spring lamb is milk-fed, coming from animals only three to five months old. The meat should be pale pink; anything darker is not true spring lamb, and will lack its perfect tenderness and delicate flavor. Serve this dish when you want a glorious center-piece for a celebration dinner, garnishing the sliced meat with sprigs of the season's abundant fresh mint.*

### FOR THE LAMB:

6 cloves garlic, thinly sliced
1 tablespoon chopped fresh mint
½ teaspoon chopped fresh rosemary
salt and freshly ground pepper
1 leg of lamb, 5–6 lb (2.5–3 kg),
    trimmed of excess fat
2 tablespoons olive oil

### FOR THE MINT SAUCE:

2 cups (2 oz/60 g) lightly packed fresh
    mint leaves
½ cup (4 fl oz/125 ml) extra-virgin
    olive oil
2 tablespoons white wine vinegar
1 large clove garlic, minced
salt and freshly ground pepper

fresh mint sprigs

To prepare the lamb, in a small bowl, mix together the garlic, chopped mint, rosemary and salt and pepper to taste. Using a sharp paring knife, make incisions 1 inch (2.5 cm) deep all over the meat and insert the garlic mixture into the slits. Rub the meat evenly with the olive oil.

❧ Position a rack in the bottom of an oven and preheat to 450°F (230°C).

❧ Place the lamb, fat side up, on a rack in a large roasting pan and season with salt and pepper. Roast the lamb for 30 minutes. Turn the lamb over and reduce the heat to 325°F (165°C). Continue to roast until an instant-read thermometer inserted into the thickest part of the leg away from the bone registers 130°–135°F (54°–57°C) for medium-rare, or the meat is pink when cut into with a sharp knife, about 45 minutes.

❧ Meanwhile, make the mint sauce: Place the mint leaves, extra-virgin olive oil, vinegar and garlic in a blender or in a food processor fitted with the metal blade. Process on high speed until smooth. Transfer to a bowl and season to taste with salt and pepper.

❧ When the lamb is done, transfer it to a cutting board; reserve the juices in the pan. Cover the lamb loosely with aluminum foil and let rest for 10 minutes before carving. Using a large spoon, skim the fat from the pan juices and strain the juices through a fine-mesh sieve into the mint sauce. Stir until incorporated.

❧ To serve, cut the lamb across the grain into thin slices. Arrange the slices on a warmed platter and garnish with mint sprigs. Pass the mint sauce at the table to add to taste.

*As for the garden of mint, the very smell of it alone recovers and refreshes our spirits, as the taste stirs up our appetite for meat.*
*—Pliny the Elder*

## VEAL STIR-FRY WITH SNOW PEAS AND SNOW PEA SHOOTS

SERVES 6

*Both snow peas and their leafy green shoots are edible. The pods should be harvested when they are flat and crisp, and the peas inside are still smaller than peppercorns.*

1 lb (500 g) top round of veal, cut into slices ¼ inch (6 mm) thick

⅓ cup (3 fl oz/80 ml) soy sauce

2 teaspoons cornstarch (cornflour)

3 tablespoons peeled and grated fresh ginger

6 cloves garlic, minced

1 tablespoon Asian sesame oil

¼ cup (2 fl oz/60 ml) unseasoned rice vinegar

1 fresh jalapeño chili pepper, seeded and finely diced

2 tablespoons vegetable oil, or as needed

¾ lb (375 g) snow peas (mangetouts), ends trimmed

½ cup (4 fl oz/125 ml) chicken stock or water

6 cups (6 oz/185 g) lightly packed snow pea shoots

Place each slice of veal between 2 sheets of plastic wrap or waxed paper. Using a meat pounder, pound to an even ⅛-inch (3-mm) thickness. Cut the veal into strips 1 inch (2.5 cm) wide.

❧ In a bowl, combine the soy sauce, cornstarch, ginger, garlic, sesame oil, vinegar and jalapeño. Mix well. Add the veal, toss to coat evenly, cover and let marinate in the refrigerator for 2 hours. In a wok or large, deep frying pan over medium-high heat, warm 1 tablespoon of the vegetable oil. Add the snow peas

and toss and stir constantly until tender but still crisp, 1–2 minutes. Transfer to a bowl and set aside.

❧ Remove the veal from the marinade and reserve the marinade. Add the remaining 1 tablespoon vegetable oil to the wok or frying pan and place over high heat until the pan is very hot and the oil is rippling. Add half of the veal and toss and stir constantly until pale gold, about 2 minutes. Using a slotted spoon, transfer to the bowl holding the snow peas. Repeat with the remaining

veal, adding more oil if needed, and transfer to the bowl.

❧ Reduce the heat to medium and add the reserved marinade and the chicken stock or water to the pan. Cook, stirring, until the liquid thickens slightly, about 1 minute. Return the veal and snow peas to the pan and add the snow pea shoots. Toss and stir until the shoots wilt, 1–2 minutes.

❧ Transfer to a warmed serving dish and serve immediately.

# SHRIMP CAKES WITH JALAPEÑO TARTAR SAUCE

SERVES 6

### FOR THE JALAPEÑO TARTAR SAUCE:

1 cup (8 fl oz/250 ml) mayonnaise
1 teaspoon Dijon mustard
2 teaspoons fresh lemon juice
¼ cup (1¼ oz/37 g) minced gherkins
1 fresh jalapeño chili pepper, seeded
    and finely diced
salt and freshly ground pepper

### FOR THE SHRIMP CAKES:

½ cup (4 fl oz/125 ml) bottled clam
    juice or water
1½ lb (750 g) shrimp (prawns), peeled
    and deveined
4 tablespoons (2 oz/60 g) unsalted
    butter, or as needed
1 celery stalk, finely diced
8 green (spring) onions, sliced
1¼ cups (3½ oz/105 g) finely crushed
    saltine crackers
1 teaspoon hot-pepper sauce
2 eggs, well beaten
⅓ cup (3 fl oz/80 ml) mayonnaise
¼ cup (⅓ oz/10 g) finely snipped
    fresh chives
salt and freshly ground pepper
about 3 cups (6 oz/185 g) fresh
    bread crumbs

To make the sauce, in a small bowl, combine the mayonnaise, mustard, lemon juice, gherkins and jalapeño and stir to mix well. Season to taste with salt and pepper. Set aside.

❧ To make the shrimp cakes, bring the clam juice or water to a boil in a frying pan. Add the shrimp, reduce the heat to low, cover and simmer for 1 minute. Uncover, stir lightly, re-cover and cook until the shrimp curl and are firm to the touch, about 1 minute longer. Using a slotted spoon, transfer the shrimp to a bowl and let cool slightly, then chop finely and reserve.

❧ In a large frying pan over low heat, melt 2 tablespoons of the butter. Add the celery, cover and cook, stirring occasionally, until soft, about 10 minutes. Add the green onions and cook, stirring occasionally, until soft, about 4 minutes. Transfer to a bowl and let cool. Set the pan aside.

❧ Add the saltines, hot-pepper sauce, eggs, mayonnaise, chives, shrimp and salt and pepper to taste to the celery mixture; mix well. If the mixture is too wet to hold its shape, add bread crumbs as needed (about ½ cup/1 oz/30 g) to absorb the excess moisture. Shape into 12 cakes, each 2–2½ inches (5–6 cm) in diameter and ½ inch (12 mm) thick. Spread the remaining bread crumbs in a shallow bowl and dredge the cakes in them, coating evenly.

❧ In the same frying pan over medium heat, melt the remaining 2 tablespoons butter. Add half of the shrimp cakes and sauté, turning once, until golden on both sides, about 6 minutes total. Transfer to a paper towel–lined plate and keep warm. Sauté the remaining cakes in the same way, adding more butter if needed.

## ARTICHOKE AND LEEK LASAGNA

SERVES 8–10

½ lb (250 g) dried semolina lasagna
 noodles
2 cups (16 oz/500 g) ricotta cheese
¾ cup (3 oz/90 g) freshly grated
 Parmesan cheese
salt and freshly ground pepper
2 tablespoons olive oil
12 baby leeks, including 3 inches
 (7.5 cm) of green, or 5 large leeks,
 including 1 inch (2.5 cm) of green,
 cut into ½-inch (12-mm) dice
juice of 1 lemon
4 large or 20 baby artichokes
½ cup (4 fl oz/125 ml) water
5 cloves garlic, minced
3 cups (24 fl oz/750 ml) milk
3 tablespoons unsalted butter
¼ cup (1½ oz/45 g) all-purpose (plain)
 flour
freshly grated nutmeg
½ lb (250 g) whole-milk mozzarella
 cheese, shredded

Bring a large pot three-fourths full of
salted water to a boil. Add the noodles
and cook until al dente, 8–12 minutes.
Drain, immerse in cold water to cool,
drain again and lay on a baking sheet.
Cover with plastic wrap.

❧ In a small bowl, stir together the
ricotta, Parmesan and salt and pepper
to taste; set aside. In a frying pan over
medium-low heat, warm the 2 tablespoons olive oil. Add the leeks and sauté
until very soft and lightly golden, about
30 minutes. Transfer to a bowl; set the
pan and leeks aside.

❧ Have ready a large bowl of water to
which you have added the lemon juice.
Cut off the top half of each artichoke
and remove the tough outer leaves
down to the pale green leaves. Cut off
the base of the stems and peel away
the dark green outer layer. If using large
artichokes, cut in half lengthwise and
scoop out the prickly chokes. Cut the
artichokes, large or small, lengthwise
into thin slices. As each is cut, drop it
into the bowl of lemon water.

❧ Drain the artichokes and add to
the frying pan along with the ½ cup
(4 fl oz/125 ml) water and a large
pinch each of salt and pepper. Cover
and cook over medium heat until the
liquid evaporates and the artichokes
are tender, about 15 minutes. Add the
garlic and cook for 1 minute. Stir into
the leeks. Set aside.

❧ Pour the milk into a saucepan and
bring to just below a boil. In another
saucepan over medium-high heat, melt
the butter. Stir the flour into the butter;
cook, stirring, for 2 minutes. Remove
from the heat and gradually whisk in
the hot milk. Return to medium-low
heat and cook, stirring, until thick and
smooth, 3–4 minutes. Season to taste
with salt, pepper and nutmeg.

❧ Position a rack in the upper part of
an oven and preheat to 375°F (190°C).
Grease a 9-by-13-inch (23-by-33-cm)
baking dish with olive oil. Cover the
bottom with a layer of the noodles.
Spoon one-third of the ricotta mixture
over the noodles. Top with one-third
of the leek-artichoke mixture and then
one-third of the sauce. Repeat the
layering twice. Sprinkle the mozzarella
evenly over the top. Bake until golden
and bubbling, 40–50 minutes. Let stand
for 15 minutes, then cut into squares
to serve.

*Cold in the earth—and
fifteen wild Decembers
From those brown hills
have melted into spring.
—Emily Brontë*

## PARCHMENT-BAKED SCALLOPS AND ASPARAGUS

SERVES 6

*Baking in parchment is an ideal cooking method for springtime, as it accentuates the flavors of the season's fresh ingredients. These packets can be assembled several hours ahead and refrigerated until you bake them. Salmon or sea scallops can be substituted for the bay scallops, and green (spring) onions, sugar snap peas or snow peas can replace all or some of the asparagus.*

1½ lb (750 g) asparagus spears
½ teaspoon grated orange zest
1 tablespoon fresh orange juice
¼ cup (2 oz/60 g) unsalted butter,
   at room temperature
salt and freshly ground pepper
2 lb (1 kg) bay scallops

Preheat an oven to 425°F (220°C).
❧ Cut or snap off the tough stem ends from the asparagus spears and discard. Cut the spears into 1½-inch (4-cm) lengths. Bring a large saucepan three-fourths full of salted water to a boil. Add the asparagus and boil until bright green, about 1 minute. Drain well and set aside.
❧ In a small bowl, using a fork, mash together the orange zest, orange juice, butter and salt and pepper to taste.
❧ Cut out 6 hearts from parchment paper, each one 12 inches (30 cm) high and 12 inches (30 cm) wide at its widest point. Spread the 6 parchment hearts in a single layer on a work surface. Divide the scallops and asparagus evenly among them, placing them on the right half of

each heart. Season to taste with salt and pepper and dot with the orange butter. Fold the left half of each heart over the filling and, beginning at one end, fold and crease the edges together securely so no juices will escape. Place in a single layer on a large baking sheet.
❧ Bake until the packets have puffed considerably, 7–10 minutes. Remove from the oven and place on warmed individual plates. Cut open the top of each packet with scissors and serve immediately.

## PANFRIED SOFT-SHELL CRABS WITH LEMON

SERVES 6

*Soft-shell crabs, a wonderful seasonal sea-food delicacy, are crabs that have molted their hard shells, leaving just the thin, edible casing of their yet-to-develop new shells. If possible, choose meatier female crabs for this recipe: the tips of their claws are redder, and the "aprons"—the flaps of shell on the bellies—are broader than those of male crabs.*

12 soft-shell crabs
2 cups (10 oz/315 g) all-purpose (plain)
   flour
½ teaspoon salt
¼ teaspoon freshly ground pepper
6 tablespoons (3 oz/90 g) unsalted
   butter
lemon wedges
fresh flat-leaf (Italian) parsley sprigs

First, clean the crabs: Place each crab on its back and twist or cut off the small, triangular apron-shaped shell flap; turn the crab over, lift up the shell and,

using your fingers, remove and discard the gray gills. Using scissors, cut off the crab's eyes and mouth. There will be some soft matter just inside this cut. Scoop it out and discard. Rinse the crab and lightly pat it dry with paper towels.
❧ Place the flour in a wide bowl and season it with the salt and pepper. Dredge the crabs lightly in the seasoned flour, tapping off the excess.
❧ Place 2 large frying pans over medium-high heat and add half of the butter to each pan. When it has melted and is foaming, add half of the crabs to each pan in a single layer; do not crowd the pans. Cook until the crabs are reddish brown on the first side, about 3 minutes. Turn them over and cook on the second side until reddish brown, about 3 minutes longer. Using tongs or a slotted spoon, transfer the crabs to paper towels to drain briefly.
❧ Place 2 crabs on each warmed individual plate and garnish with lemon wedges and parsley sprigs. Serve immediately.

# Spring Side Dishes

The fresh produce that now beckons to us from every garden plot, farmers' market and produce store carries the promise of a myriad of side dishes produced with incomparable ease. What could be faster than briefly boiling baby peas or tender asparagus and finishing them with a pat of butter and a sprinkling of herbs? Or what about a rapid sauté of plump mushrooms, glistening with olive oil and scented with garlic? New potatoes, a prized seasonal specialty, need only a short time in a steamer and subtle seasoning to highlight their sweet taste and tender texture.

Even relatively more complicated recipes are actually quite simple. Oven baking and a sour-sweet sauce intensify the rich flavor of Roasted Red and Yellow Beets with Balsamic Glaze (page 61). And chicken stock, fresh parsley and cream lend complex character to the Wild Mushroom Ragout shown at right.

## WILTED SPRING GREENS

SERVES 6

1 bunch broccoli rabe, about
   1¼ lb (625 g)
1 bunch kale, about 1 lb (500 g)
1 bunch Swiss chard, about 1 lb
   (500 g)
2 tablespoons extra-virgin olive oil
2 tablespoons balsamic vinegar
2 cloves garlic, minced
¼ teaspoon red pepper flakes
salt and freshly ground pepper

Trim away any tough stem ends from the broccoli rabe, then cut the stalks crosswise into 2-inch (5-cm) pieces. Trim off the tough kale stems and cut the leaves crosswise into strips 1 inch (2.5 cm) wide. Cut off the white ribs from the Swiss chard and discard. Cut the green leaves crosswise into strips 1 inch (2.5 cm) wide.

❧ In a large frying pan over medium heat, warm the olive oil. Add the broccoli rabe and kale and toss with tongs until they just begin to wilt, about 3 minutes. Add the Swiss chard and continue to toss until the broccoli rabe, kale and Swiss chard have wilted completely but are still bright green, 3–5 minutes longer.

❧ Raise the heat to high and add the balsamic vinegar, garlic and red pepper flakes. Continue to cook, tossing constantly, until the ingredients are well mixed, about 1 minute. Season to taste with salt and pepper.

❧ Transfer to a warmed serving dish and serve immediately.

## WILD MUSHROOM RAGOUT

SERVES 6

1 cup (8 fl oz/250 ml) chicken stock
2 tablespoons chopped fresh flat-leaf
   (Italian) parsley, plus parsley sprigs
   for garnish
2 cloves garlic, minced
2 teaspoons unsalted butter
2 teaspoons extra-virgin olive oil
1 lb (500 g) fresh button mushrooms,
   brushed clean and halved
1 lb (500 g) mixed fresh wild and/or
   cultivated mushrooms, such as
   morels, oyster mushrooms and
   shiitakes, trimmed, brushed clean
   and cut into bite-size pieces
¼ cup (2 fl oz/60 ml) heavy (double)
   cream
salt and freshly ground pepper

In a small saucepan, bring the chicken stock to a boil and boil until reduced by half, 3–5 minutes. Remove from the heat and set aside.

❧ Combine the chopped parsley and garlic on a cutting board and continue to chop together until very finely minced. Set aside.

❧ In a large frying pan over medium-high heat, melt the butter with the olive oil. Add all the mushrooms and sauté, stirring occasionally, until golden and tender, 5–6 minutes. Add the reduced chicken stock, the cream and the garlic-parsley mixture and simmer over medium heat until reduced by half or until nicely thickened, 3–4 minutes. Season to taste with salt and pepper.

❧ To serve, transfer the mushrooms to a warmed serving dish, garnish with parsley sprigs and serve immediately.

## ROASTED RED AND YELLOW BEETS WITH BALSAMIC GLAZE

SERVES 6

*Most beet varieties are available in markets in late spring. Although the most common type sold are deep garnet-red, you'll also find golden beets and even ones with concentric red and white stripes reminiscent of a candy cane. To insure freshness and tenderness, choose small or medium beets with their greens still attached. Remove the greens as soon as you get home, as they will leach moisture from the roots if stored intact over long periods.*

1½ lb (750 g) red beets, with greens attached (see note)
1½ lb (750 g) yellow beets, with greens attached (see note)
2 tablespoons olive oil
¼ cup (2 fl oz/60 ml) water
½ cup (4 fl oz/125 ml) balsamic vinegar
3 tablespoons firmly packed brown sugar
salt and freshly ground pepper

Preheat an oven to 400°F (200°C).

✌ Trim off the beet greens and reserve for another use. Rinse the beets well, but do not peel, and place in a shallow baking dish. In a small bowl, stir together the olive oil and water. Pour the mixture over the beets and toss to coat them completely.

✌ Cover with aluminum foil and bake until the beets are tender when pierced with a skewer, 45–55 minutes. Remove from the oven, uncover and let cool for 10 minutes.

✌ Meanwhile, in a small saucepan, stir together the balsamic vinegar and brown sugar. Bring to a boil over medium heat, stirring to dissolve the sugar. Continue to boil until reduced by one-third, about 10 seconds. Remove from the heat.

✌ Peel the beets by slipping off the skins, then cut them crosswise into thin slices. Place in a warmed serving bowl and drizzle with the balsamic glaze. Season to taste with salt and pepper, toss to coat and serve at once.

## FENNEL AND NEW POTATO GRATIN

SERVES 6

*At their best in early spring, new potatoes are immature tubers measuring only about 1 inch (2.5 cm) in diameter. Their youth gives them thin, soft skins and, because their sugars have not yet turned into starch, a sweet flavor and crisp, waxy texture. Use feathery fennel fronds as a garnish, if you wish.*

1½ lb (750 g) red new potatoes, unpeeled and well scrubbed
3 fennel bulbs
salt and freshly ground pepper
2 cups (16 fl oz/500 ml) heavy (double) cream, or as needed
1 tablespoon Dijon mustard
¾ cup (3 oz/90 g) freshly grated Parmesan cheese

Cut the potatoes crosswise into slices ¼ inch (6 mm) thick. Bring a large saucepan three-fourths full of salted water to a boil. Add the potatoes and boil until tender yet crisp, 10–12 minutes. Drain well.

✌ Meanwhile, cut off the feathery tops and stems from the fennel bulbs and discard. Trim away any yellowed or bruised outer leaves. Cut in half lengthwise and cut out the tough core portions. Then cut crosswise into slices ¼ inch (6 mm) thick.

✌ Bring a large saucepan three-fourths full of salted water to a boil. Add the fennel and boil until tender, 5–10 minutes. Drain well.

✌ Position a rack in the upper part of an oven and preheat to 375°F (190°C). Butter a 9-by-13-inch (23-by-33-cm) baking dish.

✌ Arrange a row of fennel slices along one short end of the prepared baking dish. Arrange a row of potato slices slightly overlapping the fennel. Continue to form overlapping rows of the fennel and potato slices until the vegetables are used up and the dish is filled. Season to taste with salt and pepper. In a bowl, whisk together 2 cups (16 fl oz/500 ml) cream and the mustard. Pour as much of the cream mixture as needed over the fennel and potatoes to bring the liquid almost level with the vegetables. If the liquid is not deep enough, add more cream as needed. Sprinkle evenly with the cheese.

✌ Bake until most of the cream has been absorbed and the top is golden, 30–40 minutes. Remove from the oven and serve immediately.

# Spring Desserts

Although the season provides only a limited selection of good-quality fruits, those that can readily be found possess remarkable versatility. Take the citrus fruits, for example. Their zesty flavor adds delightful appeal to the delicate version of lemon meringue pie featured on this page, as well as to Lemon-Lime Cheesecake (page 70), and lemon curd-layered Spring Celebration Cake (page 66).

Tropical fruits, reasonable in price even though they've traveled to our markets from distant locales, lend intrigue to an equally diverse selection of recipes, including Tropical Fruit Trifle (page 73) and Warm Pineapple Compote (page 75).

The strawberries that begin to enter markets as spring progresses bring with them delightful hints of summer. Rhubarb and Strawberry Crisp (page 65) and White Chocolate Mousse with Strawberries (page 64) offer the first glimpse of the rich, fruity flavors usually associated with the warmer months.

## LEMON CLOUD TART

SERVES 8

*Lemon meringue pie is a favorite recipe of spring, when lemons and eggs are in abundance. This recipe introduces an intriguing variation.*

### FOR THE SHORT-CRUST TART SHELL:
1½ cups (7½ oz/235 g) all-purpose (plain) flour
1½ tablespoons sugar
pinch of salt
¾ cup (6 oz/185 g) unsalted butter, out of the refrigerator for 15 minutes, cut into pieces
about 1½ tablespoons water

### FOR THE LEMON FILLING:
4 egg yolks
⅓ cup (3 oz/90 g) sugar
3 tablespoons grated lemon zest
juice of 2 lemons
3 tablespoons unsalted butter, melted
⅓ cup (1½ oz/45 g) lightly toasted and finely ground blanched almonds

### FOR THE MERINGUE:
3 egg whites, at room temperature
¾ cup (6 oz/185 g) sugar
½ teaspoon vanilla extract (essence)

sugared violets or other spring blossoms (recipe on page 66), optional

To make the tart shell, in a food processor fitted with the metal blade, combine the flour, sugar and salt, and pulse a few times to mix. Add the butter and pulse until the mixture resembles coarse meal. With the motor running, add water as needed to bind the ingredients. Gather into a ball, flatten into a disk 6 inches (15 cm) in diameter and wrap in plastic wrap. Refrigerate for 30 minutes.

❧ Preheat an oven to 400°F (200°C). Gently press the pastry into the bottom and sides of a 9-inch (23-cm) tart pan with a removable bottom, forming a slightly thicker layer on the sides. Place the shell in the freezer for 30 minutes.

❧ Line the pastry with aluminum foil and fill with pie weights. Bake for 10 minutes. Remove the weights and foil and reduce the temperature to 375°F (190°C). Continue to bake until lightly golden, 15–20 minutes longer.

❧ Meanwhile, make the filling: In a bowl, using an electric mixer, beat together the egg yolks and sugar until they form a stiff ribbon that leaves a trail atop the batter when the beater is lifted, about 1 minute. Stir in the lemon zest and juice, then the melted butter and finally the ground almonds.

❧ Remove the tart shell from the oven and immediately pour the filling into it. Return it to the oven and bake until a skewer inserted into the center comes out clean, 20–30 minutes. Transfer to a rack and let cool completely.

❧ Raise the oven temperature to 450°F (230°C). To make the meringue, using an electric mixer, beat the egg whites until soft peaks form. Slowly add the sugar while continuing to beat until stiff peaks form. Fold in the vanilla. Spoon the meringue over the cooled filling, spreading it to the edges of the pastry and forming peaks.

❧ Bake until the meringue is golden brown, about 7 minutes. Let cool and chill until set, about 1 hour. Garnish each serving with sugared blossoms, if desired. Serve chilled.

## WHITE CHOCOLATE MOUSSE WITH STRAWBERRIES

SERVES 6

*Strawberries are members of the rose family and have long grown wild in Europe and the Americas. Today, they are cultivated almost year-round, although they are sweetest and juiciest during their peak, from April to June. White chocolate marries especially well with their wonderful flavor.*

2 cups (8 oz/240 g) strawberries, stems removed

¼ cup (2 oz/60 g) sugar

1 tablespoon kirsch or framboise

6 oz (185 g) white chocolate, finely chopped

¼ cup (2 fl oz/60 ml) milk, warmed

1 cup (8 fl oz/250 ml) heavy (double) cream

2 egg whites, at room temperature

pinch of cream of tartar

¾ teaspoon vanilla extract (essence)

In a blender or in a food processor fitted with the metal blade, combine 1½ cups (6 oz/180 g) of the strawberries with the sugar. Purée until smooth. Strain through a fine-mesh sieve into a bowl. Add the kirsch or framboise and stir until blended. Cut the remaining ½ cup (2 oz/60 g) strawberries lengthwise into thin slices and stir into the purée. Set aside.

❧ Place the chocolate in a heatproof bowl set over a pan of gently simmering water; do not allow the bowl to touch the water. Heat the chocolate, stirring occasionally, until it is melted and smooth and registers 140°F (60°C) on an instant-read thermometer. Gradually add the warm milk to the chocolate, stirring constantly until smooth. Re-move the bowl from the pan of water and let the mixture cool until it is almost at room temperature.

❧ In a bowl, using an electric mixer on high speed, beat the cream just until soft peaks form. In another bowl, using clean beaters, beat together the egg whites and cream of tartar on high speed until stiff peaks form. Using a rubber spatula, fold half of the whites into the chocolate mixture to lighten it. Fold the remaining whites, whipped cream and vanilla into the chocolate mixture just until combined and no white drifts remain. Do not overmix. (At this point, you may cover and refrigerate the mousse for up to 1 day.)

❧ To serve, spoon about half of the mousse into 6 parfait glasses, half filling each glass. Top with the strawberry sauce, again using about half and dividing it equally. Repeat with the remaining mousse and strawberry sauce.

# RHUBARB AND STRAWBERRY CRISP

SERVES 8

*Over two centuries ago, English cooks first recognized the culinary potential of rhubarb, until then regarded as an ornamental plant. Although actually a hardy perennial vegetable, rhubarb is generally treated as a fruit and often combined with strawberries, which are also harvested in the spring. Be sure to trim off the toxic leaves from the stalks before using. Serve this sprightly crisp à la mode and garnish with long-stemmed fraises des bois, if you like.*

### FOR THE CRISP TOPPING:

¾ cup (3 oz/90 g) pecan halves

1½ cups (7½ oz/235 g) all-purpose (plain) flour

½ cup (3½ oz/105 g) firmly packed brown sugar

1½ teaspoons grated orange zest

¼ teaspoon ground nutmeg

½ cup (4 oz/125 g) unsalted butter, at room temperature

### FOR THE FRUIT FILLING:

1½ lb (750 g) rhubarb

2 cups (8 oz/250 g) strawberries, stems removed and halved lengthwise

3 tablespoons all-purpose (plain) flour

½ cup (4 oz/125 g) granulated sugar, or as needed

To make the topping, preheat an oven to 350°F (180°C). Spread the pecans on a baking sheet and place in the oven until lightly toasted and fragrant, 5–7 minutes. Remove from the oven and let cool. Raise the oven temperature to 375°F (190°C).

❧ Place the nuts in a food processor fitted with the metal blade and pulse several times to form ¼-inch (6-mm) pieces. Transfer the nuts to a small bowl and set aside. In another bowl, stir together the flour, brown sugar, orange zest and nutmeg. Add the flour mixture and butter to the food processor and pulse until the mixture just begins to hold together. Add the nuts and pulse 3 or 4 more times until well mixed.

❧ To make the filling, trim the tough ends and the leaves from the rhubarb stalks and then cut crosswise into 1-inch (2.5-cm) pieces. Place in a bowl with the strawberries, flour and ½ cup (4 oz/125 g) sugar, adding more sugar if the strawberries are not particularly sweet. Toss until well mixed. Place the fruit in a 2–2½-qt (2–2.5-l) gratin dish or other shallow baking dish and sprinkle evenly with the topping.

❧ Bake until a skewer inserted into the center enters without any resistance and the top is golden and bubbling around the edges, 35–40 minutes. Remove from the oven and let cool for 20 minutes before serving.

❧ To serve, spoon the crisp into individual dishes.

## SPRING CELEBRATION CAKE

SERVES 10

*Tart ribbons of lemon curd separate the dense layers of this delightful cake. For a seasonal flourish, garnish with a sprinkling of sugared violets, or substitute rose petals, pansies or any of your other favorite edible flower varieties.*

**FOR THE VANILLA CAKE:**
6 eggs
1 cup (8 oz/250 g) granulated sugar
1 teaspoon vanilla extract (essence)
1⅓ cups (5½ oz/170 g) sifted
    all-purpose (plain) flour
pinch of salt
1 tablespoon grated lemon zest

**FOR THE SUGARED VIOLETS (OPTIONAL):**
40 pesticide-free violets
2 egg whites, at room temperature
2 teaspoons water
2 cups (14 oz/440 g) superfine (castor)
    sugar

**FOR THE LEMON CURD:**
3 egg yolks
¼ cup (2 oz/60 g) granulated sugar
2 tablespoons grated lemon zest
5 tablespoons (2½ fl oz/75 ml) fresh
    lemon juice
3 tablespoons unsalted butter, cut
    into 6 equal pieces

**FOR THE LEMON SUGAR SYRUP:**
⅓ cup (3 oz/90 g) granulated sugar
⅓ cup (3 fl oz/80 ml) water
3 tablespoons fresh lemon juice

1 cup (8 fl oz/250 ml) heavy (double)
    cream
2 tablespoons confectioners' (icing)
    sugar
½ teaspoon vanilla extract

To make the cake, preheat an oven to 350°F (180°C). Butter two 8-inch (20-cm) round cake pans and line the bottoms with parchment paper.

❧ In a bowl, using an electric mixer, beat together the eggs, sugar and vanilla until a stiff ribbon forms that leaves a trail atop the batter when the beater is lifted, about 1 minute. Sift together half of the flour and the pinch of salt over the eggs and sugar. Add the lemon zest and fold the wet and dry ingredients together partially. Sift the remaining flour over the top and fold in until mixed. Pour the batter into the prepared pans, dividing it evenly.

❧ Bake until a skewer inserted into the center of a cake comes out clean and the top springs back when lightly pressed, 30–35 minutes. Transfer to a rack and let cool for 15 minutes. Run a knife blade around the edges of the cakes, invert onto the rack and remove the pans and parchment.

❧ To make the sugared violets, if desired, carefully snip off the stem from each violet, then rinse gently and place on paper towels to dry. In a bowl, beat together the egg whites and water until frothy. Using some of the sugar, spread a thin layer over a large plate. Holding each flower by its base and using a pastry brush, paint each violet on both sides with a thin coating of egg white. Then sprinkle lightly on both sides with sugar. Place in a single layer on the sugared plate and let dry for 2 hours before using. (You can store the violets in single layers between sheets of waxed paper in an airtight container at room temperature for up to 2 weeks before serving.)

❧ To make the lemon curd, in a heat-proof bowl, whisk together the egg yolks, sugar and lemon zest and juice until blended. Place over (not touching) simmering water in a pan and whisk vigorously until the foam disappears and the mixture is very thick, about 10 minutes. Whisk in the butter until melted. Reduce the heat to low and continue to cook, stirring constantly, until very thick, about 5 minutes longer. Remove from the heat and whisk for 2 minutes. Cover with plastic wrap placed directly on the curd; set aside to cool.

❧ To make the sugar syrup, in a saucepan over medium heat, bring the sugar, water and lemon juice to a boil, stirring to dissolve the sugar. Boil for 30 seconds. Remove from the heat and let cool for at least 15 minutes.

❧ Place 1 cake layer, top side up, on a serving plate. Puncture in several places with a fork and drizzle with half of the sugar syrup. Spread the lemon curd evenly onto the cake. Place the second cake layer, top side up, over the first and repeat with the fork and remaining sugar syrup. In a bowl, beat together the cream, confectioners' sugar and vanilla until almost-stiff peaks form. Spread over the top and sides of the cake. Chill for at least 30 minutes or for up to 2 hours. Sprinkle with violets just before serving.

*Can words describe the fragrance of the very breath of spring?*
—*Neltje Blanchan*

# MARZIPAN CAKE

SERVES 8–10

*In countries where almonds are grown, the harvest begins in late spring and the fresh nuts are much prized. Drying, however, makes this versatile nut available year-round, and the almond-sugar paste known as marzipan extends the range of its uses. Top slices of this moist cake with fresh strawberries and softly whipped cream, or offer it plain with tea or coffee.*

1 cup (8 oz/250 g) sugar
6 oz (185 g) marzipan
¾ cup (6 oz/185 g) unsalted butter, at
    room temperature
¼ teaspoon almond extract (essence)
5 eggs, at room temperature
¾ cup (4 oz/125 g) plus 2 tablespoons
    all-purpose (plain) flour
1¼ teaspoons baking powder
¼ teaspoon salt

Preheat an oven to 350°F (180°C). Butter an 8½-by-4½-by-2½-inch (21-by-11-by-6-cm) loaf pan and then dust with flour. Tap out the excess flour.
❧ Using an electric mixer or a food processor fitted with the metal blade, pulverize together the sugar and marzipan until the mixture is in fine pieces. If a food processor was used, transfer the mixture to a large bowl. Add the butter and almond extract and mix until light and fluffy, 1–2 minutes. Add the eggs, one at a time, beating well after each addition until thoroughly combined. Sift together the flour, baking powder and salt over the egg mixture and beat in just until thoroughly blended.
❧ Pour the batter into the prepared pan. Bake until a toothpick inserted into the center comes out clean and the top springs back when lightly pressed, about 1¼ hours. Transfer the pan to a rack and let cool for 15 minutes. Run a knife blade around the edge of the cake and invert onto the rack. Lift off the pan and cool the cake upright on the rack for at least 30 minutes before serving.

# BLOOD ORANGE AND MANGO SHERBET

SERVES 6

*Blood oranges are so abundant in Sicily that it is not uncommon to greet each morning with a big glass of their fresh-squeezed juice. Today, they are also propagated in the United States, and are in season from January through late spring. You may substitute limes, lemons (especially the Meyer variety), oranges or grapefruit. For a fanciful presentation, scrape any remaining pulp from the orange halves after juicing, then freeze and use as frosted serving cups.*

4 large ripe mangoes
3 lb (1.5 kg) blood oranges
about 1 cup (8 oz/240 g) sugar
candied citrus zest (recipe on page 70),
    optional

Working with 1 mango at a time, cut off the flesh from each side of the large, flat pit to form 2 large pieces. Trim any remaining flesh from around the edge of the pit then discard the pit. Using a knife, peel away and discard the skin. Place in a food processor fitted with the metal blade or in a blender.
❧ Finely grate the zest from 2 blood oranges and set aside. Juice all the oranges and strain through a coarse-mesh sieve into the food processor or blender, pushing as much of the pulp through the sieve as possible. Process until smooth. Add the grated zest and process briefly to mix.
❧ Measure the fruit purée; you should have about 4 cups (32 fl oz/1 l). For each 1 cup (8 fl oz/250 ml) fruit purée, measure out ¼ cup (2 oz/60 g) sugar. To dissolve the sugar, pour approximately one-fourth of the fruit purée into a small saucepan and add the measured sugar. Stir well and place over medium-high heat, stirring constantly, until the sugar dissolves, 3–4 minutes. Pour the contents of the saucepan back into the fruit purée and stir to distribute evenly. Cover and place in the refrigerator until well chilled, about 2 hours.
❧ Freeze in an ice cream maker according to the manufacturer's instructions. To serve, spoon into individual serving dishes and garnish with candied citrus zest, if you wish.

# LEMON-LIME CHEESECAKE

SERVES 12

*If you like, make a glaze for this rich dessert by whisking together 1 tablespoon fresh lemon juice and 3 tablespoons sifted confectioners' (icing) sugar. Brush the glaze over the cake just before serving. Arrange candied citrus zest on the top, if you like.*

**FOR THE CRUST:**

3 tablespoons granulated sugar

¼ cup (2 oz/60 g) unsalted butter, at room temperature

1½ teaspoons grated lemon zest

1 egg yolk

1 cup (5 oz/155 g) all-purpose (plain) flour

¼ teaspoon baking powder

pinch of salt

**FOR THE LEMON-LIME FILLING:**

1¼ lb (625 g) cream cheese, at room temperature

¾ cup (6 oz/185 g) granulated sugar

¾ cup (6 fl oz/180 ml) sour cream

1 tablespoon grated lemon zest

1 tablespoon grated lime zest

2 tablespoons fresh lemon juice

2 tablespoons fresh lime juice

4 eggs

**FOR THE CANDIED CITRUS ZEST (OPTIONAL):**

2 oranges, blood oranges or tangerines

1 lemon

1 lime

1 grapefruit

3½ cups (1½ lb/750 g) superfine (castor) sugar

¾ cup (6 fl oz/180 ml) water

Preheat an oven to 325°F (165°C). Butter the bottom of a 9-inch (23-cm) springform cake pan and line the bottom with parchment paper cut to fit precisely. Wrap aluminum foil around the outside of the pan to prevent seepage during baking.

To make the crust, in a food processor fitted with the metal blade, combine the sugar and butter and process until light and fluffy. Add the lemon zest and yolk and process until smooth. In a bowl, sift together the flour, baking powder and salt and add to the processor. Pulse a few times until mixed but still crumbly.

Gather the dough together and press it evenly over the bottom of the prepared pan. Bake until golden, 25–30 minutes. Let cool on a rack.

Meanwhile, make the filling: Using an electric mixer, beat the cream cheese on low speed until smooth. Slowly beat in the sugar. Add the sour cream and lemon and lime zest and juice and beat until blended. Add the eggs, one at a time, beating after each addition only until each has been absorbed. Scrape down the sides of the bowl and beat just until blended.

Pour the filling over the crust and place the pan inside a larger baking pan. Pour hot water into the larger pan to a depth of ½ inch (12 mm). Bake until golden brown and firm to the touch, 1–1¼ hours. Transfer the cheesecake pan to a rack and let cool. Cover with foil and chill overnight.

To make the candied citrus zest, using a vegetable peeler, remove the zest from all the fruits, making the longest strips possible. Place the strips on a work surface, pith side up, and, using a sharp paring knife, scrape away any white pith. Cut the zest into very thin strips about 2 inches (5 cm) long.

In a saucepan over medium heat, combine 1½ cups (10 oz/310 g) of the sugar and the water. Cover and bring to a simmer. Simmer, stirring, for 30 seconds to dissolve the sugar. Add all the zests, cover and simmer for 3 minutes. Let cool.

Using a slotted spoon, transfer the zests to paper towels to drain. Place the remaining 2 cups (14 oz/440 g) sugar on a baking sheet. Toss the zest in the sugar, separating the pieces. (To store, layer the candied zest in additional sugar in a covered container in the refrigerator; it will keep indefinitely.)

To serve, remove the foil and pan sides and carefully slide the cake off the pan bottom onto a serving plate. Serve chilled, cut into wedges.

# TROPICAL FRUIT TRIFLE

SERVES 10

**FOR THE SPONGE CAKE:**

6 eggs, separated, at room temperature

¾ cup (6 oz/185 g) sugar

1 teaspoon vanilla extract (essence)

⅔ cup (3½ oz/105 g) all-purpose (plain) flour

⅓ cup (1½ oz/45 g) cake (soft-wheat) flour

pinch of salt

¾ cup (6 fl oz/180 ml) heavy (double) cream

6 egg yolks

1 cup (8 oz/240 g) sugar

½ cup (4 fl oz/125 ml) orange liqueur such as Grand Marnier or Mandarin Napoleon

3 cups (12 oz/375 g) strawberries, hulled

4 mangoes, peeled and pitted

½ cup (4 fl oz/125 ml) pineapple juice

¼ cup (2 fl oz/60 ml) dark rum

seeds and juice from 6 passion fruits

To make the sponge cake, preheat an oven to 350°F (180°C).

❧ Butter and lightly flour an 11½-by-17½-inch (28.5-by-44-cm) jelly-roll pan. Line the bottom with parchment paper. In a bowl, using an electric mixer, beat together the egg yolks, sugar and vanilla until thick and tripled in volume, about 1 minute. Sift half of the flours and salt over the eggs and sugar and, using a rubber spatula, fold together partially. Sift the remaining flour mixture over the top and fold in until mixed. In another bowl, beat the egg whites to soft peaks. Fold half of the whites into the batter to lighten it. Then fold in the remaining whites. Spread the batter evenly into the prepared pan.

❧ Bake until the top springs back when lightly pressed, about 15 minutes. Let cool in the pan on a rack. Invert onto the rack and remove the pan and parchment. Cut into 4 equal sections and let stand until dry, 12–24 hours.

❧ In a bowl, beat the cream to soft peaks. Cover and refrigerate.

❧ Fill a bowl one-fourth full with ice water. In a heatproof bowl, combine the egg yolks, 6 tablespoons (3 oz/90 g) of the sugar and the liqueur. Place over (not touching) simmering water in a pan; whisk vigorously until tripled in volume and soft mounds form, about 5 minutes. Nest the bowl in the ice water; whisk until cold. Fold in the whipped cream, cover and refrigerate.

❧ In a blender, combine the strawberries and 5 tablespoons (2½ oz/75 g) of the remaining sugar; purée until smooth. Strain into a bowl; set aside. Put the mangoes and the remaining 5 tablespoons (2½ oz/75 g) sugar in the blender; purée until smooth. Strain into another bowl; set aside.

❧ To assemble the trifle, spread one-fourth of the strawberry purée over the bottom of a 2½-qt (2.5-l) straight-sided glass bowl. Trim 1 of the cake sections to fit in the bowl and place it and the trimmed pieces over the purée. In a small bowl, combine the pineapple juice and rum and sprinkle 3 tablespoons of the mixture over the cake. Drizzle with one-fourth of the passion fruit seeds and juice, then with one-fourth of the mango purée, and top with one-fourth of the orange cream. Repeat the layering three more times, starting with the berry purée. Cover and refrigerate for at least 8 hours before serving.

*Let my beloved come*
*to his garden,*
*And eat its choicest fruits.*
*—Song of Solomon*

## COCONUT MACAROONS

MAKES ABOUT 3½ DOZEN

*These rich, chewy cookies are inspired by a recipe from Lindsey Shere, the former pastry chef at Chez Panisse in Berkeley, California, and the author of* Chez Panisse Desserts. *Served alongside choco-late eggs and other springtime confections, they are the perfect conclusion to an Easter brunch. Drizzle them with melted chocolate before serving, if you like.*

¾ cup (4 oz/125 g) blanched almonds
2 cups (6 oz/185 g) unsweetened,
    flaked dried coconut
2 egg whites, at room temperature
¼ teaspoon cream of tartar
¾ cup (6 oz/185 g) sugar

Preheat an oven to 350°F (180°C). Spread the almonds on a baking sheet and place in the oven until lightly toasted and fragrant, 5–7 minutes. Remove from the oven, let cool and chop finely. Set aside.

~❧ Raise the oven temperature to 375°F (190°C). Line the same baking sheet with parchment paper.

~❧ Spread the coconut evenly on the parchment-lined baking sheet and bake, stirring often, until golden, 5–10 minutes. Remove from the oven and transfer to a bowl to cool. Reduce the oven temperature to 325°F (165°C). Leave the parchment paper on the baking sheet.

~❧ In another bowl, combine the egg whites and cream of tartar. Using an electric mixer on high speed, beat until stiff peaks form. Gradually add the sugar and continue beating until stiff peaks form again. Using a rubber spatula, gently fold in the nuts and coconut, distributing them as evenly as you can. Be careful not to deflate the mixture.

❧ For each cookie, scoop up about 1 teaspoon of the egg white mixture and shape it into a 1-inch (2.5-cm) ball with your fingers. Place the balls on the parchment-lined baking sheet, spacing them about 1 inch (2.5 cm) apart.

❧ Bake until lightly golden, 14–16 minutes. Remove from the oven, transfer to a rack and let cool. Store in an airtight container at room temperature for up to 2 days.

## WARM PINEAPPLE COMPOTE

SERVES 6

*Pineapples are available year-round with peak season from March through June. This warm compote is also delicious served with pound cake and softly whipped cream or atop a generous scoop of vanilla ice cream.*

1 pineapple, about 4 lb (2 kg)

¼ cup (2 fl oz/60 ml) dark rum

½ cup (3 oz/90 g) golden raisins (sultanas)

3 tablespoons unsalted butter

¼ cup (2 oz/60 g) firmly packed dark brown sugar

½ cup (4 fl oz/125 ml) pineapple juice

Grasp the leafy top of the pineapple and twist it off. Using a sharp knife, cut off the top just below the crown. Cut a slice ½ inch (12 mm) thick off the bottom. Place the pineapple upright and, using a sharp knife, cut off the peel in vertical strips. Using the knife tip, cut out the round "eyes" on the pineapple sides. Cut the pineapple lengthwise into quarters and cut out the core. Cut each quarter in half lengthwise, then cut each piece crosswise into slices ½ inch (12 mm) thick.

❧ In a saucepan over medium heat, heat the rum until bubbles appear along the pan edges, about 1 minute. Add the raisins, stir once or twice and remove from the heat. Set aside, stirring occasionally, until cool, about 30 minutes. Drain the raisins, reserving the rum and raisins separately.

❧ In a large frying pan over high heat, melt 1 tablespoon of the butter. When hot, add half of the pineapple slices and cook until golden on the first side, about 2 minutes. Turn over the pineapple slices and cook on the second side until golden, about 2 minutes longer. Using a slotted spoon, transfer to a plate. Repeat with the remaining pine-

apple and another tablespoon of the butter and set aside with the first batch. Wash and dry the pan.

❧ Place the pan over medium-high heat and add the remaining 1 tablespoon butter. When it melts, add the brown sugar and heat, stirring, until the sugar melts, 1–2 minutes. Add the pineapple juice and cook until reduced by half, 1–2 minutes. Add the raisins, 1 tablespoon of the reserved rum and the pineapple. Mix together gently and cook until the pineapple is heated through, 1–2 minutes.

❧ To serve, spoon into individual serving bowls and serve at once.

# Summer

❧

# Summer Openers

The summer harvest is one of sun-ripened flavors ideal for tempting appetites at the start of a meal. Vegetable fruits, which grow plump and sweet during the long, warm days, capture attention in such specialties as Fettuccine with Golden Tomatoes (page 82), Stuffed Zucchini Flowers (page 85) or the Tomato and Onion Tart shown at right. Summer's succulent fruits, too, take their rightful turn in recipes like Figs, Prosciutto and St. André Cheese and Sparkling Fruit Wine (both on page 86).

The sweet corn crop is at its best right now. Crisp, juicy kernels of gold and white explode with sweet flavor in Corn and Red Pepper Fritters and Smoked Shellfish Quesadillas with Fresh Corn Salsa (both on page 81). If possible, buy your corn from a farm stand or farmers' market to be assured of recently picked ears whose natural sugars have not had time to turn to starch.

## TOMATO AND ONION TART

MAKES ONE 10-INCH (25-CM) TART; SERVES 6–8

*In France, simple country tarts like this one often form the centerpiece of a sunny picnic lunch. If you are short of time, ¾ pound (375 g) store-bought puff pastry can be substituted for the homemade.*

3 ripe but firm tomatoes, 8–10 oz (250–315 g) total, cut into slices ¼ inch (6 mm) thick
1 cup (5 oz/155 g) all-purpose (plain) flour, frozen for 1 hour
⅓ cup (1½ oz/45 g) cake (soft-wheat) flour, frozen for 1 hour
¼ teaspoon salt
¾ cup (6 oz/185 g) unsalted butter, cut into pieces, frozen for 1 hour
2 teaspoons fresh lemon juice, chilled
¼ cup (2 fl oz/60 ml) ice water
1 cup (4 oz/125 g) shredded mozzarella cheese
½ cup (2 oz/60 g) freshly grated Parmesan cheese
1½ tablespoons chopped fresh oregano
¼ cup (1 oz/30 g) thinly sliced yellow onion, separated into rings

Place the tomato slices on paper towels and let drain for 1 hour.

❧ Place both flours, the salt and butter in a food processor fitted with the metal blade and pulse until the mixture resembles pea-size crumbs. Transfer to a bowl. In a small cup, combine the lemon juice and ice water and add to the bowl. Using a fork, mix until the dough almost holds together.

❧ Turn out the dough onto a lightly floured work surface and press together to form a rough rectangle shape. Large chunks of butter will be visible. Using a rolling pin, roll out into a rectangle about 8 by 12 inches (20 by 30 cm) and ½ inch (12 mm) thick. Fold in the 8-inch (20-cm) sides to meet in the center. Then fold in half to make a rough square forming 4 layers. This is your first turn.

❧ Turn the dough a quarter of a turn and roll out again into a rectangle 8 by 12 inches (20 by 30 cm) and ½ inch (12 mm) thick. Repeat the folding. This is your second turn. Again make a quarter turn and roll out into the same-sized rectangle. Now fold into thirds as you would a business letter. Wrap in plastic wrap and chill for 1 hour.

❧ Position a rack in the top part of an oven. Preheat to 400°F (200°C).

❧ Roll out the dough on a lightly floured work surface into a round 12 inches (30 cm) in diameter. Trim the edges so that they are even, and then crimp to form sides ½ inch (12 mm) thick. Transfer to an ungreased baking sheet and sprinkle evenly with the mozzarella, ¼ cup (1 oz/30 g) of the Parmesan and the oregano. Arrange the tomato slices in concentric circles, overlapping slightly, on the cheese. Scatter the onion rings and then the remaining ¼ cup (1 oz/30 g) Parmesan over the tomatoes.

❧ Bake until the crust is golden and the top is crispy, 25–35 minutes. Serve immediately.

## SMOKED SHELLFISH QUESADILLAS WITH FRESH CORN SALSA

SERVES 6

### FOR THE SALSA:

2 cups (12 oz/375 g) corn kernels
    (from 3 ears)
5 tablespoons (½ oz/15 g) chopped
    fresh cilantro (fresh coriander)
3 green (spring) onions, thinly sliced
3 tablespoons fresh lime juice
½–1 fresh jalapeño or serrano chili
    pepper, seeded and minced
salt and freshly ground pepper

### FOR THE QUESADILLAS:

6 oz (185 g) smoked shellfish such as
    mussels, shrimp (prawns) or scallops
5 green (spring) onions, thinly sliced
¾ cup (3 oz/90 g) shredded pepper
    Jack cheese
¾ cup (3 oz/90 g) shredded mozzarella
    cheese
¾ cup (3 oz/90 g) shredded white
    Cheddar cheese
6 flour tortillas, each 8–9 inches
    (20–23 cm) in diameter

To make the salsa, bring a saucepan
three-fourths full of water to a boil. Add
the corn kernels and cook for 1 minute.
Drain and let cool. In a bowl, combine
the corn, cilantro, green onions, lime
juice and chili pepper. Mix well and
season to taste with salt and pepper.
You should have about 2½ cups
(15 oz/470 g). Set aside.

❧ To make the quesadillas, in a bowl,
combine the shellfish, green onions and
Jack, mozzarella and Cheddar cheeses.
Toss to mix. Distribute the mixture
evenly over 3 tortillas and top with the
remaining 3 tortillas.

❧ Place a nonstick frying pan over
medium heat. When hot, add the

tortillas and cook, turning once, until
the cheese is melted throughout,
4–6 minutes total.

❧ Transfer to a cutting board and cut
each quesadilla into 6 wedges. Place on
a serving plate and serve with the salsa.

## CORN AND RED PEPPER FRITTERS WITH RED PEPPER COULIS

MAKES ABOUT 24 FRITTERS; SERVES 6

1 cup (5 oz/155 g) all-purpose (plain)
    flour
½ teaspoon salt, plus salt to taste
2 eggs, separated
2 tablespoons olive oil
¾ cup (6 fl oz/180 ml) flat beer, at
    room temperature
5 red bell peppers (capsicums)
6 tablespoons (3 fl oz/90 ml) heavy
    (double) cream
2 tablespoons sour cream
1 teaspoon balsamic vinegar
cayenne pepper and freshly ground
    black pepper
canola oil for frying
2 cups (12 oz/375 g) corn kernels
    (from 3 ears)
⅓ cup (½ oz/15 g) snipped fresh chives

In a bowl, sift together the flour and
the ½ teaspoon salt. Make a well in the
center. In a small bowl, beat the egg
yolks and add to the well along with the
olive oil and beer. Whisk to blend. Let
stand at room temperature for 1 hour.

❧ Preheat a broiler (griller). Cut
each bell pepper in half lengthwise and
remove the stem, seeds and ribs. Place,
cut sides down, on a baking sheet and
broil (grill) until the skins are blackened
and blistered. Remove from the broiler
and cover loosely with aluminum foil.
Let steam for about 10 minutes, then

peel off the skins. Finely dice 4 of the
pepper halves and set aside.

❧ To make the coulis, place the remaining peppers in a blender and purée
until smooth. In a bowl, mix the heavy
cream and sour cream. Add the pepper
purée and whisk until the cream
thickens slightly. Add the vinegar and
season to taste with cayenne pepper, salt
and black pepper. Cover and refrigerate
until needed.

❧ Pour canola oil into a deep, heavy
sauté pan to a depth of 1 inch (2.5 cm).
Heat to 375°F (190°C) on a deep-
frying thermometer.

❧ Meanwhile, add the corn, diced
peppers, chives and salt and black
pepper to taste to the prepared batter.
Using a whisk or an electric mixer, beat
the egg whites until stiff peaks form.
Using a spatula, fold the whites into the
batter just until no white drifts remain.

❧ Working in batches, drop the batter
by heaping tablespoonfuls into the oil;
do not crowd the pan. Cook, turning
once, until golden brown, 1–2 minutes
total. Using a slotted spoon, transfer
to paper towels to drain briefly, then
arrange on a warmed platter. Drizzle
the coulis over the fritters. Serve hot.

# FETTUCCINE WITH GOLDEN TOMATOES AND BREAD CRUMBS

SERVES 6

*Wedges of large yellow tomatoes or halved yellow pear-shaped cherry tomatoes make an attractive and tasty addition to this dish. Just before serving the pasta, mix the tomatoes with 1 tablespoon extra-virgin olive oil in a frying pan over high heat and stir constantly until warm, 1–2 minutes. Then toss with the hot pasta and fresh tomato sauce.*

**FOR THE YELLOW TOMATO SAUCE:**

5 lb (2.5 kg) yellow tomatoes, cored
    and quartered
1 small red (Spanish) onion, peeled
    but left whole
3 fresh basil sprigs
4 cloves garlic
salt and freshly ground pepper

1 cup (2 oz/60 g) very coarse fresh
    bread crumbs
2 tablespoons extra-virgin olive oil
salt and freshly ground pepper
¾ lb (375 g) dried fettuccine
½ cup (2 oz/60 g) freshly grated
    Parmesan cheese

To make the yellow tomato sauce, in a large pot over medium-high heat, combine the tomatoes, onion, basil and garlic. Bring to a boil, reduce the heat to medium-low and simmer, uncovered, until much of the liquid has evaporated, about 2 hours.

❧ Remove the onion and discard. Pass the sauce through a food mill fitted with the fine disk into a clean bowl. Alternatively, let cool slightly and purée the sauce in a food processor fitted with the metal blade, then strain through a coarse-mesh sieve into a clean bowl. You should have about 3 cups (24 fl oz/ 750 ml). Season to taste with salt and pepper. Use immediately, or let cool completely, cover and refrigerate for up to 3 days or freeze for up to 3 months.

❧ Preheat an oven to 375°F (190°C).

❧ Spread the bread crumbs on a baking sheet. Drizzle with the olive oil and toss to distribute the oil evenly. Season to taste with salt and pepper. Bake, tossing occasionally, until golden brown, 8–10 minutes. Remove from the oven and let cool.

❧ Bring a large pot three-fourths full of salted water to a rolling boil over high heat. Add the pasta, stir well and cook until al dente (tender but firm to the bite), 10–12 minutes or according to the package directions.

❧ Meanwhile, heat the tomato sauce in a saucepan over medium-high heat, stirring occasionally, until hot, 3–5 minutes.

❧ When the pasta is done, drain and transfer to a warmed serving bowl. Pour on the tomato sauce, toss well and season to taste with salt and pepper. Toss the bread crumbs with the Parmesan cheese and sprinkle over the top. Serve immediately.

*In a summer season when soft was the sun.*
*— William Langland*

# RISOTTO WITH OVEN-DRIED TOMATOES AND BASIL

SERVES 6

*Oven-drying is an excellent way to prolong the shelf life of a bumper crop of tomatoes. Plum tomatoes are the best choice because their flesh is dense. Once dried, they can be stored in a cool, dark place for up to 7 days or frozen for up to 2 months. Purchased dried tomatoes can be substituted; use 3 ounces (90 g) and add them just before the risotto is removed from the heat.*

1½ lb (750 g) ripe but firm plum
    (Roma) tomatoes
1 teaspoon kosher salt
3 cups (24 fl oz/750 ml) chicken stock
3 cups (24 fl oz/750 ml) water
1½ cups (9 oz/280 g) peeled, seeded
    and chopped tomatoes
3 tablespoons extra-virgin olive oil
1 yellow onion, finely chopped
1½ cups (10½ oz/330 g) Arborio rice
1½ tablespoons balsamic vinegar
2 cloves garlic, finely chopped
3 tablespoons finely chopped fresh
    flat-leaf (Italian) parsley
salt and freshly ground pepper
20 fresh basil leaves, cut into thin strips,
    or basil sprigs for garnish

Core the whole tomatoes and cut in half lengthwise. Place, cut sides up, on a baking sheet and sprinkle with the kosher salt. Let stand for 1 hour.

❧ Preheat an oven to 275°F (135°C). Bake the tomatoes until dry, yet still soft, 5–6 hours. Let cool, then set aside.

❧ In a saucepan, combine the stock, water and chopped tomatoes and bring to a boil. Reduce the heat to low and maintain a gentle simmer.

❧ In a large, heavy frying pan over medium heat, warm the olive oil. Add the onion and sauté, stirring, until soft, about 10 minutes. Add the rice and stir constantly until the edges of the grains are translucent, about 4 minutes.

❧ Increase the heat to medium-high, add a ladleful of the simmering stock mixture and cook, stirring constantly. When the liquid is almost fully absorbed, add another ladleful. Stir steadily to keep the rice from sticking and continue to add more liquid, a ladleful at a time, as soon as each previous ladleful is almost absorbed. The risotto is done when it is creamy and the rice is tender but firm, 20–25 minutes total. If you run out of stock before the rice is tender, use hot water.

❧ Remove the risotto from the heat, cover and let stand for 5 minutes. Stir in 1 ladleful stock (or water), the vinegar, garlic, parsley and oven-dried tomatoes. Season to taste with salt and pepper. Transfer to a large warmed platter or individual shallow bowls and garnish with basil. Serve immediately.

# STUFFED ZUCCHINI FLOWERS

SERVES 6

*Zucchini flowers (pictured on pages 280–281) enjoy a short season during the summer months when zucchini plants begin to bloom.*

24 zucchini (courgette) flowers
2 cups (16 fl oz/500 ml) water, or
    as needed
1⅔ cups (9 oz/280 g) all-purpose
    (plain) flour, or as needed
½ teaspoon salt, plus salt to taste
⅛ teaspoon freshly ground pepper
6 anchovy fillets packed in olive oil,
    drained and chopped
olive oil for frying
10 oz (315 g) mozzarella cheese, diced
lemon wedges

Detach the green stems and leaves from the zucchini flowers and gently remove any pistils. Wash the flowers quickly under cold running water and dry gently with paper towels.

❧ Pour the 2 cups (16 fl oz/500 ml) water into a bowl. In another bowl, sift together the flour, the ½ teaspoon salt and the pepper. Then sift the flour mixture into the water while stirring constantly. The batter should be the consistency of thick heavy (double) cream. If it is too thin, add additional flour; if it is too thick, add additional water. Let stand for 30 minutes.

❧ Meanwhile, place the anchovies in a small bowl and add water to cover; let soak for 10 minutes, then drain.

❧ Pour olive oil into a deep, heavy sauté pan to a depth of 1 inch (2.5 cm). Heat to 375°F (190°C) on a deep-frying thermometer.

❧ Meanwhile, make the filling: In a small bowl, combine the mozzarella and anchovies. Carefully open the flowers and fill each one with an equal portion of the filling. Twist the petals together slightly to close the tops.

❧ When the oil is ready, dip a few flowers into the batter and slip them into the oil; do not crowd the pan. Deep-fry, turning once, until golden and crisp, 1–2 minutes total. Using a slotted spoon, transfer to paper towels to drain briefly. Repeat with the remaining flowers.

❧ Arrange the flowers on a platter or individual plates. Sprinkle with salt to taste. Garnish with lemon wedges and serve immediately.

# SPARKLING FRUIT WINE

MAKES 4 CUPS (32 FL OZ/1 L); SERVES 6

*The best part of this sparkling summer cooler is the wine-marinated fruit at the bottom of each glass; be sure to offer spoons so guests can eat the fruit once they have drunk the wine.*

½ bottle (1½ cups/12 fl oz/375 ml)
   Gewürztraminer, chilled
1 cup (8 fl oz/250 ml) peach nectar,
   chilled
1 lime, cut into 8 thin slices
1 peach or nectarine, halved, pitted
   and cut into small wedges
1 plum, halved, pitted and cut into
   small wedges
½ cup (2 oz/60 g) blackberries
½ bottle (1½ cups/12 fl oz/375 ml)
   sparkling wine, chilled
ice cubes

In a large pitcher, stir together the Gewürztraminer and peach nectar. Reserve 6 lime slices for a garnish. Add the remaining lime slices, peach or nectarine wedges, plum wedges and blackberries to the pitcher. Chill for 1 hour.

❧ Just before serving, stir in the sparkling wine and ice cubes. Pour into glasses, distributing some of the fruit into each glass. Place a lime slice on the rim of each glass and serve well chilled.

# FIGS, PROSCIUTTO AND ST. ANDRÉ CHEESE

SERVES 6

*California's Spanish missionaries were the first to grow figs in North America, resulting in the naming of the purple-black variety known as the Black Mission. Other figs can be used for this recipe, including the large, fat, white-fleshed, green-skinned Calimyrna, and the small, thick-skinned, green Kadota. Or consider an assortment of all three.*

⅓ cup (3 fl oz/80 ml) crème fraîche
2 teaspoons chopped fresh mint,
   plus mint sprigs for garnish
2 teaspoons fresh lemon juice
2–3 teaspoons milk
salt and freshly ground pepper
12 ripe figs, a single variety or a mixture
   (see note)
6 oz (185 g) St. André or other triple-
   cream cheese such as Explorateur,
   cut into 12 wedges
3 oz (90 g) thinly sliced prosciutto

In a small bowl, whisk together the crème fraîche, chopped mint, lemon juice and as much of the milk as needed to form a thick, creamy consistency. Season to taste with salt and pepper.

❧ Halve the figs and arrange them on individual plates or a platter. Intersperse the wedges of cheese among the figs. Drape the prosciutto around the figs and drizzle with the crème fraîche mixture. Garnish with mint sprigs.

# FLAT BREAD WITH TOMATO, MOZZARELLA AND BASIL SALAD

SERVES 6

### FOR THE FLAT BREAD:

1 package (2½ teaspoons) active dry yeast

¾ cup (6 fl oz/180 ml) lukewarm water (110°F/43°C)

2 cups (10 oz/315 g) all-purpose (plain) flour, plus flour as needed

¾ teaspoon salt

3 tablespoons extra-virgin olive oil

### FOR THE SALAD:

1½ tablespoons extra-virgin olive oil

1½ tablespoons balsamic vinegar

1 clove garlic, minced

salt and freshly ground pepper

¾ lb (375 g) cherry tomatoes, stemmed and halved

1 ball fresh mozzarella cheese, about 6 oz (185 g), quartered and then sliced ¼ inch (6 mm) thick

½ cup (½ oz/15 g) loosely packed fresh small basil leaves

To make the flat bread, in a large bowl, combine the yeast, ¼ cup (2 fl oz/ 60 ml) of the lukewarm water and ¼ cup (1½ oz/45 g) of the flour. Let stand until bubbly and slightly risen, about 20 minutes. Add the remaining 1¾ cups (8½ oz/270 g) flour, the salt, olive oil and the remaining ½ cup (4 fl oz/120 ml) water and mix well. When the dough comes together into a ball, transfer it to a lightly floured work surface. Knead until soft, smooth and elastic, about 10 minutes, adding flour as needed to prevent sticking. Place in an oiled bowl and turn the dough to oil the top. Cover the bowl with plastic wrap and let the dough rise in a warm place until doubled in bulk, about 1 hour.

❧ Meanwhile, position a rack in the bottom part of an oven and place a pizza stone on it, or line with unglazed quarry tiles. Set the oven temperature to 500°F (260°C) and preheat for 30 minutes.

❧ Punch down the dough and transfer to a lightly floured work surface.

❧ Roll out into an oval 9 by 13 inches (23 by 33 cm) in diameter and ½ inch (12 mm) thick. Transfer to a flour-dusted pizza peel or rimless baking sheet, then slide the dough onto the heated stone or tiles. Bake until golden and crisp, 8–10 minutes. Using the pizza peel or baking sheet, transfer to a cutting board. Cut into 6 pieces and arrange them on a platter.

❧ To make the salad, in a large bowl, whisk together the olive oil, balsamic vinegar, garlic and salt and pepper to taste. Add the tomatoes and mozzarella and carefully mix together. Spoon the salad atop the flat bread and garnish with the basil. Serve immediately.

# LINGUINE WITH PESTO AND BORAGE FLOWERS

SERVES 6

### FOR THE BASIL PESTO:

1 teaspoon olive oil

¼ cup (1¼ oz/37 g) pine nuts

1½ cups (1½ oz/45 g) packed fresh basil leaves, carefully rinsed and well dried

¼ cup (¼ oz/7 g) flat-leaf (Italian) parsley leaves, carefully rinsed and well dried

4 cloves garlic, minced

½ cup (4 fl oz/125 ml) extra-virgin olive oil

¾ cup (3 oz/90 g) freshly grated Parmesan cheese

salt and freshly ground pepper

1 teaspoon extra-virgin olive oil

¼ cup (1¼ oz/37 g) pine nuts

1 lb (500 g) dried linguine or fettuccine

small handful borage flowers or other edible blossoms, optional

To make the pesto, in a frying pan over medium heat, warm the olive oil. Add the pine nuts and cook, stirring constantly, until golden, 3–4 minutes. Remove from the heat and let cool.

❧ In a blender or a food processor fitted with the metal blade, combine the basil, parsley, pine nuts, garlic, extra-virgin olive oil and Parmesan. Process at high speed until well mixed, about 1 minute. Stop and scrape down the sides, then continue to process until smooth, about 1 minute longer, stopping to scrape down the sides as needed. Season to taste with salt and pepper. You should have about 1¼ cups (10 fl oz/310 ml).

❧ In a frying pan over medium heat, warm the olive oil. Add the pine nuts and cook, stirring constantly, until a light golden brown, 3–4 minutes. Remove from the heat and set aside.

❧ Bring a large pot three-fourths full of salted water to a rolling boil over high heat. Add the pasta, stir well and cook until al dente (tender but firm to the bite), 10–12 minutes or according to the package directions.

❧ When the pasta is done, scoop out ¼ cup (2 fl oz/60 ml) of the pasta water and set aside. Immediately drain the pasta and transfer to a large bowl.

❧ Add the pasta water, pesto and pine nuts to the pasta and toss well. Transfer to a warmed serving bowl, garnish with the borage flowers, if desired, and serve immediately.

# Summer Soups & Salads

Just as they do in first courses, summer's abundant vegetable fruits shine brightly in its soups and salads. Some signature soups of the season beat the heat by being served cold, from Chilled Cucumber Soup (page 100) to Cool Honeydew-Mint Soup (page 99) to Golden Gazpacho (page 95). Still other soups are served hot to accentuate their myriad seasonal flavors, as in the mix of green beans, Swiss chard and fresh herbs found in Summer Vegetable Soup with Mint Pesto (page 99).

Many summer salads offer refreshing alternatives to more traditional lunch or dinner main courses. From Tuscan-Style Bread Salad with Tomatoes and Lemon Cucumbers (page 96) to French Salade Niçoise (page 103), from Pasta Salad with Summer Beans and Herbs (page 100) to the Couscous Salad with Grilled Summer Vegetables on this page, such warm-weather plates are incomparably light, yet undeniably satisfying.

## COUSCOUS SALAD WITH GRILLED SUMMER VEGETABLES

SERVES 6

*If your garden or farmers' market has orange or purple bell peppers, use them for this colorful salad; otherwise red, yellow or green bell peppers will do. For a heartier dish, add ¾ pound (375 g) grilled shrimp (prawns) or grilled chicken, cut into strips, with the tomatoes.*

2½ cups (20 fl oz/625 ml) water
1¼ cups (6½ oz/200 g) couscous
2 bell peppers (capsicums) (see note)
1 red or green chili pepper such as
    serrano or jalapeño
1 Asian (slender) eggplant (aubergine),
    cut crosswise into slices
1 zucchini (courgette), cut crosswise
    into slices
7 tablespoons (3½ fl oz/105 ml)
    extra-virgin olive oil
2 large red tomatoes, diced
2 tablespoons chopped fresh flat-leaf
    (Italian) parsley
⅓ cup (½ oz/15 g) chopped fresh
    cilantro (fresh coriander), plus
    cilantro sprigs for garnish
6 tablespoons (3 fl oz/90 ml) fresh
    lemon juice
1 teaspoon ground cumin
3 cloves garlic, minced
salt and freshly ground pepper
6 lemon wedges

In a saucepan, bring the water to a boil. Add the couscous, cover, remove from the heat and let stand for 10 minutes. Dump the couscous onto a paper towel–lined baking sheet, spread it out, and let stand at room temperature for 30 minutes. Transfer to a bowl, cover and chill for 30 minutes.

Meanwhile, prepare a fire in a charcoal grill.

Cut each bell pepper and the chili pepper in half lengthwise and remove the stems, seeds and ribs. Place the bell pepper and chili halves, cut sides up, on the grill rack and grill until the skins are blackened and blistered.

Remove from the grill and cover loosely with aluminum foil. Let steam until cool enough to handle, about 10 minutes, then peel off the skins. Cut the bell pepper into 1-inch (2.5-cm) squares and mince the jalapeño. Add to the couscous.

While the peppers are steaming, brush the eggplant and zucchini slices on both sides with 2 tablespoons of the olive oil and place on the grill rack. Grill, turning occasionally, until golden brown and tender when pierced with a fork, 6–8 minutes for the zucchini and 8–12 minutes for the eggplant. Add to the couscous along with the tomatoes, parsley and chopped cilantro.

In a small bowl, whisk together the remaining 5 tablespoons (3 fl oz/80 ml) olive oil, the lemon juice, cumin, garlic and salt and pepper to taste. Drizzle over the couscous and vegetables and toss to mix.

Transfer the salad to a serving platter and garnish with the lemon wedges and cilantro sprigs.

## GREEN GARDEN SALAD WITH SUMMER FLOWERS

SERVES 6

*In the south of France, this combination of garden lettuces is called* mesclun, *Provençal dialect for "mixed," and generally refers to an assortment of young shoots and plants. Try a mixture of frisée, mâche, lamb's lettuce, Bibb (Boston) lettuce, garden cress and red leaf.*

¼ baguette, thinly sliced on the diagonal
6 tablespoons (3 fl oz/90 ml)
   extra-virgin olive oil
2 cloves garlic
2 tablespoons balsamic vinegar
1½ teaspoons red wine vinegar
1 shallot, minced
salt and freshly ground pepper
9 cups (9 oz/280 g) loosely packed
   salad greens (see note), carefully
   rinsed and dried
¾ cup (¾ oz/20 g) assorted pesticide-
   free edible flowers such as pansies,
   nasturtiums, borage and rose petals,
   carefully rinsed and dried

Preheat an oven to 350°F (180°C).

❧ Brush the baguette slices on both sides with 2 tablespoons of the olive oil and place in a single layer on a baking sheet. Bake until crisp and lightly golden, 8–10 minutes. Remove from the oven. When cool enough to handle, lightly rub the toasts on both sides with the garlic cloves. Set aside.

❧ In a small bowl, whisk together the remaining 4 tablespoons (2 fl oz/60 ml) olive oil, the balsamic vinegar, red wine vinegar, shallot and salt and pepper to taste to make a vinaigrette.

❧ To serve, place the greens in a large salad bowl and drizzle with the vinaigrette. Toss well and sprinkle the flowers over the top. Serve with the toasts on the side.

## SPICY GRILLED CHICKEN SALAD WITH PEPPERS AND TOMATOES

SERVES 6

*In Italy, this salad is called* pollo forte, *meaning "strong chicken," a name derived from the fiery hot peppers that season the bird. The amount of heat is up to you: add or subtract the chili peppers as you wish. The salad serves six as a light first course or as an accompaniment to a bowl of chilled gazpacho (page 95). As a luncheon main course, the recipe serves four.*

4 skinless, boneless chicken breast
   halves, about 6 oz (185 g) each
1 tablespoon olive oil
2 red, green, yellow or orange bell
   peppers (capsicums), or a mixture,
   seeded, deribbed and very thinly
   sliced
1 fresh pasilla chili pepper, seeded and
   very thinly sliced
½ fresh jalapeño pepper, seeded and
   minced
1 small red (Spanish) onion, thinly
   sliced
salt and freshly ground pepper
2 cloves garlic, minced
½ teaspoon red pepper flakes
3 tablespoons red wine vinegar
2 tablespoons balsamic vinegar
5 tablespoons (2½ fl oz/75 ml)
   extra-virgin olive oil
½ lb (250 g) assorted cherry tomatoes
   such as red, yellow, green, orange
   and yellow pear, halved
½ cup (2½ oz/75 g) brine-cured black
   olives, preferably Niçoise or Kalamata
40 fresh small basil leaves

Prepare a fire in a charcoal grill.

✒ Brush the chicken breasts with the 1 tablespoon olive oil. Place the chicken breasts on the grill rack about 4 inches (10 cm) from the fire and grill until golden brown on the first side, 4–5 minutes. Turn the chicken and continue to grill until golden brown on the second side and opaque in the center, 4–5 minutes longer. Transfer to a cutting board and let cool for 20 minutes, then cut across the grain into very thin strips.

✒ Place the chicken strips in a large bowl and add the bell, pasilla and jalapeño peppers and the onion. Mix well and season to taste with salt and pepper. Cover and refrigerate until needed.

✒ In a small bowl, whisk together the garlic, red pepper flakes, red wine vinegar, balsamic vinegar and extra-virgin olive oil. Season to taste with salt and pepper. Pour over the chicken mixture, toss to mix and return to the refrigerator for 15 minutes.

✒ To serve, add the cherry tomatoes, olives and basil to the chicken mixture. Toss well and transfer to a serving bowl or individual plates. Serve chilled or at room temperature.

# GOLDEN GAZPACHO

SERVES 6

*In Spain, there are over 30 distinct versions of the famed cold soup known as gazpacho. It was first introduced in southern Spain by the Moors, who originally made it with garlic, bread, olive oil, lemon, water and salt. When the tomato was introduced to Spanish cooks in the early 16th century, gazpacho took on its familiar rosy hue. Yellow tomatoes give this version of the soup its marvelous golden color.*

1 slice coarse white bread
3 lb (1.5 kg) yellow tomatoes, peeled, seeded and chopped
1 green bell pepper (capsicum), seeded, deribbed and chopped
1 red (Spanish) onion, coarsely chopped
1 large English (hothouse) cucumber, peeled and coarsely chopped
6 tablespoons (3 fl oz/90 ml) red wine vinegar
3 large cloves garlic, minced
1¼ cups (10 fl oz/310 ml) tomato juice
3 tablespoons extra-virgin olive oil

**FOR THE GARNISH:**
1 tablespoon unsalted butter
1 tablespoon olive oil
3 cloves garlic, crushed
6 slices coarse white bread, crusts removed, cut into small cubes
salt and freshly ground pepper
¼ cup (1¼ oz/37 g) diced green bell pepper (capsicum)
¼ cup (1¼ oz/37 g) peeled, seeded and diced cucumber
¼ cup (1 oz/30 g) diced red (Spanish) onion
1½ cups (9 oz/280 g) red cherry tomatoes, quartered

Remove the crust from the bread slice and place in a shallow bowl with water to cover. Let stand until the bread is fully soaked, then remove and squeeze dry. In a bowl, combine the soaked bread, yellow tomatoes, bell pepper, onion, cucumber, vinegar, garlic, tomato juice and olive oil. Stir well. Working in batches, transfer the mixture to a blender and process on high speed until very smooth, about 3 minutes for each batch. Strain through a coarse-mesh sieve into a clean bowl. Cover and chill for 1 hour.

❧ To prepare the garnish, in a frying pan over medium heat, melt the butter with the olive oil. Add the garlic and cook, stirring, until golden brown, about 1 minute. Remove the garlic and discard. Add the bread cubes and stir to coat with the butter and oil. Cook slowly, stirring occasionally, until golden, 10–12 minutes. Remove the croutons from the heat and let cool.

❧ Before serving, season the soup to taste with salt and pepper. Ladle the soup into chilled individual bowls and garnish each serving with bell pepper, cucumber, onion, cherry tomatoes and croutons. Serve well chilled.

⅓ cup (3 fl oz/80 ml) extra-virgin
   olive oil
salt and freshly ground pepper
½ cup (½ oz/15 g) loosely packed fresh
   basil leaves, torn into small pieces

Spread the diced cucumbers on paper
towels and sprinkle with coarse salt.
Let stand for 15 minutes. Place the
cucumbers in a colander and rinse with
cold water. Pat dry with paper towels.
❧ Meanwhile, cut the bread into slices
1 inch (2.5 cm) thick and place in a
shallow dish. Sprinkle the bread with
the water and let stand for 2 minutes.
Then carefully squeeze the bread
until it is dry. Tear into rough 1-inch
(2.5-cm) pieces and place on paper
towels. Let stand for 10 minutes.
❧ In a bowl, combine the cucumbers,
tomatoes, onion and bread; toss gently.
❧ In a large bowl, whisk together
the vinegar and olive oil. Season to taste
with salt and pepper. Add the bread
mixture and the basil, mix gently and
refrigerate for at least 1 hour, or for
up to 4 hours.
❧ Transfer to a platter. Serve chilled.

## BREAD SALAD WITH TOMATOES AND LEMON CUCUMBERS

SERVES 4–6

*This rustic Tuscan salad, called* panzanella,
*is best when made with a chewy, coarsely
textured white bread. The bread must be
at least 3 days old to provide the correct
texture when mixed with tomatoes and
vinaigrette. Round, light yellow lemon
cucumbers deliver a sweet, mild flavor to
the salad.*

3 lemon cucumbers or 1 English
   (hothouse) cucumber, peeled,
   halved, seeded and diced
coarse salt
½ lb (250 g) stale coarse-textured
   white bread (see note)
½ cup (4 fl oz/125 ml) water
5 ripe tomatoes, 1½–2 lb (750 g–1 kg)
   total, seeded and diced
1 red (Spanish) onion, diced
4–5 tablespoons (2–2½ fl oz/60–80 ml)
   red wine vinegar

## FARMERS' MARKET TOMATO SALAD

SERVES 6

*Most farmers' markets provide a variety of
fresh red, yellow and orange summer tomatoes, all of which need little embellishment
to highlight their sweet, sun-ripened flavor.*

1 very small yellow onion, cut into
   paper-thin slices
salt
½ cup (4 fl oz/125 ml) milk
½ cup (4 oz/125 g) plain yogurt
1–2 tablespoons fresh lemon juice
1 clove garlic, minced
1 tablespoon chopped fresh oregano
1½ tablespoons chopped fresh basil
2 teaspoons extra-virgin olive oil
freshly ground pepper
6 ripe tomatoes, thinly sliced
1 English (hothouse) cucumber, peeled
   and cut crosswise into thin slices
handful of fresh basil leaves
handful of fresh cherry tomatoes

Place the onion slices in a bowl and
sprinkle with salt. Pour the milk over
the onion and let stand for 30 minutes.
❧ Meanwhile, in a small bowl, whisk
together the yogurt, lemon juice, garlic,
oregano, basil, olive oil and salt and
pepper to taste to form a vinaigrette.
Cover and refrigerate until needed.
❧ Arrange the tomato and cucumber
slices on a plate. Drain the onion slices
and pat dry with paper towels. Scatter
the onions atop the tomatoes and
cucumbers. Drizzle with the vinaigrette,
top with the basil leaves and cherry
tomatoes and serve.

## SUMMER VEGETABLE SOUP WITH MINT PESTO

SERVES 6

*A traditional basil pesto laced with mint brings out the fresh flavors of this hearty soup. Spoon it directly onto the top of each bowl just before serving, or pass it at the table for guests to help themselves.*

½ cup (3½ oz/105 g) dried small
    white (navy) beans
2 tablespoons extra-virgin olive oil
1 small yellow onion, chopped
2 small carrots, peeled and diced
2 small celery stalks, diced
2 cups (12 oz/375 g) peeled, seeded
    and chopped tomatoes
4 cups (32 fl oz/1 l) chicken stock or
    vegetable stock
3 cups (24 fl oz/750 ml) water
½ lb (250 g) green beans, trimmed
    and cut on the diagonal into
    1-inch (2.5-cm) lengths
¼ lb (125 g) dried penne or small
    elbow pasta
3 cups (3 oz/90 g) loosely packed
    Swiss chard (silverbeet) leaves (about
    1 small bunch), coarsely chopped
salt and freshly ground pepper
½ recipe pesto (recipe on page 89),
    substituting ½ cup (½ oz/15 g)
    packed fresh mint leaves for the
    ¼ cup parsley
⅓ cup (1½ oz/45 g) freshly grated
    Parmesan cheese

Pick over the beans and discard any damaged beans or stones. Rinse well and place in a bowl with water to cover generously. Let soak for 3 hours. Drain and place in a saucepan with water to cover by 2 inches (5 cm). Bring to a boil, reduce the heat to low and simmer gently, uncovered, until slightly tender, 30–40 minutes. Drain, discarding the liquid. Set the beans aside.

❧ In a large soup pot over medium-low heat, warm the olive oil. Add the onion, carrots and celery and cook uncovered, stirring occasionally, until the vegetables are soft, about 20 minutes. Add the tomatoes, stock, water and drained white beans and continue to cook, uncovered, until the beans are very tender and quite soft, about 45 minutes longer.

❧ About 15 minutes before the beans are ready, add the green beans and pasta. Cover and simmer until the pasta is tender to the bite, 8–10 minutes. Add the Swiss chard and cook until it wilts, about 2 minutes. Season to taste with salt and pepper.

❧ Ladle the soup into warmed individual bowls and place a spoonful of the pesto on top of each serving. Sprinkle with the Parmesan and serve hot.

## COOL HONEYDEW-MINT SOUP

SERVES 6

*Melons thrive in warm climates during the summer months. The honeydew melon, available both with green skin and flesh and with yellow skin and orange flesh, is principally grown in the hot reaches of California, the Mediterranean, Africa, the Caribbean, Central and South America. Persian, Crenshaw, Casaba or cantaloupe melons can be substituted with equally pleasing results.*

½ large honeydew melon, 2 lb (1 kg),
    seeded, peeled and cut into pieces
¼ cup (¼ oz/7 g) loosely packed
    fresh mint leaves, plus mint sprigs
    for garnish
3 tablespoons fresh lime juice, or
    as needed
1 tablespoon honey
salt
paper-thin lime slices

Working in batches, place the melon, mint leaves, 3 tablespoons lime juice, and honey in a blender. Process on high speed until smooth and light, about 2 minutes for each batch.

❧ Transfer to a container, cover and chill for at least 1 hour.

❧ Before serving, season to taste with more lime juice, if needed, and salt. Ladle the soup into chilled individual bowls and garnish with lime slices and mint sprigs. Serve well chilled.

## PASTA SALAD WITH SUMMER BEANS AND HERBS

SERVES 6

*Shell beans can be found fresh in the late summer months, before the pods begin to show signs of drying. Because most shell beans, such as the kidney, cannellini, scarlet runner, lima, cranberry and black-eyed pea varieties, are used dry, few cooks realize the distinctive quality they add when included fresh in summer dishes. Select any type you like for this recipe.*

¾ lb (375 g) dried fusilli
6 tablespoons (3 fl oz/90 ml)
    extra-virgin olive oil
1 lb (500 g) assorted snap beans such
    as green, yellow and haricot vert,
    trimmed
2 lb (1 kg) fresh shell beans of choice,
    shelled (see note)
5 tablespoons (3 fl oz/80 ml) red wine
    vinegar
2 cloves garlic, minced
2 tablespoons chopped fresh flat-leaf
    (Italian) parsley, plus parsley sprigs
    for garnish

1 tablespoon chopped fresh mint, plus
    mint sprigs for garnish
2 teaspoons chopped fresh oregano,
    plus oregano sprigs for garnish
salt and freshly ground pepper

Bring a large pot three-fourths full of salted water to a rolling boil over high heat. Add the fusilli, stir well and boil until al dente (tender but firm to the bite), 12–15 minutes or according to the package directions. Drain and transfer to a large bowl. Immediately add 1 tablespoon of the olive oil and toss well. Cover and place in the refrigerator to cool.

❧ Refill the pot three-fourths full with salted water and bring to a boil over high heat. Add the snap beans and boil until tender, 4–6 minutes. Drain and rinse under cold water to halt the cooking. Add to the pasta in the refrigerator.

❧ Again refill the pot three-fourths full with salted water and bring to a boil over high heat. Add the shell beans and boil until tender, 5–10 minutes, depending upon the variety. Drain, add to the pasta and snap beans; let cool completely in the refrigerator for at least 1 hour or for up to 24 hours.

❧ In a large bowl, whisk together the remaining 5 tablespoons (3 fl oz/80 ml) olive oil, the vinegar and garlic. Pour over the pasta and beans and add the chopped parsley, mint and oregano. Toss together well. Season to taste with salt and pepper.

❧ To serve, transfer the salad to a large serving dish and garnish with parsley, mint and oregano sprigs.

## CHILLED CUCUMBER SOUP

SERVES 6

*Cucumbers are native to Asia, where they have been eaten for thousands of years. They contain a great deal of water, which makes them particularly refreshing in the hot summer months. When choosing cucumbers, avoid the waxed variety sold in grocery stores year-round, and instead seek out the long, thin-skinned English, or hothouse, variety. It has a superior flavor, less water and far fewer seeds. Three lemon cucumbers can be substituted for the single English (hothouse) cucumber, if you like.*

3 cups (1½ lb/750 g) plain yogurt
1 large English (hothouse) cucumber,
    peeled, halved, seeded and coarsely
    grated, plus 6 paper-thin cucumber
    slices with skin intact for garnish
2 cloves garlic, minced
1 tablespoon extra-virgin olive oil
1½ tablespoons chopped fresh mint
2½ tablespoons chopped fresh dill,
    plus 6 dill sprigs for garnish
2 cups (16 fl oz/500 ml) milk
3 tablespoons white wine
    vinegar or fresh lemon juice
salt and freshly ground pepper

Line a sieve with cheesecloth (muslin) and place over a large bowl. Spoon the yogurt into the sieve and let drain in the refrigerator for 4 hours. Discard the captured liquid and place the yogurt in the bowl.

❧ Add the grated cucumber, garlic, olive oil, mint, chopped dill and milk. Mix well. Stir in the vinegar or lemon juice. Cover and chill for 1 hour.

❧ Before serving, season to taste with salt and pepper. Ladle the soup into chilled individual bowls and garnish each serving with a cucumber slice and a dill sprig. Serve well chilled.

## SALADE NIÇOISE

SERVES 6

2 cloves garlic, minced

3 tablespoons red wine vinegar

5 tablespoons (2½ fl oz/75 ml)
  extra-virgin olive oil

salt and freshly ground pepper

2 red or yellow bell peppers
  (capsicums), or a mixture

¾ lb (375 g) fingerling or small Yukon
  Gold potatoes, unpeeled

¾ lb (375 g) assorted snap beans such
  as green, yellow and haricot vert,
  trimmed

1¼ lb (625 g) fresh tuna steaks, about
  ¾ inch (2 cm) thick, cut into
  6 equal pieces

½ lb (250 g) red or yellow cherry
  tomatoes or a mixture, halved

½ cup (2½ oz/75 g) brine-cured black
  olives, preferably Niçoise

3 hard-cooked eggs, peeled and
  quartered lengthwise

3 tablespoons drained capers

1 can (2 oz/60 g) anchovy fillets packed
  in olive oil, drained, soaked in cold
  water for 10 minutes, drained, patted
  dry and cut in half crosswise

2 teaspoons chopped fresh parsley

1 tablespoon snipped fresh chives

1 teaspoon chopped fresh thyme

If grilling the tuna, prepare a fire in a
charcoal grill.

❧ In a small bowl, whisk together
the garlic, vinegar and 4 tablespoons
(2 fl oz/60 ml) of the olive oil. Season
to taste with salt and pepper. Set aside.

❧ Cut each bell pepper in half lengthwise and remove the stem, seeds and
ribs. Place the peppers cut sides down
on a baking sheet and slip under a
broiler (griller), or place cut sides up
over the charcoal fire. Broil or grill until
the skins are blackened and blistered.

Remove from the broiler or grill and
cover loosely with aluminum foil. Let
steam until cool enough to handle,
about 10 minutes, then peel off the
skins. Cut lengthwise into strips 1 inch
(2.5 cm) wide. Set aside.

❧ Bring a large saucepan three-fourths
full of salted water to a boil over high
heat. Add the potatoes and boil until
tender, 10–15 minutes. Using a slotted
spoon, transfer to a cutting board and
let cool. Add the beans to the same
pan and boil until tender, 4–6 minutes.
Drain and rinse under cold running
water to halt the cooking. Cut the
cooled potatoes lengthwise into
quarters.

❧ If grilling the tuna, brush the pieces
on both sides with the remaining 1
tablespoon olive oil and place on the
grill rack about 4 inches (10 cm) above
the fire. If panfrying, heat the remaining
1 tablespoon olive oil in a wide frying
pan over medium heat, then add the
tuna. Grill or panfry, turning once, until
golden on the outside but still slightly
pink at the center, 3–4 minutes on
each side, or until done to your liking.
Season to taste with salt and pepper.

❧ To serve, arrange the tuna, potatoes
and beans on a platter or individual
plates. Garnish with the pepper strips,
tomatoes, olives, eggs, capers and
anchovies. Drizzle with the vinaigrette
and sprinkle with the herbs.

## CREAMY POTATO SALAD

SERVES 6

3 lb (1.5 kg) red potatoes, unpeeled

⅓ cup (2½ oz/75 g) plain yogurt

¼ cup (2 fl oz/60 ml) mayonnaise

¼ cup (2 fl oz/60 ml) sour cream

1 tablespoon Dijon mustard

3 tablespoons fresh lemon juice

8 green (spring) onions, thinly sliced

2 celery stalks, finely chopped

3 tablespoons chopped fresh flat-leaf
  (Italian) parsley, plus parsley sprigs
  for garnish

3 tablespoons chopped fresh mint,
  plus mint sprigs for garnish

3 tablespoons chopped fresh basil,
  plus basil sprigs for garnish

salt and freshly ground pepper

Bring a large pot three-fourths full of
salted water to a boil over high heat.
Add the potatoes and boil until tender
when pierced with a fork, 15–20
minutes. Drain and let cool in the
refrigerator for at least 1 hour. Cut the
potatoes into ¾-inch (2-cm) dice.

❧ In a large bowl, stir together the
yogurt, mayonnaise, sour cream,
mustard, lemon juice, green onions,
celery and the chopped parsley, mint
and basil. Add the potatoes. Season
to taste with salt and pepper and toss
gently to mix.

❧ To serve, place the salad in a large
serving bowl and garnish with parsley,
mint and basil sprigs.

# Summer Main Courses

Warm, sunny days and breezy nights lure us outdoors to cook on the grill. Many of the main course recipes that follow provide ample inspiration for any grill cook, taking advantage of some of the season's most popular ingredients. This is prime time for all kinds of tuna, perfect for Tuna Burgers with Ginger-Mustard Mayonnaise (page 115). Shrimp (prawns) are widely available as well and are delicious skewered with lemons and bay leaves (also on page 115). From leg of lamb (page 112) to chicken (page 107) to flank steak (page 108), numerous favorites benefit from a lick of fire and smoke.

But not all summertime cooking needs to take place outdoors. You'll also find such dishes as Silver-Baked Salmon with Salsa Verde (page 111), Chicken Rolled with Pesto (page 108) or the Summer Vegetable Calzone on this page, all designed for indoor cooking, whether you're assembling a meal at home or in the kitchen of your vacation getaway.

# Summer Vegetable Calzone

MAKES 2 CALZONES; SERVES 6

### FOR THE DOUGH:

1 package (2½ teaspoons) active
   dry yeast
1 cup (8 fl oz/250 ml) lukewarm water
   (110°F/43°C)
3 cups (15 oz/470 g) all-purpose (plain)
   flour, plus flour as needed
¾ teaspoon salt
3 tablespoons extra-virgin olive oil

### FOR THE FILLING:

5 Asian (slender) eggplants, 1 lb (500 g)
   total, cut on the diagonal into
   thin slices
3 tablespoons extra-virgin olive oil
salt and freshly ground pepper
2 red bell peppers (capsicums), seeded,
   deribbed and cut lengthwise into
   narrow strips
2 tablespoons balsamic vinegar
¼ cup (1¼ oz/37 g) pine nuts
20 large fresh basil leaves, coarsely
   chopped, plus basil sprigs for garnish
1½ cups (6 oz/185 g) shredded
   Fontina cheese
1½ cups (6 oz/185 g) shredded
   mozzarella cheese
¾ cup (4 oz/125 g) crumbled goat
   cheese

To make the dough, in a large bowl, combine the yeast, ¼ cup (2 fl oz/60 ml) of the lukewarm water and ¼ cup (1½ oz/45 g) of the flour. Let stand until bubbly and slightly risen, about 20 minutes. Add the remaining flour, the salt, oil and the remaining water and mix until the dough comes together into a ball. Transfer to a floured surface and knead until smooth and elastic, about 10 minutes, adding flour as needed to prevent sticking. Place in an oiled bowl and turn the dough to oil the top. Cover with plastic wrap and let rise in a warm place until doubled in bulk, about 1 hour.

❧ Meanwhile, position a rack in the top part of an oven and preheat to 400°F (200°C).

❧ To make the filling, brush the eggplant slices with 2 tablespoons of the olive oil. Place on a baking sheet and bake, turning once, until golden and tender, 15–20 minutes. Season to taste with salt and pepper; set aside.

❧ Position the rack in the bottom part of the oven and place a pizza stone on it, or line with unglazed quarry tiles. Raise the oven temperature to 500°F (260°C) and preheat for 30 minutes.

❧ In a frying pan over medium-high heat, warm the remaining 1 tablespoon oil. Add the bell peppers and cook, stirring occasionally, until soft, about 10 minutes. Add the vinegar and cook until it evaporates, 1–2 minutes. In a bowl, combine the peppers, eggplant, pine nuts, chopped basil and the 3 cheeses.

❧ Punch down the dough and transfer to a floured work surface. Divide in half. Cover one-half with plastic wrap. Roll out the other half into a round 12 inches (30 cm) in diameter and ¼ inch (6 mm) thick. Transfer to a flour-dusted pizza peel or rimless baking sheet. Spread half of the eggplant mixture over half of the round, leaving a 1-inch (2.5-cm) border. Moisten the border with water, fold the uncovered dough over the filling and seal the edges well.

❧ Slide onto the stone or tiles and bake until golden and crisp, 10–12 minutes. Assemble and bake a second calzone from the remaining ingredients. Garnish with basil sprigs and cut into wedges to serve.

# BARBECUED CHICKEN

SERVES 6

*Serve this summertime classic with chili-rubbed corn on the cob (recipe on page 121) and creamy potato salad (page 103). To give the sauce an even spicier edge, add 1 teaspoon each ground cumin and paprika and 1 tablespoon chili powder with the allspice and ginger.*

**FOR THE BARBECUE SAUCE:**
1 tablespoon vegetable oil
1 small yellow onion, minced
1 cup (8 fl oz/250 ml) tomato purée
3 tablespoons Dijon mustard
¼ cup (2 fl oz/60 ml) fresh lemon juice
¼ cup (2 oz/60 g) firmly packed
   brown sugar
2 tablespoons Worcestershire sauce
2 tablespoons hot-pepper sauce
¼ teaspoon ground allspice
¼ teaspoon ground ginger
¼ cup (2 fl oz/60 ml) water
salt and ground pepper

6 chicken breast halves, about ½ lb
   (250 g) each, excess fat removed
6 chicken drumsticks, about ¼ lb
   (125 g) each, excess fat removed
6 chicken thighs, 5–6 oz (155–185 g)
   each, excess fat removed
salt and freshly ground pepper

Prepare a fire in a charcoal grill.
❧ To make the barbecue sauce, in a saucepan over medium heat, warm the oil. Add the onion and sauté until soft, about 10 minutes.
❧ Add the tomato purée, mustard, lemon juice, brown sugar, Worcestershire sauce, hot-pepper sauce, allspice, ginger, water and salt and pepper to taste. Stir well. Bring to a boil, reduce the heat to low and simmer slowly, uncovered, until the sauce thickens, 5–10 minutes.

❧ Remove from the heat and let cool. You should have about 2 cups (16 fl oz/500 ml). Use immediately, or cover and refrigerate for up to 4 days or freeze for up to 4 months.
❧ To prepare the chicken, sprinkle the chicken pieces with salt and pepper on all sides and place them, skin side down, on the grill rack about 6 inches (15 cm) from the fire. Grill, turning frequently, until well browned on all sides, 20–25 minutes. If the fire flares up, spritz with water from a spray bottle. If the chicken pieces are getting too dark, place them around the perimeter of the grill rack over less direct heat.
❧ After 20–25 minutes, brush the chicken with the sauce and cook for another 5 minutes. Turn over the pieces, brush with more sauce and continue to cook until the chicken is no longer pink when cut at the bone, about 5 minutes longer.
❧ To serve, place the chicken on a warmed platter. Pass the remaining sauce at the table.

# BARBECUED PORK RIBS

SERVES 6

*Grilling over mesquite imparts a smoky flavor to meats. Watch the ribs closely, turning to brown evenly and removing them as soon as they are ready. For a smokier flavor, the grill is partially covered during cooking. Serve with corn on the cob and coleslaw for a traditional summer barbecue.*

6 lb (3 kg) pork spareribs, in 2 racks
salt and freshly ground black pepper
barbecue sauce (recipe at left)
¼ teaspoon cayenne pepper
¼ cup (3 oz/90 g) honey

Preheat an oven to 350°F (180°C).
❧ Arrange the spareribs in a single layer on a baking sheet. Season on all sides with salt and black pepper. Cover with aluminum foil and bake until tender, 1¼–1½ hours.
❧ Prepare a fire in a charcoal grill.
❧ While the coals are heating, prepare the barbecue sauce, adding the cayenne pepper with the allspice and substituting the honey for the brown sugar.
❧ Remove the ribs from the oven and discard the foil. Place the ribs on the grill rack about 5 inches (13 cm) from the fire and brush with half of the barbecue sauce. Partially cover the grill and cook the ribs for 5–10 minutes. Turn the ribs and baste them with additional sauce. Re-cover the grill partially and continue to cook until golden brown, 5–10 minutes longer.
❧ Transfer the ribs to a cutting board and cut between the ribs into individual pieces. Serve immediately.

# GRILLED FLANK STEAK WITH GORGONZOLA BUTTER

SERVES 6

*Grilled flank steak is perfect for summer entertaining. If you like, you can make the butter up to a few days in advance so that the only task that remains is grilling the steak. Serve with grilled "thick-slice" red onions (recipe on page 125) and grilled Yukon Gold potatoes with garlic and herbs (page 122).*

**FOR THE GORGONZOLA BUTTER:**

3 tablespoons unsalted butter, at room
  temperature
3 oz (90 g) Gorgonzola cheese, at room
  temperature
2 green (spring) onions, minced
1 tablespoon chopped fresh flat-leaf
  (Italian) parsley
salt and freshly ground pepper

1 flank steak, about 2½ lb (1.25 kg),
  trimmed of excess fat

Prepare a fire in a charcoal grill.

❧ While the coals are heating, make the butter: In a bowl, using a fork, mash together the butter and Gorgonzola. Add the green onions and parsley and continue to mash until well mixed. Season to taste with salt and pepper. Mound the mixture in the center of a large piece of plastic wrap. Drape one side of the plastic wrap over the mixture and roll the butter into a sausage shape about 1½ inches (4 cm) in diameter. Wrap completely in the plastic wrap and twist the ends to seal. Refrigerate until ready to serve.

❧ Place the steak on the grill rack about 4 inches (10 cm) from the fire and grill on the first side until browned, about 5 minutes. Season the meat with salt and pepper, turn and continue to grill until browned on the second side, 5–6 minutes longer, or until an instant-read meat thermometer inserted into the thickest part of the steak registers 135°F (57°C) for medium-rare or until done to your liking. Remove from the grill and transfer to a cutting board. Cover loosely with aluminum foil and let stand for 10 minutes before carving.

❧ To serve, cut the meat on the diagonal and across the grain into thin slices. Arrange the meat slices on a warmed platter. Cut the butter into thin slices and place them on top of the meat and between the slices, distributing them evenly. Serve immediately.

# CHICKEN ROLLED WITH PESTO

SERVES 6

*This dish is equally delicious when served cold or at room temperature. For easy outdoor serving, cut the rolls into slices as directed and omit the sauce. The pesto must be thicker than is customary, so less olive oil is used when making it.*

6 skinless, boneless chicken breast
  halves, about 6 oz (185 g) each
salt and freshly ground pepper
½ recipe basil pesto (recipe on page 89),
  made with ¼ cup (2 fl oz/60 ml)
  olive oil
¼ cup (½ oz/15 g) fresh bread crumbs
6 cups (48 fl oz/1.5 l) chicken stock
1 tablespoon unsalted butter, at room
  temperature, cut into pieces

One at a time, place the chicken breasts between 2 pieces of waxed paper and, using a meat pounder, pound to an even ¼-inch (6-mm) thickness. Season to taste on both sides with salt and pepper.

❧ Cut out six 8-inch (20-cm) squares of aluminum foil. In a small bowl, combine the pesto and bread crumbs and stir well. Divide the pesto among the chicken breasts, spreading it evenly and leaving a ¼-inch (6-mm) border uncovered. Starting at a short end, roll up each chicken breast, enclosing the stuffing completely. Wrap each chicken roll tightly in a square of the foil and seal the ends closed.

❧ In a frying pan over medium-high heat, bring the chicken stock to a boil. Reduce the heat to medium-low, add the foil rolls and simmer in a single layer, turning occasionally, until slightly firm to the touch, about 20 minutes. Remove the rolls and set aside.

❧ Increase the heat to high, bring the stock to a boil and boil until reduced to about 1 cup (8 fl oz/250 ml), 10–15 minutes. Remove from the heat and whisk in the butter pieces.

❧ To serve, unwrap the rolls and discard the foil. Cut the rolls on the diagonal into slices ¼ inch (6 mm) thick. Arrange on warmed individual plates and spoon the sauce over the top. Serve immediately.

## SILVER-BAKED SALMON WITH SALSA VERDE

SERVES 6–8

*This method provides a wonderful way to bake whole salmon and works equally well with a 4-pound (2-kg) center-cut fillet.*

1 whole salmon, 6 lb (3 kg), cleaned
1 tablespoon kosher salt
¼ teaspoon ground pepper
½ lemon, thinly sliced, plus lemon
    wedges for garnish
4 fresh parsley sprigs
4 fresh thyme sprigs
4 fresh oregano sprigs
2 tablespoons extra-virgin olive oil

**FOR THE SALSA VERDE:**
1 cup (2 oz/60 g) chopped fresh
    flat-leaf (Italian) parsley
½ cup (1 oz/30 g) chopped fresh chives
2 teaspoons chopped fresh oregano
1 teaspoon chopped fresh thyme
½ teaspoon chopped fresh rosemary
¼ cup (2 oz/60 g) drained capers,
    chopped
4 cloves garlic, minced
¾ cup (6 fl oz/180 ml) extra-virgin
    olive oil
½ cup (4 fl oz/125 ml) fresh lemon
    juice
salt and ground pepper

Preheat an oven to 375°F (190°C).
❧ Rinse the fish and pat dry with paper towels. Rub all over with the kosher salt and pepper. On a baking sheet large enough to hold the fish flat, lay an 18-inch (45-cm) square of heavy-duty aluminum foil. Place the fish in the center of the foil. Stuff the cavity with the lemon slices and herb sprigs. Close the cavity and rub the outside surface with the olive oil. Cover with a piece of foil of the same size and fold and crimp the edges to make an airtight package.

❧ Bake until the fish flakes easily with a fork or an instant-read thermometer inserted into the thickest part of the fish registers 140°F (60°C), 50–60 minutes.
❧ Meanwhile, make the salsa: In a bowl, mix together all the ingredients. Set aside.
❧ Remove the salmon from the oven. Cut off a corner of the foil package and pour ½ cup (4 fl oz/125 ml) liquid from the package into a frying pan. Crimp the corner closed again to retain the juices. Place the pan over high heat and boil until only 2 tablespoons liquid remain, 1–2 minutes. Remove from the heat and let cool for 5 minutes. Add to the salsa mixture. Mix well.
❧ To serve, place the foil package on a platter and cut open the top. Garnish with lemon wedges. Serve the salsa on the side.

## NUT-CRUSTED TROUT WITH ROMESCO SAUCE

SERVES 6

**FOR THE ROMESCO SAUCE:**
5 tablespoons (3 fl oz/80 ml)
    extra-virgin olive oil
1 slice coarse-textured white bread
¼ cup (1½ oz/45 g) blanched almonds
1 cup (6 oz/185 g) peeled, seeded and
    chopped tomatoes
1 clove garlic, minced
2 teaspoons sweet paprika
¼ teaspoon red pepper flakes
3 tablespoons red wine vinegar
salt and freshly ground pepper

**FOR THE TROUT:**
2 cups (11 oz/345 g) plain almonds
½ cup (2½ oz/75 g) all-purpose (plain)
    flour
3 eggs
salt and freshly ground pepper

6 whole trout, 10 oz (315 g) each,
    cleaned
1 tablespoon unsalted butter
1 tablespoon olive oil

To make the sauce, in a frying pan over medium heat, warm 1 tablespoon of the olive oil. Add the bread and fry, turning occasionally, until golden on both sides, 2–3 minutes. Transfer the bread to a food processor. Add the blanched almonds to the same frying pan and cook over medium heat, stirring often, until golden, about 2 minutes. Remove from the heat and transfer to the processor. Add the tomatoes, garlic, paprika and red pepper flakes to the processor. Process until a rough paste forms, about 1 minute. With the motor running, pour in the vinegar and the remaining 4 tablespoons (2 fl oz/60 ml) olive oil in a slow, steady stream and process until barely fluid, about 1 minute longer. Season to taste with salt and pepper. Pour into a bowl and let stand at room temperature for 1 hour before using.
❧ To prepare the trout, rinse and dry the processor bowl. Add the plain almonds and process to chop finely. Transfer to a shallow bowl. Place the flour and eggs in separate shallow bowls. Whisk the eggs until blended and season with salt and pepper. Season the flour as well. One at a time, dip the trout into the flour, patting off the excess, then into the egg and then lightly into the almonds. Set aside on a platter.
❧ In a large, heavy frying pan over medium heat, melt the butter with the oil. Add the trout and cook, turning once, until golden on both sides and cooked through, 8–10 minutes total.
❧ Serve the trout on individual plates with the sauce alongside.

## SWORDFISH STEAKS WITH MANGO AND AVOCADO SALSA

SERVES 6

*A nice alternative to traditional tomato salsa, this exotic mix offers an irresistible blend of fruitiness and richness. It is also good with grilled tuna steaks, halibut, snapper or chicken.*

2 large, ripe mangoes
1 ripe avocado, halved, pitted, peeled
    and diced
½ fresh jalapeño chili pepper, seeded
    and minced
⅓ cup (1½ oz/45 g) diced red (Spanish)
    onion
1 teaspoon grated lime zest
3 tablespoons fresh lime juice
¼ cup (2 fl oz/60 ml) fresh orange juice
¼ cup (⅓ oz/10 g) chopped fresh
    cilantro (fresh coriander), plus
    cilantro sprigs for garnish
2 tablespoons olive oil
salt and freshly ground pepper
6 swordfish steaks, about 6 oz (185 g)
    each and 1 inch (2.5 cm) thick
lime wedges

Working with 1 mango at a time, cut off the flesh from each side of the big, flat pit to form 2 large pieces. Discard the pit. Using a knife, score the flesh lengthwise and then crosswise into ½-inch (12-mm) squares, cutting through to the skin. Then, holding the mango over a bowl, slip the blade between the skin and flesh to cut away the flesh, allowing the cubes to fall into a bowl. Add the avocado, jalapeño, onion, lime zest, lime juice, orange juice, chopped cilantro and 1 tablespoon of the olive oil. Mix well and season to taste with salt and pepper. Set aside.

❧ In 1 or 2 frying pans large enough to hold the swordfish steaks in a single layer without crowding, warm the remaining 1 tablespoon olive oil over medium-high heat. Add the swordfish and cook until lightly golden on the first side, about 5 minutes. Turn the fish, season to taste with salt and pepper and continue to cook until lightly golden on the second side and opaque throughout when cut with a knife, about 5 minutes longer.

❧ Place the swordfish steaks on warmed individual plates and top with the salsa. Garnish with lime wedges and cilantro sprigs and serve.

## GRILLED LEG OF LAMB WITH LAVENDER-ROSEMARY RUB

SERVES 6–8

1 leg of lamb, 5–6 lb (2.5–3 kg), boned,
    trimmed of excess fat and butterflied
3 cloves garlic, thinly sliced
¼ cup (¼ oz/7 g) dried or fresh
    lavender flowers
3 tablespoons chopped fresh rosemary
3 tablespoons extra-virgin olive oil

salt and freshly ground pepper
fresh lavender sprigs or fresh rosemary
    sprigs

Make 20 small incisions at regular intervals in the lamb meat. Tuck a garlic slice into each incision.

❧ In a small bowl, combine the lavender flowers, rosemary and olive oil. Rub the mixture over the lamb. Cover and let stand at room temperature for 2 hours or overnight in the refrigerator.

❧ Preheat a broiler (griller), or prepare a fire in a charcoal grill.

❧ Place the lamb on a broiler pan under the broiler or on an oiled grill rack, each about 4 inches (10 cm) from the heat source. Broil or grill until the first side is browned, about 15 minutes. Turn, season well with salt and pepper, and continue to cook until browned on the second side and an instant-read thermometer inserted into the thickest portion registers 130–135°F (54–57°C) for medium-rare or the meat is pink when cut into with a sharp knife, about 15 minutes longer. Transfer to a cutting board, cover with aluminum foil and let rest for 10 minutes before carving.

❧ Cut the lamb across the grain into thin slices and arrange on a warmed platter. Garnish with lavender or rosemary sprigs and serve immediately.

## SHRIMP KABOBS WITH LEMONS AND BAY LEAVES

SERVES 6

*A great summertime treat, kabobs can be assembled ahead of time and grilled at the last minute. These lemony shrimp-filled skewers are delicious accompanied with steamed couscous or rice.*

36 extra-large shrimp (prawns), about
   2 lb (1 kg), peeled and deveined
6 tablespoons (3 fl oz/90 ml)
   extra-virgin olive oil
24 bay leaves
3 lemons, each cut into 8 wedges
2½ tablespoons fresh lemon juice
1 small clove garlic, minced
1 teaspoon chopped fresh oregano, plus
   oregano sprigs for garnish
salt and freshly ground pepper

Soak 12 bamboo skewers in water to cover for 30 minutes.

❧ Prepare a fire in a charcoal grill.

❧ While the coals are heating, place the shrimp in a bowl and add 2 tablespoons of the olive oil. Toss to coat the shrimp evenly. Drain the skewers. Working with 1 skewer at a time, thread a shrimp onto it, piercing each shrimp through the body and again through the tail. Next thread a bay leaf and a lemon wedge diagonally onto the skewer, making sure the skewer pierces the lemon rind. Continue in this manner, ending with a shrimp, until the skewer holds 3 shrimp in all. Repeat with the remaining skewers and ingredients. Set aside until ready to grill.

❧ In a small bowl, whisk together the remaining 4 tablespoons (2 fl oz/60 ml) olive oil, the lemon juice, garlic and chopped oregano and season to taste with salt and pepper to form a vinaigrette. Set aside.

❧ Place the kabobs on an oiled grill rack about 4 inches (10 cm) from the fire. Grill, turning every few minutes, until the shrimp are almost firm to the touch, 5–7 minutes.

❧ Transfer to a warmed platter, drizzle with the vinaigrette and garnish with oregano sprigs.

## TUNA BURGERS WITH GINGER-MUSTARD MAYONNAISE

SERVES 6

*Fresh tuna fillets offer a healthful alternative to regular hamburgers. This classy grilled sandwich can also be made with swordfish, snapper or salmon. Slices of tomato or avocado can be added along with the lettuce.*

⅓ cup (3 fl oz/80 ml) mayonnaise
2 teaspoons fresh lemon juice
1 teaspoon Asian sesame oil
1½ teaspoons peeled and grated
   fresh ginger
1 tablespoon whole-grain mustard
1 clove garlic, minced
salt and freshly ground pepper
6 good-quality hamburger rolls, split
2 lb (1 kg) tuna fillets, about ¾ inch
   (2 cm) thick, cut into 6 equal pieces
olive oil
6 large lettuce leaves
6 thin slices red onion

Prepare a fire in a charcoal grill.

❧ In a small bowl, whisk together the mayonnaise, lemon juice, sesame oil, ginger, mustard, garlic and salt and pepper to taste. Set aside.

❧ Lightly brush the cut sides of the rolls with the mayonnaise mixture. Lightly oil the grill rack. Place the rolls, cut sides down, on the grill rack about

4 inches (10 cm) from the fire and grill until lightly golden. Set the rolls around the perimeter of the grill rack, away from the coals, to keep warm. Lightly brush the tuna with olive oil and place on the grill rack. Grill until golden on the first side, about 4 minutes. Turn, season to taste with salt and pepper, and continue to cook until golden on the second side but still slightly pink at the center, 3–4 minutes longer, or until done to your liking.

❧ Remove from the grill, placing each piece of tuna on the bottom half of a roll. Top each with an equal amount of the mayonnaise mixture, a lettuce leaf and an onion slice and the other half of the roll. Serve immediately.

## GRILLED FONTINA AND EGGPLANT CAVIAR SANDWICH

SERVES 6

*Eggplant caviar is the American version of a Mediterranean eggplant preparation often served as an accompaniment to bread or pita chips, or as a spread for sandwiches. The name* caviar *is derived from the nubby texture of the coarsely chopped mixture.*

2 large eggplants (aubergines), 2½ lb (1.25 g) total
2 tablespoons fresh lemon juice
2 cloves garlic, minced
1 teaspoon ground cumin
½ teaspoon sweet paprika
⅛ teaspoon cayenne pepper
1 tablespoon extra-virgin olive oil
salt and freshly ground black pepper
2 tablespoons unsalted butter, at room temperature
12 slices coarse-textured white bread
6 oz (185 g) Fontina cheese, thinly sliced

Prepare a fire in a charcoal grill. Preheat an oven to 400°F (200°C).

When the fire is ready, place the eggplants on an oiled grill rack about 4 inches (10 cm) from the fire and grill, turning occasionally, until soft and black, 10–15 minutes. Transfer the eggplants to a baking sheet and bake until very soft, 15–20 minutes. Remove from the oven and let cool slightly.

Cut the eggplants in half and scoop out the pulp onto a cutting board. Discard the skin. Chop the eggplant coarsely. In a large bowl, combine the eggplant, lemon juice, garlic, cumin, paprika, cayenne pepper and olive oil. Mix well. Season to taste with salt and black pepper.

Place a large frying pan over medium heat. While the pan is heating, spread 1 tablespoon of the butter on one side of 6 bread slices, dividing it evenly, and place them buttered side down on a work surface. Top the slices with half of the Fontina, distributing it evenly, then spread each sandwich with one-sixth of the eggplant mixture. Top with the remaining cheese. Spread the remaining 6 bread slices with the remaining 1 tablespoon butter and place, buttered side up, on the sandwiches.

Place the sandwiches in the hot pan and cook until golden on the first side and the cheese is almost melted, 2–3 minutes. Turn the sandwiches and continue to cook until golden on the second side and the cheese is melted completely, 2–3 minutes longer. Remove from the pan.

Transfer to individual plates and cut in half on the diagonal. Serve at once.

*I know I am but summer to your heart,
And not the full four seasons of the year.*
—Edna St. Vincent Millay

# Summer Side Dishes
*ନ*

The irresistibly casual nature of summertime cooking comes across in the collection of accompaniments on the following pages. Although created primarily to arrive alongside main dishes, many of them could just as effectively be pressed into service as a first course, with Orzo-and-Feta-Stuffed Tomatoes (page 122) an excellent example.

Every one of these side dishes is a model of effortless preparation as well, most welcome at a time of year when we'd rather be relaxing outdoors than working in the kitchen. Scan the photographs for these recipes and you'll see telltale signs of this ease in the grill marks that score the season's tomatoes, peppers (capsicums), onions, egg-plants (aubergines) and buttery golden tubers. From Grilled Yukon Gold Potatoes with Garlic and Herbs (page 122) to Chili-Rubbed Corn on the Cob (page 121) to the Grilled Vegetable Ratatouille on this page, these recipes can be set next to the main course as it cooks above a glowing fire.

## GRILLED VEGETABLE RATATOUILLE

SERVES 6

*Throughout Provence, there are many versions of this thick vegetable ragout. In this recipe, the vegetables are first grilled separately and then stewed together. Ratatouille often tastes even better the next day, so you may wish to make it a day in advance, then reheat it on the stove top before serving. If you have leftover ratatouille, pair it with sliced grilled chicken in a sandwich.*

olive oil for the grill rack, plus
    2 tablespoons olive oil
2 eggplants (aubergines), 1 lb (500 g)
    each, cut crosswise into slices
    1 inch (2.5 cm) thick
4 small zucchini (courgettes), ¾ lb
    (375 g) total, cut crosswise into slices
    1 inch (2.5 cm) thick
2 yellow onions, cut into slices
    1 inch (2.5 cm) thick
3 red, yellow, orange or green bell
    peppers (capsicums), or a mixture
5 tomatoes, 1–1¼ lb (500–625 g) total
4 cloves garlic, minced
¼ cup (⅓ oz/10 g) chopped fresh
    flat-leaf (Italian) parsley
½ teaspoon chopped fresh thyme
2 tablespoons red wine vinegar
salt and freshly ground pepper
20 fresh basil leaves, cut into thin strips

Prepare a fire in a charcoal grill.
ନ When the fire is ready, brush the grill liberally with olive oil. Place the egg-plant, zucchini and onion slices, the bell peppers and the tomatoes on the grill rack about 4 inches (10 cm) from the fire. Grill, turning frequently, until lightly golden, about 5 minutes. As the vegetables are ready, remove all of them, except the bell peppers; keep the vegetables separate. Continue to cook the bell peppers until the skin is black-ened and blistered, then remove from the grill, cover with aluminum foil and let steam until cool enough to handle, about 10 minutes. Peel off the skins and cut the peppers in half lengthwise. Remove the stems, seeds and ribs and cut the peppers into strips. Cut the eggplant and onion slices and the whole tomatoes into 1-inch (2.5-cm) dice. Keep all of the vegetables separate.
ନ In a large, heavy pot over medium heat, warm the 2 tablespoons olive oil. Add the onions and cook, stirring, until soft, about 7 minutes. Add the eggplant, bell peppers, zucchini, and tomatoes and cook uncovered, stirring occasionally, until all the vegetables are tender, 30–40 minutes. Add the garlic, parsley, thyme and vinegar, stir well and cook for 5 minutes longer to blend the flavors. Season to taste with salt and pepper.
ନ Transfer to a platter and garnish with the basil. Serve warm or at room temperature.

# GREEN AND YELLOW BEANS WITH SUMMER SAVORY

SERVES 6

*Few herbs complement fresh snap beans better than summer savory. With a flavor resembling a cross between mint and thyme and masked with a slightly peppery taste, savory's assertiveness offers an ideal foil for the beans' sun-ripened mellowness and the chili's mild heat.*

1 lb (500 g) green beans, trimmed
1 lb (500 g) yellow beans, trimmed
1 fresh poblano chili pepper
1 teaspoon unsalted butter
1 teaspoon olive oil
2 tablespoons chopped fresh summer savory, plus summer savory sprigs for garnish
salt and freshly ground pepper

Bring a large saucepan three-fourths full of salted water to a boil over medium-high heat. Add the green and yellow beans and cook until tender, 4–6 minutes. Drain and rinse under cold running water to halt the cooking. Set aside.

❧ Preheat a broiler (griller). Cut the chili pepper in half lengthwise and remove the stem, seeds and ribs. Place the pepper halves, cut sides down, on a baking sheet. Broil (grill) until the skins are blackened and blistered. Remove from the broiler and cover loosely with aluminum foil. Let steam until cool enough to handle, about 10 minutes, then peel off the skin. Cut the pepper halves lengthwise into strips about ¼ inch (6 mm) wide.

❧ In a large frying pan over medium heat, melt the butter with the olive oil. Add the beans, chili pepper strips and chopped savory and cook, stirring frequently, until hot, about 2 minutes. Season to taste with salt and pepper.

❧ Transfer to a warmed platter and garnish with savory sprigs. Serve immediately.

# CHILI-RUBBED CORN ON THE COB

SERVES 6

*Corn on the cob celebrates the very soul of summer. Some purists will go so far as to eat corn only if it was picked less than half a dozen hours before serving. To test for freshness, stick the nail of your index finger into a kernel. If the center of the kernel shoots into the air, the corn is truly fresh.*

6 ears of corn with husks intact
½ teaspoon salt
¼ teaspoon freshly ground black pepper
1 teaspoon chili powder
½ teaspoon ground cumin
⅛ teaspoon cayenne pepper
2 tablespoons unsalted butter, melted

Pull back the husks from each ear of corn but leave them attached to the base of the cob. Pull off and discard the silks. Rinse the ears under running water and then place in a sink with cold water to cover. Let soak for 20 minutes to saturate the corn husks and add moisture to the kernels.

❧ Meanwhile, prepare a fire in a charcoal grill.

❧ In a small bowl, stir together the salt, black pepper, chili powder, cumin, cayenne pepper and butter. Brush the ears of corn with the butter mixture and rewrap the husks around them. Then wrap each ear of corn in aluminum foil.

❧ Place the corn on a grill rack about 4 inches (10 cm) from the fire. Grill, turning occasionally, until the corn is tender, about 15 minutes. To test, open a package; the corn kernels should be tender when pierced with a fork.

❧ Remove the foil and arrange the corn cobs on a warmed platter. Serve immediately.

## GRILLED YUKON GOLD POTATOES WITH GARLIC AND HERBS

SERVES 6

*Yukon Golds are yellow-gold potatoes with an assertive flavor and a creamy texture. Whole cloves of garlic, scattered over the potatoes in the roasting pan, add to their memorable flavor. For those who like extra garlic taste, the browned sheaths can be removed and the whole garlic cloves enjoyed with the grilled potatoes.*

2½ lb (1.25 kg) small Yukon Gold
   potatoes
3 heads garlic
2 tablespoons extra-virgin olive oil
salt and freshly ground pepper
15 fresh thyme sprigs, coarsely chopped
6 fresh rosemary sprigs, coarsely
   chopped

Preheat an oven to 375°F (190°C).

❧ Rinse the potatoes but do not dry them. Cut them in half and place in a 9-by-13-inch (23-by-33-cm) baking dish. Remove the outer papery sheaths from the garlic heads. Cut each garlic head in half through the stem end. Break up the garlic and sprinkle the cloves over the potatoes. Drizzle with the olive oil and season to taste with salt and pepper. Toss the potatoes to coat them with the oil, then sprinkle with the thyme and rosemary.

❧ Cover tightly with aluminum foil. Bake until the potatoes are tender when pierced with a knife, about 1 hour.

❧ Meanwhile, prepare a fire in a charcoal grill.

❧ Remove the potatoes from the pan and place on the grill rack about 4 inches (10 cm) from the fire; reserve the garlic cloves in the pan until ready to serve. Grill the potatoes, turning once, until golden on both sides and hot throughout, 6–8 minutes total.

❧ Transfer the potatoes to a platter and sprinkle the reserved garlic cloves over the top. Serve immediately.

## ORZO-AND-FETA-STUFFED TOMATOES

SERVES 6

*Stuffed tomatoes are a wonderful partner to grilled meats, and can also be served alone as a first course or even a light main course for an al fresco lunch.*

1¼ cups (8½ oz/265 g) dried orzo
1 tablespoon extra-virgin olive oil
ice water as needed
6 ripe but firm tomatoes, any color
6 oz (185 g) feta cheese, crumbled
½ cup (2½ oz/75 g) finely diced
   English (hothouse) cucumber
½ cup (2½ oz/75 g) finely diced
   red (Spanish) onion
1½ tablespoons fresh lemon juice
3 tablespoons chopped fresh dill
3 tablespoons chopped fresh mint
salt and freshly ground pepper

Bring a large saucepan three-fourths full of salted water to a rolling boil over high heat. Add the orzo and cook until al dente (tender but firm to the bite), 5–8 minutes or according to the package directions. Drain and place in a bowl. Immediately add the olive oil and toss well. Cover and refrigerate until well chilled, at least 1 hour or for up to 24 hours.

❧ Meanwhile, have ready a large bowl of ice water. Bring another large saucepan three-fourths full of water to a boil. Add the tomatoes and blanch for no more than 15 seconds. Using a slotted spoon, transfer to the ice water to cool completely. Cut a slice ¾ inch (2 cm) thick off the stem end of each tomato and set aside. Using a spoon, carefully scoop out the pulp, leaving sturdy shells; discard the pulp or reserve for another use. Place, cut sides down, on paper towels to drain until ready to use.

❧ In a large bowl, mix together the chilled orzo, feta, cucumber, onion, lemon juice, dill and mint. Season to taste with salt and pepper.

❧ Place each tomato, cut side up, on a serving plate. Spoon the orzo and feta mixture into the tomatoes, distributing it evenly. Place the tomato tops over the filling, cover and chill for 30 minutes.

❧ Place the tomatoes on individual plates and serve.

## SUMMER SQUASH SAUTÉ

SERVES 6

*Squashes, members of the gourd family, are native to the Western Hemisphere. There are two basic types of squash: summer and winter. Summer varieties have thin, edible skin, tender seeds and a high water content, while winter squashes have tough, hard skin and seeds.*

5 small zucchini (courgettes), 1 lb
    (500 g) total
4 small yellow summer or crookneck
    squashes, 1 lb (500 g) total
4 pattypan (custard) squashes, ¾ lb
    (375 g) total
2 tablespoons extra-virgin olive oil
2 cloves garlic, minced
2 tablespoons chopped fresh basil
1 teaspoon chopped fresh oregano
½ teaspoon chopped fresh marjoram
salt and freshly ground pepper
zucchini (courgette) blossoms, optional
fresh herb sprigs, optional

Cut the zucchini and the summer or crookneck squashes crosswise into rounds ½ inch (12 mm) thick. Cut the pattypan squash in half horizontally and then crosswise into pieces ½ inch (12 mm) thick.

❧ In a frying pan over medium-high heat, warm the olive oil. Add all of the squashes and cook, stirring occasionally, until tender when pierced with a fork, 10–12 minutes. Stir in the garlic, basil, oregano and marjoram. Season to taste with salt and pepper.

❧ To serve, place the squash in a serving bowl and garnish with squash blossoms and herb sprigs, if desired.

## GRILLED "THICK-SLICE" RED ONIONS

SERVES 6

6 large red (Spanish) onions, cut into
    slices ¾ inch (2 cm) thick
1 tablespoon olive oil
3 tablespoons extra-virgin olive oil
1½ tablespoons balsamic vinegar
1 teaspoon chopped fresh summer
    savory, thyme or oregano, plus
    summer savory, thyme or oregano
    sprigs for garnish
salt and freshly ground pepper

Prepare a fire in a charcoal grill.

❧ While the coals are heating, brush each onion slice on both sides with the 1 tablespoon olive oil.

❧ In a small bowl, whisk together the extra-virgin olive oil, vinegar, chopped herb and salt and pepper to taste to form a vinaigrette.

❧ Place the onions on the grill rack about 5 inches (13 cm) from the fire. Grill until golden on the first side, 5–6 minutes. Carefully turn the onions and continue to grill until tender and golden on the second side, 5–6 minutes longer.

❧ Transfer to a warmed platter, drizzle with the vinaigrette and garnish with herb sprigs.

# $\mathscr{S}$ummer Desserts

Many of summer's most delightful desserts are memorable for the magical ways in which they capture a precious moment in time, showcasing succulent tree fruits or berries that appear for a month or two and then are gone: a Latticed Cherry Pie (page 132) bubbling over with red juices; a Fig and Raspberry Clafouti (page 128) featuring two of the season's most irresistible fruits; and a Summer Berry Gratin (page 129) showcasing whichever berries—blueberries, blackberries, raspberries, boysenberries—are at their best when you make it.

Other fruits provide more constant opportunities for assembling colorful summertime desserts. Fresh melons remain reliably available, making it possible to prepare a Watermelon Granita (page 137) or Summer Melons in Spiced White Wine (page 139) almost on a whim. And a Fresh Fruit Tart (also on page 139) is versatility itself, allowing you to use whatever combination of fresh summer fruits are at their finest when you visit the market.

## MIXED PLUM SHORTCAKE

SERVES 8

*There are more varieties of plums than any other stone fruit. The common Santa Rosa has red skin and tart yellow flesh, while the El Dorado is large, heart shaped and almost black. The Laroda has reddish yellow skin and sweet, firm yellow flesh, and the Kelsey is dark green, turning yellow when ripe.*

**FOR THE SHORTCAKES:**
2½ cups (12½ oz/390 g) all-purpose (plain) flour
¼ teaspoon salt
1 tablespoon baking powder
½ cup (4 oz/125 g) unsalted butter, at room temperature, cut into pieces
1 cup (8 fl oz/250 ml) buttermilk, at room temperature

**FOR THE FILLING:**
2¾ lb (1.4 kg) assortment of any 3 plum varieties (see note)
⅔ cup (5 fl oz/160 ml) water
¼ cup (2 oz/60 g) granulated sugar
1½ tablespoons quetsch (plum liqueur) or kirsch

**FOR THE WHIPPED CREAM:**
1 cup (8 fl oz/250 ml) heavy (double) cream
1 teaspoon quetsch (plum liqueur) or kirsch
1 tablespoon confectioners' (icing) sugar

2 tablespoons confectioners' (icing) sugar for dusting

Preheat an oven to 400°F (200°C).
❧ To make the shortcakes, sift together the flour, salt and baking powder into a bowl. Add the butter and, using your fingertips, rub it in until the mixture resembles coarse meal. Using a fork,

gradually stir in the buttermilk until the mixture holds together. Gather the dough into a ball and transfer to a well-floured work surface. Using a floured rolling pin, roll out into a round ½ inch (12 mm) thick. Fold in half and roll out again ½ inch (12 mm) thick. Repeat once more. Using a round biscuit cutter 2½–3 inches (6–7.5 cm) in diameter, cut out 6 rounds. Reroll the scraps and cut out 2 additional rounds. Place on an ungreased baking sheet, spacing them well apart. Bake until the tops are lightly golden, about 10 minutes. Transfer to a rack to cool.
❧ To make the filling, halve and pit ¾ lb (375 g) of the plums and place in a blender. Process on high speed until smooth. Strain through a fine-mesh sieve into a large bowl. In a small saucepan over high heat, combine the water and granulated sugar and stir until slightly thickened, about 30 seconds. Add the sugar syrup and liqueur to the plum purée. Halve and pit the remaining 2 lb (1 kg) plums and cut into ½-inch (12-mm) wedges. Toss well with the purée.
❧ To prepare the whipped cream, using a whisk or an electric mixer, beat the cream just until it begins to thicken. Add the liqueur and confectioners' sugar and continue to beat until soft peaks form.
❧ To serve, cut each shortcake in half horizontally. Place the bottoms on individual plates, cut sides up. Spoon the plum mixture and the cream over them. Crown with the tops, cut sides down. Using a sieve or sifter, dust the tops with the confectioners' sugar. Serve immediately.

## FIG AND RASPBERRY CLAFOUTI

SERVES 6

*Most fig varieties are available from June to October. They are extremely perishable and should be eaten as soon as possible after they are picked or purchased. If you must store them, lay them on a baking sheet lined with a kitchen towel or paper towels, and place them, uncovered, in the refrigerator. Figs are at their best when the skins have cracked slightly.*

1 lb (500 g) figs, halved through the stem end

1 cup (4 oz/125 g) raspberries

¼ cup (1½ oz/45 g) whole almonds

2 tablespoons all-purpose (plain) flour

¾ cup (6 fl oz/180 ml) milk

6 tablespoons (3 oz/90 g) granulated sugar

2 eggs

1 tablespoon framboise or kirsch

pinch of salt

2 tablespoons unsalted butter, cut into small pieces

1 cup (8 fl oz/250 ml) heavy (double) cream

2 teaspoons confectioners' (icing) sugar

¼ teaspoon vanilla extract (essence)

Preheat an oven to 400°F (200°C). Butter a 2-qt (2-l) gratin or other baking dish.

❧ Arrange the figs, cut sides up, in the prepared baking dish. Sprinkle the raspberries around and on top of the figs. Set aside.

❧ In a blender or in a food processor fitted with the metal blade, combine the almonds and flour and process until finely ground. Add the milk, 4 tablespoons (2 oz/60 g) of the granulated sugar, the eggs, framboise or kirsch and salt. Process until well mixed, about

30 seconds. Pour the milk mixture over the fruit. Dot the fruit with the butter pieces and sprinkle the remaining 2 tablespoons granulated sugar over the top.

❧ Bake until the top is golden and the custard is set, 30–35 minutes. Transfer to a rack and let cool for 15 minutes.

❧ While the clafouti is cooling, pour the cream into a bowl. Using a whisk or an electric mixer, beat the cream just until it begins to thicken. Add the confectioners' sugar and vanilla and continue to beat until soft peaks form.

❧ Spoon the warm clafouti onto individual plates. Pass the cream at the table.

## SUMMER BERRY GRATIN

SERVES 6

*All kinds of summer berries or fruits can be used for this versatile dessert. Try plums, peaches or nectarines in place of the mixed berries used here. You can make the pastry cream and ready the berries several hours in advance. When it is time to serve the dessert, just assemble and broil.*

5 egg yolks
1 teaspoon cornstarch (cornflour)
⅓ cup (3 oz/90 g) granulated sugar
2 tablespoons all-purpose (plain) flour
1½ cups (12 fl oz/375 ml) milk
½ teaspoon vanilla extract (essence)
1 tablespoon kirsch, framboise or
    crème de cassis
1 tablespoon unsalted butter, at room
    temperature
½ cup (4 fl oz/125 ml) mascarpone
    cheese
4 cups (1 lb/500 g) mixed berries
    such as blueberries, blackberries,
    raspberries and boysenberries, in
    any combination
1 tablespoon confectioners' (icing) sugar

In a bowl, using a whisk or an electric mixer, beat the egg yolks until light and fluffy, 1–2 minutes. In another bowl, stir together the cornstarch, granulated sugar and flour. Add the flour mixture to the egg yolks and again beat until light and fluffy, about 1 minute.

❧ Pour the milk into a saucepan over medium heat and heat until small bubbles appear along the edges of the pan. Gradually add the milk to the egg mixture, whisking constantly. Pour the mixture back into the saucepan and place over low heat. Cook, stirring, until the mixture thickens and bubbles

around the edges, 2–3 minutes. Remove from the heat and whisk in the vanilla, liqueur and butter. Fold in the mascarpone cheese.

❧ Preheat a broiler (griller). Divide the custard mixture evenly among 6 flameproof 4-inch (10-cm) gratin or tartlet dishes. Gently press the berries into the custard mixture, dividing them evenly. Sprinkle the tops evenly with the confectioners' sugar. Slip under the broiler about 4 inches (10 cm) from the heat source and broil (grill) until the tops are golden brown, 1–2 minutes. Serve immediately.

## PEACH ICE CREAM WITH ROSE PETALS

MAKES ABOUT 1½ QT (1.5 L); SERVES 6–8

*Freestone peaches are well suited to ice cream making. Use either the O'Henry, Elberta, First Lady or floral-scented white Babcock variety here.*

**FOR THE ROSE PETALS:**

1 cup (1½ oz/45 g) very loosely packed pesticide-free rose petals, in any color
2 egg whites
2 tablespoons water
1 cup (7 oz/220 g) superfine (castor) sugar

**FOR THE ICE CREAM:**

6 egg yolks
¾ cup (6 oz/185 g) granulated sugar
1 cup (8 fl oz/250 ml) milk
2 cups (16 fl oz/500 ml) heavy (double) cream
few drops vanilla extract (essence)
5 very ripe, flavorful peaches (see note), 1¼ lb (625 g) total, blanched in boiling water for 1 minute, drained, peeled, halved and pitted

To prepare the rose petals, rinse gently and place on paper towels until dry. In a bowl, combine the egg whites and water and whisk lightly to break up the whites. Line a baking sheet with waxed paper or parchment paper. Using tweezers to hold a petal by its base, brush the egg wash on both sides. Then, holding the petal over the prepared baking sheet, sprinkle with the superfine sugar. Continue with the remaining petals, placing them in a single layer on the baking sheet. Let stand uncovered at room temperature, turning the petals occasionally, until dry and crisp, 2–4 days, depending upon the temperature and humidity.

To make the ice cream, in a saucepan, whisk together the egg yolks and ½ cup (4 oz/125 g) of the sugar until well mixed. In another saucepan, combine the milk and cream over medium heat and heat until small bubbles form along the edges of the pan. Remove from the heat and very gradually add the cream mixture to the yolk mixture, whisking constantly. Place over medium heat and heat, stirring constantly, until the mixture begins to thicken and coats the back of a wooden spoon, or until an instant-read thermometer inserted into the liquid registers 165°F (74°C), about 5 minutes. Remove from the heat and strain through a fine-mesh sieve into a bowl. Add the vanilla and whisk to cool the mixture for 1 minute, then cover and chill well, about 2 hours.

Place the peach halves in a bowl. Add the remaining ¼ cup (2 oz/60 g) sugar and, using a potato masher, mash until you have a mixture with tiny pieces of peach. Strain through a coarse-mesh sieve into another bowl. Let stand for 15 minutes, then stir into the chilled ice cream base.

Freeze in an ice cream maker according to the manufacturer's directions. Scoop the ice cream into chilled bowls and garnish with the rose petals.

*The odors of fruits waft me to my southern home, to my childhood frolics in the peach orchard.*
*—Helen Keller*

*Cherries are especially prized because they have such a short season. The first ones arrive in late spring and the last are available only into early summer.*

*A happy soul, that all the way*
*To heaven hath a summer's day.*
*—Richard Crashaw*

## LATTICED CHERRY PIE

MAKES ONE 9-INCH (23-CM) PIE; SERVES 6–8

### FOR THE PASTRY:
2 cups (10 oz/315 g) all-purpose (plain) flour, plus flour as needed
½ teaspoon salt
7 tablespoons (3½ oz/105 g) unsalted butter, chilled, cut into pieces
½ cup (4 oz/125 g) vegetable shortening, chilled, cut into pieces
3 tablespoons ice water
1 teaspoon cider vinegar

### FOR THE FILLING:
1¾ lb (875 g) sweet cherries such as Royal Ann, Bing or Rainier, pitted
¾ cup (6 oz/185 g) sugar
2 tablespoons all-purpose (plain) flour
1 teaspoon kirsch or quetsch (plum liqueur)

1 egg yolk
1 tablespoon milk
vanilla ice cream

To make the dough, in a bowl, stir together the flour and salt. Using a pastry blender or 2 knives, cut in the butter and shortening until the mixture resembles coarse meal. In a cup or small bowl, combine the water and vinegar. Sprinkle the mixture over the top and, using a fork, toss lightly to moisten evenly. Gather the dough into a ball, being careful not to work it too much, and place on a lightly floured work surface. Divide the dough in half and wrap each half in plastic wrap. Chill for at least 4 hours or for up to 24 hours.

Using a rolling pin, roll out 1 ball of dough on a lightly floured work surface into a round 12 inches (30 cm) in diameter and ⅛ inch (3 mm) thick. Fold the dough in half and then into quarters and transfer it to a 9-inch (23-cm) pie pan. Unfold and gently press into the pan. Trim the edges flush with the pan rim. Place in the freezer for 30 minutes. Position a rack in the lower part of an oven and preheat to 400°F (200°C). Meanwhile, to make the filling, toss together the cherries, sugar, flour and liqueur.

Remove the remaining dough from the refrigerator and roll out into a round about 11 inches (28 cm) in diameter. Using a small knife or a pastry wheel, cut into strips about ¾ inch (2 cm) wide. Place a large sheet of waxed paper on the work surface and dust lightly with flour. Placing the strips about ¼ inch (6 mm) apart, weave them on the waxed paper to form a lattice.

Remove the pastry shell from the freezer and turn the cherry mixture into it. Gently lift the waxed paper over the filling and carefully slide the lattice onto the pie. Trim the edges flush with the pan rim and crimp to form an attractive edge. In a small bowl, beat together the egg yolk and milk and brush over the lattice and pastry edge.

Bake until the juices bubble thickly and the crust is golden, 1–1¼ hours. Transfer to a rack to cool for 1 hour before serving. Accompany each slice with a scoop of ice cream.

# APRICOT AND BLACKBERRY COBBLER

SERVES 6

*Cobblers are a great way to utilize the bounty of summer fruits. Any combination of fruits and berries can be used for this recipe, such as peaches, plums, nectarines, boysenberries, raspberries and blueberries.*

### FOR THE TOPPING:

1½ cups (7½ oz/235 g) all-purpose (plain) flour, plus flour as needed
2 tablespoons granulated sugar
2½ teaspoons baking powder
¼ teaspoon salt
6 tablespoons (3 oz/90 g) unsalted butter, cut into pieces
6–8 tablespoons (3–4 fl oz/90–125 ml) heavy (double) cream

### FOR THE FILLING:

1¾ lb (875 g) ripe but firm apricots, quartered and pitted
1 cup (4 oz/125 g) blackberries
⅓ cup (3 oz/90 g) granulated sugar, or as needed
3 tablespoons all-purpose (plain) flour

### FOR THE WHIPPED CREAM:

¾ cup (6 fl oz/180 ml) heavy (double) cream
1 tablespoon confectioners' (icing) sugar
¼ teaspoon vanilla extract (essence)

Preheat an oven to 375°F (190°C).

❧ To make the topping, in a food processor fitted with the metal blade, combine the flour, granulated sugar, baking powder and salt. Pulse to mix. Add the butter and pulse until the mixture resembles coarse meal. Transfer the mixture to a bowl. Using a fork, gradually stir in just enough of the cream to moisten the mixture so that it holds together. Gather it into a ball and place on a well-floured work surface. Using a floured rolling pin, roll out ½ inch (12 mm) thick. Using a round biscuit cutter 2½ inches (6 cm) in diameter, cut out 12 dough rounds.

❧ To make the filling, in a bowl, toss together the apricots, blackberries, ⅓ cup (3 oz/90 g) granulated sugar and the flour. Taste the fruit to see if it is sweet enough. If not, add additional sugar as needed.

❧ Transfer the filling to a 1½-qt (1.5-l) gratin or baking dish. Arrange the dough rounds so that they are evenly spaced and almost touching on top of the fruit. Bake until the biscuits are golden brown and fruit is bubbling around the edges, 30–35 minutes.

❧ While the cobbler is baking, prepare the whipped cream: Pour the cream into a bowl. Using a whisk or an electric mixer, beat the cream just until it begins to thicken. Add the confectioners' sugar and vanilla and continue to beat until soft peaks form. Cover and refrigerate until ready to serve.

❧ To serve, spoon the fruit and biscuits onto individual plates. Top with the cream and serve immediately.

*The blushing apricot and woolly peach Hang on thy walls, that every child may reach.*
*—Ben Johnson*

## BLUEBERRY SORBET WITH BERRY AND CASSIS COMPOTE

MAKES ABOUT 1 QT (1 L) SORBET AND 2 CUPS
(16 FL OZ/500 ML) COMPOTE; SERVES 6–8

*Fraises des bois, tiny wild strawberries from the French Alps, have the scent and flavor of roses. They are easy to grow and do well as an ornamental in any spring or summer garden with part shade and part sunshine. But use them quickly after picking, for they are quite fragile. If fraises des bois are unavailable, double the amount of blueberries in the compote.*

**FOR THE COMPOTE:**

2 cups (8 oz/250 g) raspberries

½ cup (4 fl oz/125 ml) water

⅓ cup (2½ oz/75 g) sugar

1 piece lemon peel, about 2 inches
    (5 cm) long

¾ cup (3 oz/90 g) blueberries

¾ cup (3 oz/90 g) fraises des bois
    (see note)

1 tablespoon crème de cassis

1 teaspoon fresh lemon juice

**FOR THE SORBET:**

6 cups (1½ lb/750 g) blueberries

1 cup (8 oz/250 g) sugar

½ teaspoon fresh lemon juice

To make the compote, place 1 cup (4 oz/125 g) of the raspberries in a food processor fitted with the metal blade or in a blender and purée until smooth. Strain through a fine-mesh sieve into a clean bowl.

⤷ In a saucepan over medium-high heat, combine the water, sugar and lemon peel and bring to a boil. Reduce the heat to medium and add the blueberries. Cook until the blueberries just begin to crack, about 1 minute. Remove from the heat and remove the

lemon peel and discard. Stir in the fraises des bois, raspberry purée, crème de cassis, lemon juice and the remaining 1 cup (4 oz/125 g) raspberries. Cover and chill for at least 30 minutes.

❧ To make the sorbet, place the blueberries in a food processor fitted with the metal blade or in a blender and purée until smooth. Strain through a fine-mesh sieve into a clean bowl. You should have 2 cups (16 fl oz/500 ml) blueberry purée. Place approximately one-fourth of the purée in a small saucepan over medium heat. Add the sugar and stir until dissolved. Remove from the heat and stir the hot blueberry mixture into the reserved blueberry purée. Add the lemon juice, cover and chill well, about 2 hours.

❧ Freeze the blueberry purée in an ice cream maker according to the manufacturer's directions.

❧ To serve, scoop the sorbet into chilled bowls. Spoon the compote over the top.

## WATERMELON GRANITA

SERVES 6

*Granita is a cooling, icy slush made during the furnacelike summers of Italy. Like ice cream, it comes in a variety of sweet, refreshing flavors, such as melon, peach, nectarine, berry and coffee. If you like, garnish with tiny wedges of well-chilled watermelon.*

4–5 packed cups (1½ lb/750 g) seedless watermelon chunks
1 cup (8 fl oz/250 ml) water
1 cup (8 oz/250 g) sugar
1 tablespoon fresh lemon juice

Place the watermelon chunks in a blender and purée until smooth. Strain through a fine-mesh sieve into a bowl. You should have 2 cups (16 fl oz/ 500 ml) purée.

❧ In a saucepan over high heat, combine the water and sugar. Heat, stirring, just until the sugar dissolves. Add the sugar syrup and lemon juice to the watermelon purée and stir well. Pour the mixture into a shallow 9-by-13-inch (23-by-33-cm) metal or glass baking dish.

❧ Place, uncovered, in the freezer until ice crystals begin to form, 1½–2 hours. Using a fork, stir to break up the mixture. Return to the freezer and freeze, stirring with the fork every 30 minutes to prevent the mixture from forming a solid mass. It should be evenly crystallized and like slush in another 2 hours.

❧ To serve, spoon or scoop the granita into chilled serving dishes.

# FRESH FRUIT TART

MAKES ONE 9-INCH (23-CM) TART; SERVES 8

### FOR THE PASTRY:

1 cup (5 oz/155 g) all-purpose (plain)
 flour
1 tablespoon sugar
¼ teaspoon salt
½ cup (4 oz/125 g) unsalted butter, out
 of the refrigerator for 20 minutes,
 cut into pieces
1–2 tablespoons water

### FOR THE FILLING:

1¼ cups (10 fl oz/310 ml) milk
3½ tablespoons all-purpose (plain) flour
¼ cup (2 oz/60 g) sugar
4 egg yolks
1 tablespoon unsalted butter
2 teaspoons kirsch or ½ teaspoon vanilla
 extract (essence)
4 cups (about 1¼ lb/625 g) sliced
 mixed fruits such as kiwifruits,
 peaches, plums and whole blueberries
¼ cup (2½ oz/75 g) red currant jelly,
 melted

To make the pastry, in a food processor
fitted with the metal blade, combine
the flour, sugar and salt. Pulse briefly to
mix. Add the butter and process until
the consistency of coarse meal. With the
motor running, add just enough of the
water to form a ball that cleans the sides
of the bowl. Remove from the processor, wrap the dough in plastic wrap
and chill for 30 minutes.
❧ Place the pastry in a 9-inch (23-cm)
tart pan with a removable bottom and
press it gently onto the bottom and
sides of the pan, forming an even layer.
Place in the freezer for 30 minutes.
Preheat an oven to 375°F (190°C).
❧ Line the pastry shell with parchment
paper and fill with pie weights, rice or
beans. Bake until lightly golden around

the edges, 15–20 minutes. Remove
from the oven and remove the weights
and parchment. Continue to bake until
pale gold, 5–7 minutes. Remove from
the oven and let cool on a rack.
❧ To make the filling, first make the
pastry cream: Pour the milk into a
saucepan over medium heat and heat
until small bubbles appear along the
edges of the pan. Remove from the
heat. In another saucepan, stir together
the flour and sugar. In a bowl, whisk
the egg yolks until light colored. Whisk
the hot milk into the flour mixture and
place over medium heat. Cook, stirring
constantly, until the mixture boils, 1–2
minutes. Remove from the heat and
whisk one-fourth of the hot mixture
into the egg yolks. Then whisk the egg
yolks into the remaining hot mixture
and cook over medium heat, stirring
constantly, until thickened slightly and
an instant-read thermometer inserted
into the liquid registers 165°F (74°C),
2–3 minutes. Remove from the heat, stir
in the butter and strain through a fine-
mesh sieve into a clean bowl. Stir in the
kirsch or vanilla and cover with plastic
wrap, pressing it directly onto the
surface of the pastry cream. Let cool in
the refrigerator.
❧ Spread the cooled pastry cream
in the pastry shell. Arrange the fruits
attractively on top of the pastry cream
and brush with a thin coating of the
jelly. Remove the pan sides and, using
a spatula, slide the tart from the pan
bottom onto a serving plate.

# SUMMER MELONS IN SPICED WHITE WINE

SERVES 6

2 cups (16 fl oz/500 ml) late-harvest
 dessert wine such as Muscat or
 Sauternes
1 tablespoon honey
4 thin slices fresh ginger
½ vanilla bean
5 lb (2.5 kg) assorted summer melons,
 in any combination

In a saucepan, combine the wine, honey
and ginger. Split the vanilla bean in half
lengthwise and scrape the seeds into
the pan, then add the pod halves as well.
Bring to a boil over high heat. Reduce
the heat to low and simmer for 5 minutes. Remove from the heat. Discard the
vanilla pods and ginger slices. Let cool.
❧ Meanwhile, halve the melons.
Scoop out the seeds and discard. Using
a melon baller, scoop out balls of the
melon flesh and place them in a large
bowl. Pour the cooled spiced wine over
the melon, cover and chill for 1 hour.
❧ To serve, divide the melon among
chilled individual bowls, spooning some
of the wine over each portion.

*Autumn*

# Autumn Openers

Just as the foliage changes from shades of green to burnished oranges, reds, golds and browns, so does the harvest define the palette of autumn's first courses. The hard-shelled winter squashes that arrive in markets are transformed into colorful starters like Curried Pumpkin and Leek Flan (page 148) and Pizza with Winter Squash and Smoked Bacon (page 151). Equally rich in autumnal hues is a lofty Sweet Potato Soufflé (page 146).

Such dishes also possess a sustaining heartiness that is particularly welcome as the days grow shorter and the weather grows colder. "Comfort" is a prevailing theme of autumn meals, evident in the Mushroom and Stilton Galette on this page, which features some of the season's foraged treasures, or in Fried Polenta Sticks with Sage (page 147). With the holidays approaching, "celebration" also comes to mind, and any one of these dishes would open traditional feasts in true seasonal style.

## MUSHROOM AND STILTON GALETTE

SERVES 6

*During the damp autumn months, professional mushroom foragers and amateurs alike seek out prized fungi along the floors of dampened fields and forests.*

**FOR THE PASTRY:**

1¼ cups (6½ oz/200 g) all-purpose (plain) flour

¼ teaspoon salt

½ cup (4 oz/125 g) unsalted butter, cut into pieces

¼ cup (2 fl oz/60 ml) sour cream

2 teaspoons fresh lemon juice

¼ cup (2 fl oz/60 ml) ice water

**FOR THE FILLING:**

¼ oz (7 g) dried wild mushrooms such as chanterelles, porcini or shiitakes

1 cup (8 fl oz/250 ml) boiling water

2 tablespoons unsalted butter

¾ cup (2 oz/60 g) sliced green (spring) onions

1 clove garlic, minced

½ teaspoon chopped fresh rosemary

½ teaspoon chopped fresh thyme

½ lb (250 g) assorted fresh wild mushrooms such as chanterelles, porcini and shiitakes, brushed clean and large mushrooms thinly sliced

½ lb (250 g) fresh button mushrooms, brushed clean and thinly sliced

5 oz (155 g) Stilton or other good-quality blue cheese

To make the pastry, combine the flour and salt in a bowl. Place the butter in another bowl. Place both bowls in the freezer for 1 hour. Remove the bowls from the freezer and make a well in the center of the flour. Add the butter to the well and, using a pastry blender, cut it in until the mixture has the consist-ency of coarse meal. Make another well in the center. In a small bowl, whisk together the sour cream, lemon juice and water and add half of this mixture to the well. With your fingertips, mix in the liquid until large lumps form. Remove the large lumps and repeat with the remaining liquid and flour-butter mixture. Pat the lumps into a ball; do not overwork the dough. Wrap in plastic wrap and refrigerate for 1 hour.

Meanwhile, make the filling: Place the dried mushrooms in a small bowl and add the boiling water. Let stand for 30 minutes until softened. Drain the mushrooms and mince finely. Preheat an oven to 400°F (200°C).

In a large frying pan over medium heat, melt the butter. Add the green onions and sauté, stirring occasionally, until soft, about 5 minutes. Add the garlic, rosemary and thyme and continue to cook, stirring, for 1 minute longer. Raise the heat to high, add the fresh and rehydrated mushrooms and sauté until the mushrooms are tender and the liquid they released has completely evaporated, 8–10 minutes. Transfer to a plate and let cool.

On a floured work surface, roll out the dough into a 12-inch (30-cm) round. Transfer to an ungreased baking sheet. Crumble the blue cheese into a bowl, add the cooled mushrooms and stir well. Spread the mixture over the dough, leaving a 1½-inch (4-cm) border. Fold the border over the mushrooms and cheese, pleating the edge to make it fit. The center will be open.

Bake until golden brown, 30–40 minutes. Remove from the oven, let stand for 5 minutes, then slide the galette onto a serving plate. Cut into wedges and serve hot, warm or at room temperature.

## GRILLED BREAD WITH FRESH SHELL BEANS AND ESCAROLE

MAKES 18 PIECES; SERVES 6

*Although fresh shell beans can be found in markets during July and August, the abundance and variety increase during late summer and into the autumn months. The palette is enormous, from American varieties such as cranberry, pinto and lima to Italian borlotti and cannellini and French flageolets. They take a bit of work to shell but are well worth the effort.*

1 lb (500 g) fresh shell beans (see note)
3 cloves garlic, minced
2 tablespoons chopped fresh sage
3 tablespoons extra-virgin olive oil, plus olive oil for brushing
salt and freshly ground pepper
18 slices country-style bread, about 3 inches (7.5 cm) in diameter
½ head escarole (Batavian endive), cored and cut into strips 1 inch (2.5 cm) wide
1 tablespoon red wine vinegar
small pinch of red pepper flakes

Shell the beans. Bring a saucepan three-fourths full of water to a boil over medium-high heat. Add the beans and cook until very soft, about 20 minutes. Drain, reserving 1 cup (8 fl oz/250 ml) of the liquid.

❧ Prepare a fire in a charcoal grill or preheat a broiler (griller). In a frying pan over medium heat, combine the beans, garlic, sage and 2 tablespoons of the oil. Cook, mashing the beans with a spoon or potato masher and adding the reserved cooking liquid as needed to keep the mixture moist, until a rough paste forms, 10–15 minutes. Remove from the heat and continue mashing the beans to form a smooth paste. Alterna-tively, pulse the mixture in a food processor fitted with the metal blade or in a blender. Season to taste with salt and pepper.

❧ Lightly brush the bread slices on both sides with olive oil and place on the grill rack or on a baking sheet. Grill or broil, turning once, until golden on both sides, 30–60 seconds on each side. Remove from the heat and set aside.

❧ In another frying pan over high heat, warm the remaining 1 tablespoon oil. Add the escarole and cook, tossing frequently with tongs, until wilted, 2–3 minutes. Add the vinegar and red pepper flakes and season to taste with salt and pepper. Mix well.

❧ To serve, spread the bean purée on the grilled or toasted bread, dividing it evenly. Top with the wilted escarole and serve immediately.

## SMOKED CHEDDAR TWISTS

MAKES ABOUT 30 TWISTS

*Perfect for serving with wine or aperitifs, these crisp twists can also be made with aged Cheddar or pepper Jack in place of the smoked Cheddar.*

1 cup (5 oz/155 g) all-purpose (plain) flour
⅓ cup (1½ oz/45 g) cake (soft-wheat) flour
¼ teaspoon cayenne pepper
½ cup (2 oz/60 g) shredded smoked Cheddar cheese
¼ cup (1 oz/30 g) grated Parmesan cheese
¼ teaspoon salt
¾ cup (6 oz/185 g) unsalted butter, cut into pieces
2 teaspoons fresh lemon juice
¼ cup (2 fl oz/60 ml) ice water

In the work bowl of a food processor fitted with the metal blade, combine the all-purpose flour, cake flour, cayenne pepper, Cheddar cheese, Parmesan cheese and salt. Pulse to mix. Sprinkle the butter pieces over the flour mixture and place the work bowl in the freezer for 1 hour, then pulse again to combine.

❧ In a small bowl, mix the lemon juice and ice water. With the processor on, add just enough of the lemon juice mixture to the flour mixture for it to come together in a rough mass.

❧ Turn out the dough onto a lightly floured board and gently form into a rough rectangle; do not overwork. Using a rolling pin, roll out into a rectangle ½ inch (12 mm) thick. Fold in the narrow ends to meet in the center. Then fold in half crosswise so that there are 4 layers. Turn the dough a quarter turn and roll out again to form a rectangle ½ inch (12 mm) thick. Fold the rectangle into thirds as if you are folding a letter. Wrap the dough in plastic wrap and refrigerate for 45 minutes.

❧ Preheat an oven to 400°F (200°C). Unwrap the dough and place on a floured work surface. Roll out into a rectangle about 7 inches (18 cm) wide by 15 inches (38 cm) long by ⅛ inch (3 mm) thick. Trim the edges so that they are even. Cut the dough crosswise into sticks ½ inch (12 mm) wide and twist each one once to form a soft turn at the center. Place the twists on 2 ungreased baking sheets, spacing them about 1 inch (2.5 cm) apart.

❧ Bake until golden and crisp, about 15 minutes, switching the baking sheets about halfway through baking. Let cool. Serve immediately, or pack into an airtight container and store at room temperature for up to 1 week.

## SWEET POTATO SOUFFLÉ

SERVES 6

*Contrary to popular belief, the tuberous roots most people refer to as sweet potatoes or yams are not related to the russet potato. These natives of the New World are members of the morning glory family. Their characteristic sweetness develops even further after harvest.*

2 lb (1 kg) sweet potatoes
½ cup (2 oz/60 g) freshly grated
    Parmesan cheese
3 tablespoons unsalted butter
1 white onion, minced
1½ cups (12 fl oz/375 ml) milk
3 tablespoons all-purpose (plain) flour
¼ teaspoon freshly grated nutmeg
¼ teaspoon ground allspice
¼ teaspoon ground ginger
6 eggs, separated
1 cup (4 oz/125 g) shredded Gruyère
    cheese
salt and freshly ground pepper

Preheat an oven to 375°F (190°C).

❧ Pierce the potatoes two or three times with a fork and place on a baking sheet. Bake until easily pierced with a knife, 30–40 minutes. Remove from the oven and let cool. Cut in half and scrape out the pulp into a bowl. Using a potato masher, mash to form a smooth purée; you should have 2½ cups (1¼ lb/625 g). Leave the oven temperature set at 375°F (190°C).

❧ Butter a 2-qt (2-l) soufflé dish and dust the bottom and sides with ¼ cup (1 oz/30 g) of the Parmesan cheese.

❧ In a large saucepan over medium heat, melt the butter. Add the onion and sauté, stirring occasionally, until soft, about 10 minutes. Meanwhile, in a small saucepan over medium heat, warm the milk until small bubbles appear along the edges of the pan; remove from the heat. Add the flour to the onion and cook, stirring constantly, for 3 minutes. (Do not brown.) Whisk in the milk all at once and simmer, continuing to whisk, until thickened, 2–3 minutes. Remove from the heat and stir in the nutmeg, allspice and ginger. Add the egg yolks one at a time, beating well after each addition. Add the sweet potato purée and the Gruyère cheese and stir until well blended. Season to taste with salt and pepper.

❧ In a bowl, using an electric mixer set on high speed, beat the egg whites until they just hold stiff peaks. Using a rubber spatula, fold one-fourth of the egg whites into the sweet potato mixture to lighten it. Then gently fold in the remaining whites just until no white streaks remain. Pour into the prepared soufflé dish. Sprinkle with the remaining ¼ cup (1 oz/30 g) Parmesan cheese.

❧ Bake until puffed and golden, 45–50 minutes. Serve immediately.

# FRIED POLENTA STICKS WITH SAGE

*MAKES ABOUT 50 POLENTA STICKS; SERVES 8*

*The heartiness of polenta makes it a comforting menu addition when autumn's chill sets in. The coarse grains develop their characteristic mushiness while mixing them with simmering liquid, so reserve some stamina for stirring.*

5 cups (40 fl oz/1.25 l) water
1 teaspoon salt, plus salt to taste
1¼ cups (7½ oz/235 g) polenta
½ cup (2 oz/60 g) freshly grated
    Parmesan
2 tablespoons chopped fresh sage
3 tablespoons unsalted butter
freshly ground pepper
2 cups (10 oz/315 g) all-purpose (plain)
    flour
olive oil and safflower oil for deep-
    frying
fresh herb sprigs

In a heavy saucepan, bring the water to a boil over high heat and add the 1 teaspoon salt. Slowly add the polenta in a steady stream while whisking constantly. Continue to whisk until the mixture thickens, about 2 minutes. Switch to a wooden spoon, reduce the heat to medium and continue to simmer, stirring, until the polenta pulls away from the sides of the pan, 20–25 minutes. Add the Parmesan, sage and butter and stir to mix well. Season with salt and pepper to taste.

~ Butter a 9-inch (23-cm) square pan. Pour the hot polenta into the prepared pan and smooth the top with a rubber spatula. Let cool slightly, then cover and refrigerate until cold and set, at least 1 hour or for up to 3 days.

~ Using a sharp knife, cut the polenta into sticks 3 inches (7.5 cm) long by ½ inch (12 mm) wide. Toss them gently with the flour, dusting lightly.

~ Position a rack in the upper part of an oven and preheat to 400°F (200°C). Pour equal amounts of the olive and safflower oils into a large, deep frying pan to a depth of 2 inches (5 cm). Heat to 375°F (190°C) on a deep-frying thermometer. When hot, add the polenta sticks a few at a time and fry, turning occasionally with a slotted spoon or tongs, until golden brown, 1–2 minutes. Transfer to paper towels to drain, then keep warm in the oven until all are cooked.

~ Arrange the polenta sticks on a warmed platter and sprinkle with salt to taste. Garnish with herb sprigs and serve immediately.

## CURRIED PUMPKIN AND LEEK FLAN

SERVES 6

*Sugar pumpkins are an excellent choice for baking and work well in this recipe. If unavailable, substitute any winter squash.*

1 small pumpkin, 2 lb (1 kg) (see note)

2 tablespoons unsalted butter

6 leeks, including 1 inch (2.5 cm) of green, carefully rinsed and cut into ½-inch (12-mm) dice

3 whole eggs, plus 3 egg yolks

1½ cups (12 fl oz/375 ml) heavy (double) cream

2 tablespoons sugar

1 teaspoon curry powder

salt and freshly ground pepper

boiling water, as needed

1½ cups (12 fl oz/375 ml) chicken stock

1 tablespoon chopped fresh flat-leaf (Italian) parsley plus parsley sprigs for garnish

Preheat an oven to 375°F (190°C). Lightly oil a baking sheet.

๛ Cut the pumpkin in half through the stem end and place, cut side down, on the prepared baking sheet. Bake until easily pierced with a knife, 40–50 minutes. Remove from the oven and let cool. Leave the oven set at 375°F (190°C). Using a spoon, scoop out the seeds and fibers and discard. Spoon the flesh into a blender and purée on high speed until smooth.

๛ Meanwhile, in a large frying pan over medium heat, melt the butter. Add the leeks and cook, stirring occasionally, until they are very soft and begin to fall apart, 30–40 minutes. Remove from the heat.

๛ In a bowl, whisk together the whole eggs and egg yolks, 1 cup (8 fl oz/ 250 ml) of the cream, the sugar, curry powder and salt and pepper to taste. Add three-fourths of the pumpkin purée and all the leeks and stir well.

๛ Butter six ⅔-cup (5-fl oz/160-ml) ramekins or flan molds. Place in a large baking pan and divide the flan mixture evenly among the prepared molds. Pour boiling water into the baking pan to reach halfway up the sides of the molds. Cover the pan loosely with aluminum foil. Bake until the custards are firm in the center and browned on top, 20–25 minutes.

๛ While the flans are baking, combine the chicken stock, the remaining pumpkin purée and the remaining ½ cup (4 fl oz/125 ml) cream in a saucepan. Place over medium-high heat and bring to a boil, stirring occasionally. Boil gently until reduced by half, 5–10 minutes. Strain through a fine-mesh sieve into a clean pan. Season to taste with salt and pepper.

๛ Remove the flans from the oven and let cool for 5 minutes. Run a knife around the edge of each mold and invert onto individual plates. Ladle the sauce around the custards. Garnish with the parsley and serve.

*Any type of ⅔-cup (5-fl oz/160-ml) ramekin or flan mold can be used for this elegant first course. To help unmold the custards, run a knife around the inside edge of each mold before inverting it onto an individual plate. Use the knife to smooth any uneven edges on the custards before serving.*

## Pizza with Winter Squash and Smoked Bacon

Makes two 9-inch (23-cm) pizzas; serves 6

**For the Pizza Dough:**

¾ cup (6 fl oz/180 ml) lukewarm water (110°F/43°C)

2 teaspoons active dry yeast

2 cups (10 oz/315 g) all-purpose (plain) flour, plus flour as needed

3 tablespoons extra-virgin olive oil

½ teaspoon salt

**For the Pizza Topping:**

¼ small butternut squash, ½ lb (250 g), seeded, peeled and cut into thin slices

2 tablespoons extra-virgin olive oil

salt and freshly ground pepper

¼ lb (125 g) hickory-smoked bacon, cut into small dice

3 oz (90 g) smoked mozzarella cheese, shredded

3 oz (90 g) plain mozzarella cheese, shredded

¼ cup (⅓ oz/10 g) chopped fresh sage

To make the pizza dough, in a bowl, stir together ¼ cup (2 fl oz/60 ml) of the water, the yeast and ¼ cup (1 oz/30 g) of the flour. Let stand until bubbly, about 20 minutes. Add the remaining ½ cup (4 fl oz/120 ml) lukewarm water, the olive oil and the salt. Stir in the remaining 1¾ cups (9 oz/285 g) flour and mix well. Turn out onto a floured work surface and knead until smooth and elastic, about 10 minutes. Place in a well-oiled bowl and turn the dough to oil the top. Cover the bowl with plastic wrap and let the dough rise in a warm place until doubled in volume, about 1 hour.

❧ Position a rack in the bottom third of an oven and place a pizza stone or unglazed terracotta tiles on the rack. Preheat the oven to 500°F (260°C).

❧ To make the topping, bring a saucepan three-fourths full of salted water to a boil. Add the squash slices and boil until half-cooked, about 3 minutes. Using a slotted spoon, transfer to paper towels and drain well. In a large frying pan over high heat, warm 1 tablespoon of the oil. Add the squash and cook, turning, until golden on the edges and cooked through, about 5 minutes. Season generously with salt and pepper. Remove the squash and let cool.

❧ Add the remaining 1 tablespoon oil to the frying pan and place over medium heat. Add the bacon and cook, stirring, until it begins to turn golden, about 5 minutes. Using the slotted spoon, transfer to paper towels to drain. In a bowl, combine the mozzarella cheeses and toss to mix.

❧ Punch down the dough and turn out onto a floured work surface. Divide in half and roll out one half into a round 9 inches (23 cm) in diameter and ¼ inch (6 mm) thick. Transfer to a well-floured pizza peel or rimless baking sheet. Sprinkle on half of the cheese, leaving a ½-inch (12-mm) border uncovered around the edges. Sprinkle with half each of the bacon and sage. Top with half of the squash slices. Slide the pizza directly onto the stone.

❧ Bake until golden and crisp, 8–10 minutes. Repeat with the remaining ingredients. Serve at once.

*For man, autumn is
a time of harvest,
of gathering together.
For nature, it is
a time of sowing,
of scattering abroad.*
—*Edwin Way Teale*

# *Autumn Soups & Salads*

The soups and salads in this section present an opportunity to savor the very best that autumn has to offer. Robust greens and roots that thrive in the cool ground appear in such sustaining dishes as Vegetable Barley Soup (page 160) and Fennel, Celery, Parsley and Prosciutto Salad (page 159). Winter squash, ideal for puréeing, lends bright color, substantial body and sweet flavor to the Acorn Squash Soup with Toasted Walnut Butter on this page. And a cornucopia of autumn fruits brings a taste of the festive season to come in Salad of Figs, Pomegranates, Persimmons and Pears (page 156).

In this time of dramatic contrasts, when bright Indian summer days may be suddenly followed by blustery gray weather, our soup bowls and salad plates sometimes seem to span the seasons. How else to explain the delightful proximity of such dishes as Eggplant Soup (page 161), so summery in its ingredients and flavors, and Warm Cabbage Salad (page 156), a robust concoction capable of warding off winter's cold?

## ACORN SQUASH SOUP WITH TOASTED WALNUT BUTTER

SERVES 6

*Autumn brings the familiar sight of market stands featuring baskets piled high with winter squashes. In this recipe, butternut, Hubbard, pumpkin, butternut, or turban can be substituted for the acorn squash.*

4 acorn squashes, about 1 lb (500 g) each
1 tablespoon unsalted butter, at room temperature
2 slices bacon, about 2 oz (60 g), finely chopped
1 large yellow onion, chopped
6 cups (48 fl oz/1.5 l) chicken stock

FOR THE TOASTED WALNUT BUTTER:
3 tablespoons walnuts
2 teaspoons walnut oil
large pinch of sugar
salt and freshly ground pepper
2 tablespoons unsalted butter, at room temperature

¼ cup (2 fl oz/60 ml) heavy (double) cream
large pinch of freshly grated nutmeg
¼ cup (2 fl oz/60 ml) fresh orange juice
salt and freshly ground pepper
flat-leaf (Italian) parsley leaves

Preheat an oven to 375°F (190°C). Lightly oil a baking sheet.
❧ Cut each squash in half through the stem end and place, cut sides down, on the prepared baking sheet. Bake until easily pierced with a knife, about 45 minutes. Remove from the oven and set aside until cool enough to handle.

❧ Using a spoon, scoop out the seeds and fibers and discard. Spoon the flesh into a bowl and set aside. Leave the oven set at 375°F (190°C).
❧ In a soup pot over medium heat, melt the butter. Add the bacon and onion and sauté until the onion is soft, about 10 minutes. Raise the heat to high, add the squash and stock and bring to a gentle boil. Reduce the heat to medium and simmer, uncovered, until the squash disintegrates, about 30 minutes.
❧ Meanwhile, make the walnut butter: In a small bowl, toss together the walnuts, walnut oil, sugar and salt and pepper to taste and spread out on a baking sheet. Toast until golden, 5–7 minutes. Remove from the oven, let cool and chop finely. In a small bowl, using a fork, mash together the walnuts and butter. Season to taste with salt and pepper. Spoon out the butter onto a piece of plastic wrap and, using the plastic wrap, shape into a log about 1 inch (2.5 cm) in diameter. Wrap and refrigerate until serving.
❧ Remove the squash from the heat and let cool for 20 minutes. Using a blender and working in batches, purée the soup on high speed until smooth, 2–3 minutes for each batch. Pass through a fine-mesh sieve into a clean saucepan. Add the cream, nutmeg, orange juice and salt and pepper to taste. Reheat to serving temperature and ladle into warmed bowls. Cut the walnut butter into 6 equal slices and float a slice in each bowl. Garnish with parsley leaves and serve hot.

## WILD RICE AND WILD MUSHROOM SOUP

SERVES 6

*Wild rice isn't really a rice at all, but a semiaquatic grass native to North America. In California and Minnesota, wild rice grows throughout the summer and is harvested in September and October. Its earthy flavor makes it a perfect grain for serving during the autumn months.*

½ cup (3 oz/90 g) wild rice
3 cups (24 fl oz/750 ml) boiling water
½ teaspoon salt, plus salt to taste
½ oz (15 g) dried wild mushrooms such
    as porcini, chanterelles or shiitakes
2 tablespoons unsalted butter
1 yellow onion, finely chopped
1 celery stalk, finely chopped
½ cup (4 fl oz/125 ml) dry white wine
¾ lb (375 g) fresh button mushrooms,
    brushed clean and sliced
3 cups (24 fl oz/750 ml) chicken or
    vegetable stock
½ cup (4 fl oz/125 ml) heavy (double)
    cream
freshly ground pepper
1 tablespoon chopped fresh flat-leaf
    (Italian) parsley

Rinse the wild rice in several changes of water and drain. Place the rice in a saucepan and add 2 cups (16 fl oz/ 500 ml) of the boiling water and the ½ teaspoon salt. Place over high heat and bring to a boil. Immediately reduce the heat to low, cover and cook without stirring until tender and the water is absorbed, about 40 minutes. Remove from the heat and let cool.
❧ Meanwhile, place the dried mushrooms in a small bowl and add the remaining 1 cup (8 fl oz/250 ml) boiling water. Let stand for 30 minutes until softened. Drain, reserving the liquid, and set the mushrooms aside. Strain the liquid through a sieve lined with cheesecloth (muslin). Set aside.
❧ In a soup pot over medium heat, melt the butter. Add the onion and celery and sauté, stirring occasionally, until soft, about 10 minutes. Raise the heat to high, add the wine and cook until reduced to about 2 table-spoons, 3–4 minutes. Reduce the heat to medium, add the fresh and rehy-drated mushrooms and sauté, stirring occasionally, until the mushrooms wilt, about 15 minutes. Raise the heat to high, add the stock and the reserved mushroom liquid and bring to a boil. Reduce the heat to medium and cook, uncovered, until the mushrooms are very soft, about 20 minutes. Add the wild rice and the cream and simmer for 5 minutes longer to blend the flavors. Season to taste with salt and pepper.
❧ Ladle the soup into warmed bowls and garnish with the parsley. Serve immediately.

## ESCAROLE AND ENDIVE SALAD WITH WALNUTS AND GORGONZOLA

SERVES 6

*Escarole is part of the chicory family, along with Belgian endive and radicchio. While many vegetables are prized for their delicate flavors, members of this clan are appreciated for their slightly bitter taste. When eaten raw, they pair especially well with more strongly flavored, rich ingredients such as nuts, cheeses and fruits.*

½ cup (2 oz/60 g) walnut halves
3 tablespoons extra-virgin olive oil
1 tablespoon walnut oil
2 tablespoons red wine vinegar
1 shallot, minced
salt and freshly ground pepper
4 heads Belgian endive (chicory/
    witloof), 1 lb (500 g) total weight,
    cored and leaves separated
1 head escarole (Batavian endive),
    ½ lb (250 g), carefully rinsed and
    torn into 2-inch (5-cm) pieces
3 oz (90 g) Gorgonzola cheese,
    crumbled

Preheat an oven to 350°F (180°C). Spread the walnuts on a baking sheet and toast until lightly browned and fragrant, 5–7 minutes. Remove from the oven and let cool.
❧ In a small bowl, whisk together the olive oil, walnut oil, vinegar, shallot and salt and pepper to taste to form a vinaigrette.
❧ In a bowl, combine the endives and escarole. Drizzle on the vinaigrette and toss to coat the leaves evenly. Transfer to a serving platter and garnish with the Gorgonzola and walnuts. Serve immediately.

## WARM CABBAGE SALAD

SERVES 6

*The cabbage family is broad, with Brussels sprouts, broccoli, cauliflower, kale, bok choy and Savoy, napa and celery cabbages among the many relatives. This salad is best made with green, red, napa and Savoy cabbages, in any combination.*

2 tablespoons extra-virgin olive oil
2 large shallots, minced
2–3 lb (1–1.5 kg) assorted cabbages
   (see note), cored and cut into
   shreds ¼ inch (6 mm) wide
½ teaspoon caraway seeds
2 tart green apples such as Granny
   Smith or pippin, halved, cored and
   cut into thin slices

3 tablespoons white wine vinegar
salt and freshly ground pepper
¼ cup (¼ oz/7 g) fresh flat-leaf (Italian)
   parsley leaves

In a large frying pan over medium heat, warm the olive oil. Add the shallots and sauté, stirring occasionally, until soft, about 10 minutes. Add the cabbages and caraway seeds, cover partially and cook, stirring occasionally, until the cabbages just begin to soften, about 10 minutes. Add the apples and vinegar and stir together. Continue to cook, stirring occasionally, until the apples are warm, 1–2 minutes. Season to taste with salt and pepper.
 Stir in the parsley leaves and transfer to a warmed serving dish. Serve at once.

## SALAD OF FIGS, POMEGRANATES, PERSIMMONS AND PEARS

SERVES 6

*For this colorful autumn salad, use the tomato-shaped Fuyu persimmon, which has a tender but crisp flesh and is generally eaten raw.*

½ cup (2 oz/60 g) walnut halves
1 small pomegranate
1½ tablespoons red wine vinegar
3 tablespoons extra-virgin olive oil
salt and freshly ground pepper
2 large heads frisée, carefully rinsed
   and stems trimmed
1 Fuyu persimmon, cut into thin slices
1 red Bartlett pear, halved, cored and
   cut into thin slices
6 fresh figs, halved through the
   stem end

Preheat an oven to 350°F (180°C). Spread the walnuts on a baking sheet and toast until lightly browned and fragrant, 5–7 minutes. Remove from the oven and let cool.
 Using a small, sharp knife, score the skin of the pomegranate into quarters. Fill a bowl three-fourths full with water. Holding the pomegranate in the bowl of water, peel off the pomegranate skin, then gently pull the seeds from the membrane, letting them sink to the bottom of the bowl. Scoop out the seeds and let drain on a paper towel.
 In a small bowl, whisk together the vinegar, olive oil, and salt and pepper to taste to form a vinaigrette.
 Arrange the frisée, sliced persimmon and pear, and fig halves on individual plates, dividing them equally. Sprinkle the pomegranate seeds and walnut halves evenly over each serving. Drizzle with the vinaigrette and serve.

## White Bean Soup with Smoked Ham

SERVES 6

*Pantry staples such as beans and smoked meats are traditionally featured in the soups and stews of cold-weather months. In this recipe, a trio of hearty autumn herbs flavors the beans as they cook. Freshly baked corn bread (recipe on page 170) makes a good accompaniment.*

¾ cup (5½ oz/170 g) dried small white (navy), white kidney or cannellini beans
6 fresh parsley sprigs
2 fresh thyme sprigs
2 bay leaves
1 tablespoon olive oil
¼ lb (125 g) bacon, finely diced
1 yellow onion, minced
3 cloves garlic, minced
2 smoked ham hocks, 1 lb (500 g) total weight
1½ cups (9 oz/280 g) peeled, seeded and chopped tomatoes (fresh or canned)
6 cups (48 fl oz/1.5 l) chicken stock
3 tablespoons chopped fresh mint, plus mint sprigs for garnish (optional)
salt and freshly ground pepper

Pick over the beans and discard any impurities or damaged beans. Rinse the beans, place in a bowl and add water to cover generously. Soak for about 3 hours. Drain and place in a saucepan with the parsley and thyme sprigs, bay leaves and water to cover by about 2 inches (5 cm). Bring to a boil over medium-high heat. Reduce the heat to low and simmer, uncovered, until nearly tender, 40–50 minutes. Drain well; discard the parsley, thyme and bay leaves.
❧ While the beans are cooking, in a soup pot over medium heat, warm the olive oil. Add the bacon and onion and sauté, stirring occasionally, until the onion is soft, about 10 minutes. Add the garlic and continue to cook for 1 minute. Add the ham hocks, tomatoes and chicken stock and bring to a boil. Reduce the heat to low and cook, uncovered, until the ham just begins to fall from the bone, about 1 hour. Add the beans and continue to simmer until the ham falls from the bones and the beans are very tender, about 1 hour longer.
❧ Remove the ham hocks from the soup and set aside until cool enough to handle. Discard the skin and bones and cut the meat into ½-inch (12-mm) pieces. Add the ham and chopped mint to the soup, stir well and season to taste with salt and pepper.
❧ Ladle the soup into warmed bowls, garnish with mint sprigs if desired, and serve immediately.

## Fennel, Celery, Parsley and Prosciutto Salad

SERVES 6

*Fennel has a mild anise flavor that is more pronounced when the vegetable is eaten raw than when it is cooked. There are two varieties: Florentine, the type most often found in the market and sometimes mislabeled anise, and common fennel, which produces the brown seeds used as a spice. Look for bulbs that are unblemished and firm to the touch.*

¼ cup (2 fl oz/60 ml) extra-virgin olive oil
3 tablespoons fresh lemon juice
½ teaspoon minced garlic
salt and freshly ground pepper
3 fennel bulbs
3 celery stalks, cut on the diagonal into thin slices
1 cup (1 oz/30 g) fresh flat-leaf (Italian) parsley leaves
2 oz (60 g) prosciutto, sliced paper-thin

In a small bowl, whisk together the olive oil, lemon juice, garlic and salt and pepper to taste to form a vinaigrette.
❧ If the fennel bulbs include the stalks and feathery fronds, coarsely chop enough of the feathery fronds to measure about 2 tablespoons. Discard the remaining fronds along with the stalks, or reserve for another use. Remove any damaged outer leaves from the bulbs and discard. Cut the bulbs in half lengthwise and trim away the tough core portions. Using a sharp knife, slice the fennel bulbs lengthwise into paper-thin slices.
❧ In a bowl, combine the fennel, celery, parsley leaves, and the chopped fennel fronds, if using. Drizzle on the vinaigrette and toss to coat all the ingredients evenly. Transfer to a serving platter or individual plates and arrange the prosciutto in curly ribbons on the top. Serve immediately.

# VEGETABLE BARLEY SOUP

SERVES 6

*Pearl barley is barley from which the hard outer hull and germ have been removed, leaving small, cream-colored balls that look like the gems for which they are named. In this recipe, the tiny grains are used to thicken the soup, resulting in a pleasantly chewy texture.*

2½ qt (2.5 l) chicken or vegetable stock
½ cup (4 oz/125 g) pearl barley
2 carrots, peeled and diced
2 parsnips, peeled and diced
2 boiling potatoes, unpeeled, diced
1 rutabaga, peeled and diced
1 cup (2 oz/60 g) broccoli florets
1 teaspoon chopped fresh thyme
1 teaspoon chopped fresh oregano
1 tablespoon chopped fresh flat-leaf
    (Italian) parsley

In a large soup pot over high heat, bring the stock to a boil. Add the barley, reduce the heat to medium-low, cover and simmer until almost tender, 15–20 minutes.

❧ Raise the heat to medium-high and bring to a simmer. Add the carrots, parsnips, potatoes, rutabaga, broccoli, thyme and oregano. Simmer, uncovered, until all the vegetables are tender, about 15 minutes.

❧ Ladle into warmed bowls, garnish with the parsley and serve immediately.

## SMOKY EGGPLANT SOUP WITH RED PEPPER CREAM

SERVES 6

*Eggplants reach their peak in late summer and early autumn, when their flesh is dense, firm and sweet and only tiny seeds have developed. Use them as soon as possible after they have been harvested for the best texture and flavor.*

2 eggplants (aubergines), 1½ lb (750 g) each
1 red bell pepper (capsicum)
¼ cup (2 fl oz/60 ml) heavy (double) cream
pinch of cayenne pepper
salt and freshly ground black pepper
2 tablespoons olive oil
2 yellow onions, coarsely chopped
4 cloves garlic, minced
6 cups (48 fl oz/1.5 l) chicken stock
flat-leaf (Italian) parsley sprigs

Preheat an oven to 375°F (190°C).

❧ Using tongs, hold each eggplant over the flame of a gas stove and turn occasionally until blackened on all sides, about 10 minutes. Alternatively, blacken the skins over a charcoal fire. Place the blackened eggplants on a baking sheet. Bake until very tender when pierced with a knife, 10–15 minutes. Remove from the oven and let cool. Peel off the skin and reserve the flesh.

❧ Preheat a broiler (griller). Cut the bell pepper in half lengthwise and remove the stem, seeds and ribs. Place, cut sides down, on a baking sheet and broil (grill) until blackened and blistered. Remove from the broiler and cover loosely with aluminum foil. Let steam until cool enough to handle, 10–15 minutes, then peel off the skin. Transfer the pepper to a blender or a food processor fitted with the metal blade and purée until very smooth. In a small bowl, whisk the cream until soft peaks form. Fold in the pepper purée and season with cayenne pepper, salt and black pepper. Cover and refrigerate.

❧ In a soup pot over medium heat, warm the olive oil. Add the onions and sauté, stirring occasionally, until soft, about 10 minutes. Add the garlic and cook, stirring, for 1 minute. Add the eggplant flesh and the stock, bring to a simmer and simmer, uncovered, until the eggplant falls apart, about 30 minutes. Remove from the heat. Using a blender and working in batches, purée the soup on high speed until smooth, 3–4 minutes for each batch. Season to taste with salt. If the soup is too thick, add water until it is the consistency of heavy (double) cream.

❧ Ladle into warmed bowls and spoon some red pepper cream over each serving. Garnish with parsley sprigs and serve immediately with any remaining red pepper cream on the side.

# Autumn Main Courses

With the holiday season just around the corner, autumn's main courses naturally tend to take on a festive air. Witness Roast Turkey with Dried Apple and Corn Bread Stuffing (page 170), Braised Cornish Hens with Grapes and Late-Harvest Riesling (page 167) or the Maple-Glazed Duck on this page, all of which feature the poultry so readily and reasonably available now. The same holds true for the game meat in Oven-Braised Venison Ragout (page 178).

It doesn't take a grand presentation, however, to bring a joyous mood to the table. Even the most casual main dishes take on a celebratory air, thanks to the seasonal pantry that lends them such distinctive character. Take, for example, the golden orange filling and hazelnut topping for Squash Ravioli (page 173), the lentils that form a spicy bed for Crispy Salmon (page 174) or the dried-fruit stuffing for Pork Tenderloin with Cider Glaze (page 169). Thanks to such key ingredients, each of these dishes captures the heartwarming glow of the autumn months.

## MAPLE-GLAZED DUCK

SERVES 6–8

2 ducks, each 4½–5 lb (2.25–2.5 kg)
salt and freshly ground pepper
1 orange
1 celery stalk, cut into 2-inch (5-cm) pieces
1 carrot, cut into 2-inch (5-cm) pieces
1 large yellow onion, cut into eighths
¼ cup (3 oz/90 g) pure maple syrup
1 tablespoon balsamic vinegar
orange wedges
orange zest strip, optional

Rinse the ducks inside and out and pat dry with paper towels. Prick the ducks all over with a fork, particularly along the breast and wherever you see a deposit of fat. Season inside and out with salt and pepper.

❧ Using a vegetable peeler, peel the orange, removing only the colored zest; reserve the zest. Juice the orange and set the juice aside. Divide the orange zest, celery, carrot and onion evenly between the duck cavities. Truss the ducks by tying the legs together with kitchen string. Select a heavy pot large enough to hold the ducks side by side. Pour water into the pot to a depth of about 1 inch (2.5 cm). Cover and bring to a boil over high heat. Place the ducks in the pot, breast side up, reduce the heat to low and cover tightly. Cook until the skin of each duck is white and the meat is firm to the touch, 50–60 minutes. Meanwhile, preheat an oven to 425°F (220°C).

❧ When the ducks are ready, transfer them to a roasting pan fitted with a rack, placing them breast side up. Roast for 30 minutes.

❧ In a small bowl, stir together the orange juice, maple syrup and vinegar. Remove the ducks from the oven and brush with some of the orange juice mixture. Reduce the oven temperature to 400°F (200°C) and continue to roast the ducks, basting every 5 minutes with the remaining orange juice mixture, until they are mahogany brown, 25–30 minutes longer. Remove from the oven and transfer to a platter. Cover and let rest for 10 minutes.

❧ Uncover the ducks and garnish with orange wedges and a long strip of orange zest, if desired. Carve the ducks at the table, removing the legs, then slicing the breast meat.

## CRANBERRY AND ZINFANDEL RELISH

MAKES ABOUT 2 CUPS (1¼ LB/625 G)

*Serve this zesty relish alongside duck, chicken or turkey.*

2½ cups (20 fl oz/625 ml) red Zinfandel wine
¾ cup (6 oz/185 g) sugar
5 orange peel strips, each 2 inches (5 cm) long
4 cinnamon sticks
10 whole cloves
3 cups (12 fl oz/375 g) cranberries

In a saucepan over high heat, combine the wine, sugar, orange peel, cinnamon sticks and cloves. Bring to a boil, stirring to dissolve the sugar. Reduce the heat to medium and simmer, stirring occasionally, until the liquid thickens slightly, about 15 minutes. Strain and return the liquid to the pan.

❧ Add the cranberries and raise the heat to high. Boil until the berries pop, 5–10 minutes. Reduce the heat to low and simmer until the mixture thickens slightly, 20–30 minutes. Transfer to a bowl and let cool before serving.

# Coq au Vin with Autumn Vegetables

SERVES 6

*Root vegetables come in a range of colors, shapes and sizes. If you like, substitute baby root vegetables for the regular-sized ones called for here.*

2 tablespoons unsalted butter, at room temperature

¼ lb (125 g) bacon, cut into small dice

1 chicken, 4 lb (2 kg), cut into 12 serving pieces

salt and freshly ground pepper

4 cups (32 fl oz/1 l) dry red wine such as Cabernet Sauvignon or Côtes-du-Rhône

4 cups (32 fl oz/1 l) chicken stock

1 tablespoon tomato paste

3 cloves garlic, minced

2 bay leaves

½ teaspoon chopped fresh thyme

6 fresh parsley sprigs, tied together with kitchen string, plus 1 tablespoon coarsely chopped parsley

2 parsnips, peeled and cut into 1-inch (2.5-cm) lengths

2 carrots, peeled and cut into 1-inch (2.5-cm) lengths

1 turnip, peeled and cut into wedges

1 rutabaga (swede), peeled and cut into wedges

3 tablespoons all-purpose (plain) flour

In a large, heavy pot over medium heat, melt 1 tablespoon of the butter. Add the bacon and cook, stirring occasionally, until lightly golden, about 10 minutes. Using a slotted spoon, transfer to a plate.

❧ Rinse the chicken pieces and pat dry with paper towels. Sprinkle on all sides with salt and pepper. Raise the heat to medium-high and, working in batches, add the chicken pieces to the pot. Cook, turning as needed, until lightly golden, about 10 minutes. When all of the chicken is golden, return the pieces to the pot along with the bacon. Raise the heat to high and add the wine, stock, tomato paste, garlic, bay leaves, chopped thyme and parsley sprigs. Bring to a boil over high heat, reduce the heat to low, cover and simmer until the chicken juices run clear when a thigh is pierced, 25–30 minutes. Using tongs, transfer the chicken to a large shallow dish and keep warm.

❧ Strain the liquid through a fine-mesh sieve and return it to the pot. Place over high heat and add the parsnips, carrots, turnip and rutabaga. Bring to a boil over high heat, reduce the heat to medium-low, cover and simmer until the vegetables are tender, about 15 minutes. Using a slotted spoon, transfer the vegetables to the dish holding the chicken.

❧ In a small bowl, using a fork, mix the flour and the remaining 1 table-spoon butter to form a paste. Bring the liquid in the pot to a boil over high heat and whisk in the flour-butter mixture. Reduce the heat to medium and simmer, stirring occasionally, until the liquid lightly coats the back of a spoon, 2–3 minutes.

❧ To serve, add the chicken and vegetables to the pot and heat through. Using the slotted spoon, transfer the vegetables and chicken to a warmed platter. Drizzle with the sauce and garnish with the chopped parsley.

*For his bounty,
There was no winter in 't;
an autumn 'twas
That grew the more by reaping.*
— *William Shakespeare*

# TURKEY SANDWICH WITH TAPENADE AND FONTINA

SERVES 6

*Here is a delectable use for leftover holiday turkey. Serve this sandwich for lunch or with a soup or salad for a light dinner main course. The bread can also be grilled over a charcoal fire for a smokier flavor.*

**FOR THE TAPENADE:**

1 clove garlic, minced
½ cup (2½ oz/75 g) pitted Niçoise
 olives
1 tablespoon drained capers, chopped
2 anchovy fillets, soaked in water to
 cover for 5 minutes, drained and
 patted dry
1 tablespoon fresh lemon juice
1 tablespoon extra-virgin olive oil
freshly ground pepper

6 slices country-style bread
1 tablespoon extra-virgin olive oil
1 clove garlic
1½ lb (750 g) roasted turkey, thickly
 sliced
6 oz (185 g) Fontina cheese, shredded

To make the tapenade, place the garlic and three-fourths of the olives in a food processor fitted with the metal blade. Process until the mixture forms a chunky paste. Add the capers and anchovies and pulse 4 or 5 times to mix. Add the remaining olives and pulse 4 or 5 times until a chunky paste again forms. Transfer to a bowl. Stir in the lemon juice and the olive oil and season to taste with pepper. You should have about ⅔ cup (5 oz/155 g).

❧ Preheat a broiler (griller).

❧ Lightly brush the bread slices on both sides with the olive oil. Arrange in a single layer on a baking sheet. Place in the broiler 4–6 inches (10–15 cm) from the heat source and broil (grill), turning once, until lightly golden on both sides, 30–60 seconds on each side. Rub both sides of each piece of toast lightly with the garlic clove. Divide the tapenade evenly among the bread slices and spread to cover one side of each slice completely. Distribute the turkey evenly among the bread slices. Top with the cheese, again dividing evenly.

❧ Return the pan to the broiler and broil until the cheese melts, 30–60 seconds. Serve at once.

*Crown'd with the sickle,
and the wheaten sheaf,
While Autumn,
nodding o'er the yellow plain,
Comes jovial on.*
—*James Thomson*

## BRAISED CORNISH HENS WITH GRAPES AND LATE-HARVEST RIESLING

SERVES 6

*Late-harvest Riesling is made from grapes left on the vine a little longer than normal. They begin to resemble raisins in both sweetness and appearance, and the resulting wine has a delightful spicy-sweet quality.*

6 Cornish game hens, about 1¼ lb
   (625 g) each
8 fresh thyme sprigs, plus thyme sprigs
   for garnish
1½ cups (12 fl oz/375 ml) late-harvest
   Riesling
2 tablespoons unsalted butter
1 small yellow onion, coarsely chopped
1 carrot, peeled and coarsely chopped
4 cups (32 fl oz/1 l) chicken stock
1 teaspoon cornstarch (cornflour)
2 tablespoons water
¼ teaspoon sherry vinegar
salt and freshly ground pepper
2 cups (12 oz/375 g) green and red
   seedless grapes such as Thompson,
   Flame, Ruby and Champagne, in any
   combination

Rinse the hens, pat dry with paper towels and cut in half through the breastbone. Place them in a large, shallow nonaluminum bowl with the 8 thyme sprigs and the Riesling. Cover and refrigerate for 12 hours.

❧ Remove the hens from the marinade. Strain the marinade through a fine-mesh sieve into a bowl and set aside. Dry the hens with paper towels.

❧ In a large frying pan over medium-high heat, melt the butter. Add the onion and carrot and sauté until golden, 10–12 minutes. Using a slotted spoon, transfer to a plate. Working in batches, add the hen halves to the pan, skin side down, and cook, turning once, until golden on both sides, 8–10 minutes total. Return the onion and carrot to the pan along with the strained marinade and the stock. Bring to a boil, reduce the heat to low, cover and simmer until the hens are tender, about 25 minutes.

❧ Using tongs, transfer the hens to a warmed platter and cover to keep warm. Strain the cooking liquid through a fine-mesh sieve into a clean container and, using a spoon, skim off any fat from the surface. Return the strained liquid to the frying pan and place over high heat. Bring to a boil and boil until the liquid is reduced by half, 5–10 minutes. In a small bowl, stir together the cornstarch and water. Whisk the cornstarch-water mixture into the reduced liquid and boil, whisking constantly, until the liquid lightly coats a spoon, about 30 seconds. Add the vinegar and season to taste with salt and pepper. Reduce the heat to medium, return the hens to the pan and add the grapes. Cover and cook until heated through, 3–4 minutes.

❧ Using a slotted spoon, transfer the hens and grapes to the platter. Spoon the sauce over the top, garnish with thyme sprigs and serve.

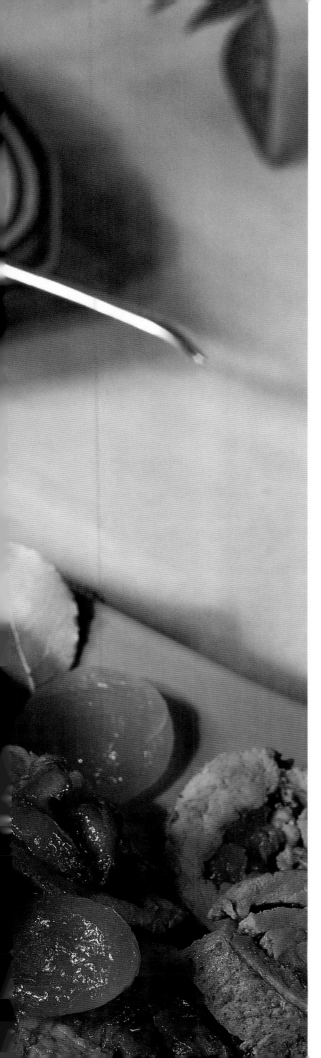

## PORK TENDERLOIN WITH CIDER GLAZE AND DRIED FRUITS

SERVES 6

*There are two types of apple cider: "sweet," which is freshly pressed, and "hard," which has fermented and has an alcohol content. Use sweet here.*

2 large pork tenderloins,
    2½ lb (1.25 kg) total weight,
    trimmed of excess fat
1 tablespoon olive oil
¼ teaspoon sweet paprika
¼ teaspoon ground cumin
large pinch of cayenne pepper
¼ teaspoon ground cloves
¼ teaspoon salt, plus salt to taste
freshly ground pepper
⅓ cup (2 oz/60 g) dried apricots,
    coarsely chopped
⅓ cup (2 oz/60 g) dried pears, coarsely
    chopped
3 tablespoons golden raisins (sultanas)
1½ tablespoons sherry vinegar or
    white wine vinegar
1 teaspoon sugar
1¼ cups (10 fl oz/310 ml) water
3 cups (24 fl oz/750 ml) apple cider
2 bay leaves
4 whole cloves
1½ cups (12 fl oz/375 ml) chicken
    stock

Butterfly the pork tenderloins: Slice each tenderloin lengthwise, cutting almost all of the way through. Open flat and then flatten slightly by pounding with a meat pounder. In a small bowl, stir together the oil, paprika, cumin, cayenne, cloves, the ¼ teaspoon salt and the pepper to taste and rub over the pork. Place in a baking dish, cover and refrigerate for 1 hour.

❧ Meanwhile, in a small saucepan, combine the apricots, pears, raisins, vinegar, sugar and water and bring to a boil. Reduce the heat to low, cover and simmer until the fruit softens, about 20 minutes. Uncover and cook over high heat until the liquid is reduced by half, about 10 minutes. Remove from the heat.

❧ Using a slotted spoon, lift out the fruits, reserving the liquid. Divide the fruits evenly between the 2 pieces of pork, spreading them over the meat in an even layer. Roll up each tenderloin into its original shape, enclosing the filling in a spiral, and tie at 1-inch (2.5-cm) intervals with kitchen string.

❧ In a sauté pan over high heat, bring the cider and the reserved poaching liquid to a boil. Boil until reduced by three-fourths, about 15 minutes. Add the bay leaves, cloves and stock and return to a boil. Add the pork tenderloins and reduce the heat to medium-low. Cover and simmer until the pork is firm to the touch and slightly pink in the center, 20–25 minutes.

❧ Transfer the tenderloins to a cutting board and cover to keep warm. Raise the heat to high and boil until the liquid is reduced by half and thickens slightly, about 5 minutes. Strain through a fine-mesh sieve into a small bowl, season to taste with salt and pepper and cover to keep warm.

❧ Snip the strings and cut the pork into slices ½ inch (12 mm) thick. Arrange on a warmed platter, drizzle with the sauce and serve.

# CORN BREAD

MAKES ONE 9-INCH (23-CM) SQUARE LOAF; SERVES 9

*This corn bread can be served as an accompaniment to main dishes or used in stuffings, as for the roast turkey at right. On its own, it is best cut into squares and served warm with lots of butter for slathering on top.*

1½ cups (7½ oz/235 g) all-purpose (plain) flour
1½ cups (7½ oz/235 g) cornmeal
2 tablespoons sugar
1 tablespoon baking powder
1 teaspoon salt
1 cup (8 fl oz/250 ml) milk
1 cup (8 fl oz/250 ml) sour cream
⅓ cup (3 fl oz/80 ml) corn oil
1 egg, lightly beaten

Preheat an oven to 375°F (190°C). Butter a 9-inch (23-cm) square cake pan.

❧ Sift together the flour, cornmeal, sugar, baking powder and salt into a bowl. In another bowl, whisk the milk, sour cream, corn oil and egg. Fold into the flour mixture; do not overmix. Pour into the prepared pan.

❧ Bake until a toothpick inserted into the center comes out clean, about 35 minutes. Remove from the oven and let stand for 10 minutes, then turn out onto a rack to cool.

# ROAST TURKEY WITH DRIED APPLE AND CORN BREAD STUFFING

SERVES 8

1 turkey, 10–12 lb (5–6 kg), with the giblets
salt and ground pepper
6 cups (48 fl oz/1.5 l) chicken stock
1 yellow onion, diced
1 carrot, peeled and diced
6 fresh parsley sprigs, ¼ teaspoon dried thyme and 1 bay leaf

**FOR THE STUFFING:**
¾ cup (6 oz/185 g) unsalted butter
2 large yellow onions, finely diced
4 celery stalks, finely diced
1 cup (3 oz/90 g) dried apples, coarsely chopped
¼ cup (⅓ oz/10 g) chopped fresh flat-leaf (Italian) parsley
1 tablespoon each chopped fresh thyme and sage
corn bread (store-bought or home-made; recipe at left), cubed and air-dried for 2 days (5–6 cups/ 10–12 oz/300–360 g)
salt and freshly ground pepper

1 tablespoon all-purpose (plain) flour
1 teaspoon cornstarch (cornflour)

Rinse the turkey and giblets and pat dry. Rub the turkey inside and out with 2 teaspoons salt. Place the giblets in a saucepan and add the stock, onion, carrot and herbs. Bring to a boil, reduce the heat to low and simmer until reduced by three-fourths, about 1½ hours. Strain through a fine-mesh sieve.

❧ To make the stuffing, in a large frying pan over medium heat, melt ½ cup (4 oz/125 g) of the butter. Add the onions and celery and sauté until soft,

about 10 minutes. Transfer to a bowl and add the apples, parsley, thyme, sage, corn bread and about 1½ cups (12 fl oz/375 ml) of the stock. Stir until well mixed, light and fluffy. Season with salt and pepper. Preheat an oven to 400°F (200°C).

❧ Stuff the body and neck cavity loosely with the stuffing, then truss as directed on page 298. Place, breast side up, on an oiled rack in a roasting pan; tuck the wing tips under the breast. Melt the remaining ¼ cup (2 oz/60 g) butter and brush 1 tablespoon on the turkey. Soak a double layer of cheese-cloth (muslin) large enough to cover the turkey in the remaining butter.

❧ Roast for 45 minutes. Reduce the heat to 325°F (165°C). Drape the soaked cheesecloth over the turkey (see page 298) and continue to roast, basting every 30 minutes, until the juices run clear when the thickest part of the thigh is pricked or an instant-read thermometer inserted into the thigh registers 180°F (82°C), 1½–2 hours longer. Remove from the oven and let stand for 20 minutes. Discard the cheesecloth and transfer the turkey to a platter.

❧ Reserve 2 tablespoons fat and drippings in the pan (discard the rest) and place over high heat. In a cup, whisk together the flour, cornstarch and ½ cup (4 fl oz/125 ml) of the stock, then whisk into the pan. Add the re-maining stock and stir until thickened, about 2 minutes. Simmer for 1 minute longer and strain through a fine-mesh sieve into a sauceboat; keep warm.

❧ Snip the trussing string. Carve the turkey (see page 298) and spoon the stuffing into a serving dish at the table. Pass the gravy.

## SQUASH RAVIOLI WITH HAZELNUT BUTTER AND PARMESAN

SERVES 6–8

1 winter squash such as Hubbard, butternut or turban, about 2 lb (1 kg)

¾ cup (1½ oz/45 g) fresh bread crumbs

2 tablespoons plus ¼ cup (1 oz/30 g) freshly grated Parmesan cheese

2 teaspoons honey

½ teaspoon chopped fresh thyme

½ teaspoon chopped fresh rosemary

½ teaspoon chopped fresh sage, plus whole leaves for garnish

1 teaspoon grated orange zest

salt and freshly ground pepper

1 teaspoon extra-virgin olive oil

2 oz (60 g) prosciutto, thinly sliced, then cut into long strips ¼ inch (6 mm) wide

1 teaspoon walnut oil or hazelnut oil

⅓ cup (2 oz/60 g) hazelnuts (filberts), chopped

6 tablespoons (3 oz/90 g) unsalted butter

pinch of freshly grated nutmeg

1 lb (500 g) purchased fresh thin egg pasta sheets

Preheat an oven to 350°F (180°C). Lightly oil a baking sheet.

❧ Cut the squash in half through the stem end and place, cut side down, on the prepared baking sheet. Bake until easily pierced with a knife, 50–60 minutes. Remove from the oven and set aside until cool enough to handle.

❧ Using a spoon, scoop out the seeds and fibers and discard. Spoon the flesh into a bowl. Mash with a potato masher (or pulse a few times in a food processor fitted with the metal blade) until

smooth. Add the bread crumbs, the 2 tablespoons Parmesan, the honey, thyme, rosemary, chopped sage and orange zest. Mix well and season to taste with salt and pepper.

❧ In a small frying pan over medium heat, warm the olive oil. Add the prosciutto and sauté until lightly golden, 4–5 minutes. Using a slotted spoon, transfer to a plate. Add the nut oil and hazelnuts to the pan and cook, stirring often, until golden, about 3 minutes. Transfer to the plate. Set aside.

❧ In a saucepan over medium-high heat, melt the butter until it turns brown and just begins to smoke, 3–4 minutes. Remove immediately from the heat and add the nutmeg. Set aside.

❧ Place a pasta sheet on a lightly floured work surface. Spoon mounds of filling onto the sheet, spacing them evenly about 1½ inches (4 cm) apart. With a spray mister filled with water, lightly mist around the mounds of filling. Place a second sheet of pasta over the first, covering the mounds, and press around the edges and between the mounds to seal. Using a fluted cutting wheel, cut between the rows of ravioli. Repeat with the remaining pasta sheets and filling.

❧ Bring a large pot three-fourths full of salted water to a boil. Add the ravioli and cook until tender, 2–3 minutes. To serve, reheat the brown butter. Drain the ravioli and place in a warmed serving bowl. Toss with the butter and sprinkle with the prosciutto, hazelnuts and the ¼ cup (1 oz/30 g) Parmesan. Garnish with the sage leaves and serve immediately.

*Days decrease,*
*And Autumn grows,*
*autumn in everything.*
*—Robert Browning*

## CRISPY SALMON WITH SPICED LENTILS

SERVES 6

*For a thousand years, tiny, lens-shaped lentils have been popular in many European countries and a staple throughout the Middle East and India. They are a natural partner to fresh salmon. Small lentils from Le Puy, France, are particularly prized, although ordinary brown lentils also work well here.*

*The rich flavor of salmon pairs well with red or white wine. For this preparation, look for a wine that matches the robust quality of the spiced lentils, such as a zesty Zinfandel or a full-bodied Chardonnay.*

1½ cups (10½ oz/330 g) lentils
8 whole cloves
1 small yellow onion
2 bay leaves
2 tablespoons extra-virgin olive oil
1 small red (Spanish) onion, minced
4 cloves garlic, minced
3 tomatoes, peeled, seeded and chopped (fresh or canned)
1½ cups (12 fl oz/375 ml) bottled clam juice
1½ teaspoons ground cumin
1½ teaspoons ground ginger
¾ teaspoon ground turmeric
¾ teaspoon sweet paprika
¼ teaspoon cayenne pepper
⅓ cup (½ oz/15 g) chopped fresh flat-leaf (Italian) parsley
⅓ cup (½ oz/15 g) chopped fresh cilantro (fresh coriander)
3 tablespoons fresh lemon juice
salt and freshly ground pepper
6 salmon fillets, each 5–6 oz (155–185 g) and ¾–1 inch (2–2.5 cm) thick, skinned
lemon wedges

Pick over the lentils and discard any impurities or damaged lentils. Rinse well and place in a large saucepan. Add water to cover by 2 inches (5 cm).

and add to the saucepan along with the bay leaves. Bring to a boil over high heat, reduce the heat to medium-low and simmer, uncovered, until the lentils are tender, 15–20 minutes. Drain and discard the onion and bay leaves. Set the lentils aside.

❧ In a large frying pan over medium heat, warm 1 tablespoon of the olive oil. Add the red onion and sauté, stirring occasionally, until soft, about 10 minutes. Add the garlic, tomatoes, clam juice, cumin, ginger, turmeric, paprika and cayenne and cook uncovered, stirring occasionally, until the tomatoes are soft, about 3 minutes. Add the parsley, cilantro and lentils and cook, stirring occasionally, until the lentils are hot, about 2 minutes. Stir in the lemon juice and season to taste with salt and pepper. Keep warm.

❧ Preheat a ridged cast-iron stove-top grill pan over high heat until very hot, about 15 minutes. Brush the salmon with the remaining 1 tablespoon olive oil and place on the pan. Cook until golden and crisp on one side, 4–5 minutes. Turn over the salmon, sprinkle with salt and pepper and continue to cook until opaque throughout, 3–4 minutes longer. Alternatively, prepare a fire in a charcoal grill. Brush the salmon with oil as directed and grill about 4 inches (10 cm) from the fire for 4–5 minutes on each side.

❧ To serve, spoon the warm lentils onto a warmed serving platter. Place the salmon fillets in the center and garnish with lemon wedges. Serve at once.

# RIGATONI WITH PANCETTA AND CARAMELIZED SHALLOTS

SERVES 6

2 tablespoons extra-virgin olive oil
¼ lb (125 g) pancetta, finely diced
30 small shallots
1 tablespoon sugar
2 cups (16 fl oz/500 ml) dry red wine
    such as Cabernet Sauvignon or
    Côtes-du-Rhône
2 cups (16 fl oz/500 ml) chicken stock
    or vegetable stock
salt and freshly ground pepper
1 lb (500 g) rigatoni
¾ cup (3 oz/90 g) freshly grated
    Parmesan cheese

In a large frying pan over medium-high heat, warm the olive oil. Add the pancetta and cook, stirring occasionally, until lightly golden, 10–12 minutes. Reduce the heat to medium-low and add the shallots. Cook uncovered, stirring occasionally with a wooden spoon and pressing on the shallots slightly to separate the layers, until golden brown, 25–30 minutes. Add the sugar, stir well and cook until the sugar dissolves, about 4 minutes. Add the wine and stock, bring to a simmer, reduce the heat to medium-low and cook gently until the shallots are very soft and only ½ cup (4 fl oz/125 g) of liquid remains, 30–40 minutes. Season to taste with salt and plenty of pepper.

❧ Just before the shallot sauce is ready, bring a large pot three-fourths full of salted water to a boil. Add the rigatoni and cook until al dente (tender but firm to the bite), 10–12 minutes or according to the package directions. Drain and return the pasta to the pot. Add the shallot sauce and mix well.

❧ To serve, transfer the sauced rigatoni to a warmed serving bowl. Sprinkle with the Parmesan and serve at once.

# POLENTA WITH TOMATO-OLIVE RAGOUT AND SAUSAGES

SERVES 6

6 cups (2¼ lb/1.1 kg) peeled, seeded
    and chopped tomatoes (fresh or
    canned)
1 small red (Spanish) onion, peeled
4 cloves garlic
salt and freshly ground pepper
2 lb (1 kg) Italian pork sausages,
    preferably flavored with fennel seeds
8½ cups (68 fl oz/2.1 l) water
2 cups (12 oz/375 g) polenta
2 teaspoons chopped fresh rosemary
3 tablespoons unsalted butter
¾ cup (4 oz/125 g) pitted brine-cured
    black olives such as Kalamata or
    Niçoise
wedge of Parmesan cheese for shaving
1½ tablespoons coarsely chopped
    fresh flat-leaf (Italian) parsley

In a heavy soup pot over high heat, combine the tomatoes, onion and garlic cloves. Bring to a boil, reduce the heat to low and simmer, uncovered, until the sauce thickens, 45–60 minutes. Remove from the heat and discard the onion. Pass the mixture through the fine disk of a food mill placed over a clean saucepan. Alternatively, purée in a food processor fitted with the metal blade, then pass through a fine-mesh sieve. Season the sauce with salt and pepper.

❧ Meanwhile, prick the sausages in several places with a fork. In a large saucepan, bring ½ cup (4 fl oz/125 ml) of the water to a boil. Add the sausages and cook over medium-high heat, turning occasionally, until golden on all sides and half-cooked, 10–12 minutes. Drain and, when cool enough to handle, cut each sausage on the diagonal into 2-inch (5-cm) pieces.

❧ In a large, heavy saucepan, bring the remaining 8 cups (64 fl oz/2 l) water to a boil over high heat. Slowly add the polenta in a steady stream while whisking constantly. Continue to whisk until the mixture thickens, 3–4 minutes. Switch to a wooden spoon, reduce the heat to medium and continue to simmer, stirring, until the polenta pulls away from the sides of the pan, 20–25 minutes. Stir in the rosemary and butter. Season to taste with salt and pepper.

❧ Meanwhile, place the sauce over medium heat and bring to a simmer. Add the sausage pieces and the olives and simmer, uncovered, until the sausages are cooked through, about 10 minutes.

❧ Divide the polenta equally among individual plates. Spoon the sauce and sausages around the edges. Using a cheese shaver or a vegetable peeler, shave a few pieces of the Parmesan cheese over each serving. Garnish with the parsley and serve immediately.

## Oven-Braised Venison Ragout

SERVES 6

*Although meats that are evenly and lightly marbled with fat are generally best for braised and stewed dishes, venison, which is quite lean, makes a tasty ragout.*

3 lb (1.5 kg) boneless venison such as rump pot roast, sirloin tip or top round, cut into 1½-inch (4-cm) cubes

2 tablespoons all-purpose (plain) flour

2 tablespoons olive oil

3 oz (90 g) pancetta, finely chopped

1 yellow onion, finely chopped

6 fresh parsley sprigs

3 fresh thyme sprigs

2 bay leaves

4 cloves garlic, minced

1½ cups (12 fl oz/375 ml) dry red wine such as Barolo, Cabernet Sauvignon or Côtes-du-Rhône

4 cups (32 fl oz/1 l) chicken, beef or veal stock

1 tablespoon tomato paste

1 lb (500 g) pearl onions

2 tablespoons unsalted butter

1 lb (500 g) small fresh button mushrooms, brushed clean

2 tablespoons chopped fresh flat-leaf (Italian) parsley

salt and freshly ground pepper

Preheat an oven to 350°F (180°C). Place the venison in a bowl, sprinkle with the flour and toss together.

❧ In a heavy stew pot over medium heat, warm 1 tablespoon of the oil. Add the pancetta and onion and sauté until the onion is soft, about 10 minutes. Using a slotted spoon, transfer to a plate. Raise the heat to medium-high and add the remaining 1 tablespoon oil. Working in batches, add the venison and cook, turning occasionally, until golden brown on all sides, 10–15 minutes. Using kitchen string, tie the herb sprigs and bay leaves into a bundle. Return the onion and pancetta to the pan along with the herb bundle and the garlic. Raise the heat to high and pour in the wine. Bring to a boil, scraping up any browned bits, and boil until the wine is reduced by half, about 5 minutes. Add the stock and the tomato paste and bring to a boil. Cover, place in the oven and cook until the venison can be easily pierced with a knife, about 1½ hours.

❧ Meanwhile, peel the pearl onions: In a saucepan, combine the onions with water to cover. Bring to a boil and boil for 2 minutes. Drain, rinse and drain again. Trim off the root end of each onion, then cut a shallow X into each trimmed end. Squeeze each onion gently to slip off the skin. Set aside.

❧ Melt 1 tablespoon of the butter in a frying pan over medium-high heat. Add the mushrooms and cook, stirring occasionally, until lightly golden, about 10 minutes. Transfer to a plate. Melt the remaining 1 tablespoon butter in the same pan. Add the pearl onions and cook over medium heat, stirring occasionally, until lightly golden, about 10 minutes. Set aside.

❧ When the venison is tender, remove it from the oven and add the onions. Place over medium heat and bring to a simmer. Cook, uncovered, until the onions are tender, about 20 minutes. Add the mushrooms and stir to heat through. Discard the herb bundle. Stir in the chopped parsley and season to taste with salt and pepper. Serve immediately.

*A runnable stag,*
*a kingly crop.*
—*John Davidson*

## LAMB CHOPS WITH PRUNE CHUTNEY

SERVES 6

*Prune plums, sometimes known as Italian plums or French plums, are picked at the height of their season during the summer months and soon after are dried into prunes. This chutney can be made up to 3 weeks in advance and stored in the refrigerator until ready to use. Any combination of dried fruits can be used in place of the prunes, including apples, figs, golden or dark raisins, pears or apricots. Garnish with shredded orange zest, if you like.*

**FOR THE PRUNE CHUTNEY:**

¼ cup (2 oz/60 g) firmly packed
   brown sugar
¼ cup (2 fl oz/60 ml) sherry vinegar
1 cup (8 fl oz/250 ml) water
½ teaspoon grated orange zest
2 tablespoons fresh orange juice
pinch of cayenne pepper
¼ teaspoon salt
1½ cups (9 oz/280 g) pitted prunes,
   stems removed
2 tablespoons crystallized ginger,
   finely diced

12 loin lamb chops, each about ¼ lb
   (125 g) and 1 inch (2.5 cm) thick
2 tablespoons olive oil
salt and freshly ground pepper

To make the chutney, in a saucepan over medium heat, combine the brown sugar, vinegar, water, orange zest, orange juice, cayenne and salt. Bring to a boil, stirring to dissolve the sugar. Reduce the heat to low and simmer, uncovered, until the mixture thickens slightly, about 20 minutes.

❧ Add the prunes and ginger and continue to cook uncovered over medium heat, stirring occasionally, until the fruit is tender but not mushy and the syrup is thick, about 1 hour. If the mixture begins to dry out during cooking, stir in a little water. Remove from the heat and let cool. You should have about 1½ cups (15 oz/470 g).

❧ Prepare a fire in a charcoal grill, or preheat a broiler (griller).

❧ Brush the lamb chops on both sides with the olive oil and sprinkle on all sides with salt and pepper. Place the lamb chops on a grill rack or on a broiler pan. Grill or broil 4 inches (10 cm) from the heat until browned on the first side, about 5 minutes. Turn and continue to cook until browned on the second side and medium-rare in the center, about 5 minutes longer, or until done to your liking. Transfer 2 lamb chops to each individual plate. Serve immediately, garnished with a spoonful of chutney on the side.

# BRAISED LAMB SHANKS WITH WHITE BEANS

SERVES 6

*Lamb shanks, white beans, tomatoes and red wine are an ideal union for a hearty autumn dinner. You can substitute the same amount of veal shanks for the lamb shanks, if you like.*

1½ cups (10½ oz/330 g) dried small
    white (navy), white kidney or
    cannellini beans
2 tablespoons extra-virgin olive oil
6 lamb shanks, ½–¾ lb (250–375 g)
    each
1 yellow onion, finely diced
1 celery stalk, finely diced
2 large carrots, peeled and finely diced
6 cloves garlic, minced
1½ cups (12 fl oz/375 ml) dry red wine
    such as Côtes-du-Rhône, Cabernet
    Sauvignon or Chianti
1½ cups (12 fl oz/375 ml) chicken
    stock
1½ cups (9 oz/280 g) peeled, seeded
    and chopped tomatoes (fresh or
    canned)
3 tablespoons tomato paste
1 teaspoon chopped fresh thyme
1 bay leaf
salt and freshly ground pepper
1 tablespoon shredded lemon zest
2 tablespoons chopped fresh flat-leaf
    (Italian) parsley

Pick over the beans and discard any impurities or damaged beans. Rinse the beans, place in a bowl and add water to cover generously. Soak for about 3 hours. Drain and place in a saucepan with water to cover by about 2 inches (5 cm). Place over medium-high heat and bring to a boil. Reduce the heat to low and simmer, uncovered, until nearly tender, 45–60 minutes. Drain well.

❧ Meanwhile, in a deep, heavy pot over medium heat, warm the olive oil. Add the lamb shanks and brown on all sides, 10–12 minutes. Transfer the shanks to a plate. Add the onion, celery and carrots to the pan and sauté over medium heat, stirring occasionally, until the onion is soft, about 10 minutes. Add the garlic and cook, stirring, for 1 minute. Add the wine, stock, tomatoes, tomato paste, thyme, bay leaf and lamb shanks. Bring to a boil over high heat. Reduce the heat to low, cover and simmer until the shanks can be easily pierced with a skewer, 1½–2 hours.

❧ Add the beans, stir well, cover and simmer gently until the lamb begins to fall from the bone and the beans are tender, about 30 minutes longer. Season to taste with salt and pepper. Remove the bay leaf and discard.

❧ In a small bowl, stir together the lemon zest and parsley. Transfer the lamb shanks and beans to individual plates and garnish with the zest-parsley mixture. Serve immediately.

# Autumn Side Dishes
*ɔⱺ*

Prepared with care and imagination from the best the season has to offer, side dishes have the power to elevate any meal from good to memorable. The accompaniments that follow accomplish that feat by highlighting standouts from the autumn harvest and cooking them in simple ways that showcase their natural qualities.

The pastalike strands of spaghetti squash (page 187), ideal for tossing with butter and cheese, are served using the squash's own hard shell as a bowl. Little pearl onions (also on page 187) shine like jewels when cooked in a cream sauce that complements their natural sweetness. Similarly sized and shaped but contrasting dynamically in color, texture and flavor, whole Brussels sprouts and chestnuts (page 184) elevate each other to new levels of sophistication. And one of the season's signature fruits ties together a medley of autumn-harvest grains in Mixed-Grain Pilaf with Cranberries and Pine Nuts (page 188).

## GOLDEN POTATO AND MUSHROOM GRATIN
SERVES 6–8

*The potato has been cultivated for thousands of years and it grows in a multitude of shapes, colors, textures and sizes. Many varieties would work well in this dish: Yukon Gold, Yellow Finn, Red, Désirée, Red LaSoda or Pink Blossom. Garnish the gratin with whole fresh wild mushrooms and fresh herb sprigs, if you like.*

½ oz (15 g) dried wild mushrooms such as porcini, chanterelle or shiitake
boiling water, as needed
8 potatoes (see note), 1¾–2 lb (875 g–1 kg)
1½ tablespoons unsalted butter
1 lb (500 g) button mushrooms, brushed clean and thinly sliced
2 teaspoons chopped fresh thyme
salt and freshly ground pepper
3 oz (90 g) blue cheese such as Gorgonzola, Stilton, Maytag or Roquefort, at room temperature
2½ cups (20 fl oz/625 ml) heavy (double) cream
½ cup (2 oz/60 g) freshly grated Parmesan cheese

Place the mushrooms in a small bowl and add boiling water to cover. Let stand for 30 minutes until softened. Drain the mushrooms, chop coarsely and set aside.

ɔ Position a rack in the upper part of an oven and preheat to 400°F (200°C). Oil a 3-qt (3-l) gratin dish or other baking dish.

ɔ Thinly slice the potatoes and place in a bowl of water to cover until ready to use.

ɔ In a large frying pan over high heat, melt the butter. Add the button mushrooms, rehydrated wild mushrooms and thyme and sauté, stirring occasionally, until the mushrooms are tender and the liquid they released has completely evaporated, 8–10 minutes. Season to taste with salt and pepper.

ɔ In a bowl, mash the blue cheese with the cream until smooth, then season to taste with salt and pepper. Place one-third of the potatoes on the bottom of the baking dish. Layer half of the mushrooms evenly over the potatoes. Add a layer of half of the remaining potatoes, and then a layer of all the remaining mushrooms. Top with the remaining potatoes and pour the cream mixture evenly over the top. Sprinkle evenly with the Parmesan cheese.

ɔ Bake until the potatoes are tender and the cream is almost fully absorbed, 40–50 minutes. Serve hot, spooning the gratin directly from the dish.

# BRUSSELS SPROUTS WITH CHESTNUTS

SERVES 6

*Brussels sprouts, which resemble miniature cabbages, grow in neat rows on long stalks. Serve this dish with roast turkey (recipe on page 170) or maple-glazed crispy duck (page 162).*

½ lb (250 g) fresh chestnuts
1½ lb (750 g) Brussels sprouts
2 tablespoons unsalted butter
salt and freshly ground pepper

Using a sharp knife, make a small incision across the flat side of each chestnut. Place the chestnuts in a saucepan, add water to cover and place over medium heat. Bring to a simmer, reduce the heat to low and cook until the nut meats can be easily pierced with a knife, 45–55 minutes. Remove from the heat. Using a slotted spoon, remove the chestnuts a few at a time from the hot water (the nuts are easier to peel when hot). Peel away the hard shells and inner sheaths and discard.

❧ Remove any damaged outer leaves from the Brussels sprouts and discard. Bring a large saucepan three-fourths full of water to a boil. Add the Brussels sprouts and simmer, uncovered, until tender, 6–8 minutes. Drain and return to the saucepan. Add the chestnuts and butter and place over medium heat until the butter melts and the chestnuts are hot, about 1 minute. Stir well and season to taste with salt and pepper.

❧ Transfer to a warmed serving dish and serve hot.

# CAULIFLOWER AND BROCCOLI WITH ROASTED GARLIC CLOVES

SERVES 6

*The word* cauliflower *comes from the Italian* cavolo a fiore, *meaning "a cabbage that blooms like a flower," and was regularly grown in the garden plots of ancient Rome. Broccoli was known by the ancient Romans as well, and its name is derived from* bracchium, *meaning "a strong branch." When purchasing broccoli or cauliflower, select those heads that are crisp and smell sweet.*

2 small heads garlic, cloves separated
   and peeled
2 tablespoons extra-virgin olive oil
salt and freshly ground pepper
1 head cauliflower, about ¾ lb (375 g),
   cut into 1½-inch (4-cm) florets
1 bunch broccoli, about ¾ lb (375 g),
   cut into 1½-inch (4-cm) florets
lemon wedges

Position a rack in the upper part of an oven and preheat to 400°F (200°C).

❧ Place the garlic cloves in a small baking dish and drizzle with 1 tablespoon of the oil. Season to taste with salt and pepper and toss to coat evenly. Cover with aluminum foil and bake until tender, 20–25 minutes. Remove the foil and continue to bake until lightly golden, 5–10 minutes longer. Remove from the oven and set aside.

❧ Bring a large pot three-fourths full of salted water to a boil. Add the cauliflower and cook until tender when pierced with a fork, 3–5 minutes. Remove with a slotted spoon and transfer to a platter to cool. Repeat with the broccoli, and again transfer to the platter to cool.

❧ In a large frying pan over medium-high heat, warm the remaining 1 tablespoon olive oil. Add the cauliflower and broccoli and cook, stirring occasionally, until warm, about 3 minutes. Add the garlic cloves and toss together until the garlic is warm, about 1 minute. Season to taste with salt and pepper.

❧ Transfer the broccoli, cauliflower and garlic cloves to a warmed serving dish. Garnish with the lemon wedges and serve immediately.

## SPAGHETTI SQUASH WITH BROWN BUTTER AND PARMESAN

SERVES 6

*Spaghetti squash derives its name from the nature of its flesh: once it is cooked and cut in half, the flesh can be separated into strands that recall the famed Italian pasta.*

1 spaghetti squash, 2½–3 lb
    (1.25–1.5 kg)
¼ cup (2 oz/60 g) unsalted butter
pinch of freshly grated nutmeg
⅓ cup (1½ oz/45 g) freshly grated
    Parmesan cheese
salt and freshly ground pepper

Place the whole squash in a large pot and add water to cover. Bring to a boil over high heat, reduce the heat to medium-low, and simmer, uncovered, until it can be easily pierced with a knife, about 45 minutes.

❧ Meanwhile, in a saucepan over medium-high heat, melt the butter and cook it until it turns brown and just begins to smoke, 3–4 minutes. Remove immediately from the heat and stir in the nutmeg.

❧ When the squash is done, drain and set aside until cool enough to handle. Cut the squash in half lengthwise and, using a fork, scrape out the seeds and discard. Place the squash halves, cut sides up, on a serving platter and, using the fork, scrape the flesh free of the skin, carefully separating it into the spaghetti-like strands that it naturally forms. Leave the strands mounded in the squash halves. If the butter has cooled, place over medium heat until hot.

❧ To serve, drizzle the butter evenly over the squash. Sprinkle with the Parmesan cheese and season to taste with salt and pepper. Serve immediately.

## CREAMY PEARL ONIONS

SERVES 6

*Creamed onions are a seasonal favorite, especially on the holiday table. Pearl onions, traditionally any white onion less than 1½ inches (4 cm) in diameter, are best for this dish. A number of different-colored pearl onions are available at well-stocked markets today, including white, yellow and purple.*

2 lb (1 kg) pearl onions (see note)
4 tablespoons (2 oz/60 g) unsalted
    butter
1 yellow onion, minced
1 teaspoon chopped fresh thyme
2½ tablespoons all-purpose (plain) flour
½ cup (4 fl oz/125 ml) milk
½ cup (4 fl oz/125 ml) heavy (double)
    cream
¼ teaspoon freshly grated nutmeg
salt and freshly ground pepper
¾ cup (3 oz/90 g) fine dried white
    bread crumbs

Bring a saucepan half full of salted water to a boil over high heat. Add the pearl onions and cook for 2 minutes. Using a slotted spoon, scoop out the onions, rinse with cold water and drain. Reserve the water in the pot. Trim off the ends of each onion, then cut a shallow X into each trimmed end. Squeeze each onion gently to slip off the skin.

❧ Bring the water back to a boil. Add the onions, reduce the heat to low and simmer, uncovered, until soft when pierced with a knife, 15–20 minutes. Using the slotted spoon, transfer the onions to a bowl. Continue to boil the cooking liquid until reduced to 1 cup (8 fl oz/250 ml), 15–20 minutes.

❧ Position an oven rack in the upper part of an oven and preheat to 375°F (190°C).

❧ In a saucepan over medium heat, melt 3 tablespoons of the butter. Add the minced onion and thyme and cook, stirring occasionally, until soft, about 7 minutes. Add the flour and cook, stirring constantly with a wooden spoon, until well mixed and bubbling, about 2 minutes. Add the reserved 1 cup (8 fl oz/250 ml) cooking liquid, the milk and the cream. Cook over medium heat until the sauce boils and thickens slightly, 3–4 minutes. Add the nutmeg and season to taste with salt and pepper. Add the pearl onions, adjust the heat to a gentle simmer and cook until the onions are hot, about 3 minutes.

❧ Transfer the onion mixture to a 2-qt (2-l) baking dish and sprinkle the bread crumbs evenly over the top. Cut the remaining 1 tablespoon butter into 6 equal pieces and dot the bread crumbs evenly with the butter. Bake until the crumbs are golden and small bubbles appear along the edges of the dish, 15–20 minutes. Serve immediately.

## BRAISED FENNEL WITH OLIVE OIL AND GARLIC

SERVES 6

*Fennel is related to a group of herbs including anise, cumin, dill, coriander and caraway. In the vegetable world, however, fennel is recognized as having a taste all its own, one often compared to licorice.*

4 fennel bulbs, about 2 lb (1 kg) total
    weight
3 tablespoons extra-virgin olive oil
3 cloves garlic, chopped
1 teaspoon ground fennel seeds
salt and freshly ground pepper
2 cups (16 fl oz/500 ml) water
1 lemon peel strip, about 2 inches
    (5 cm) long
2 tablespoons fresh lemon juice
lemon wedges

Cut off the stalks and feathery fronds from the fennel bulbs. Reserve the stalks for another use. Chop enough of the feathery fronds to measure 1 tablespoon and reserve some of the remaining fronds for garnish. Set aside. Remove any damaged outer leaves from the bulbs and discard. Cut each bulb into quarters lengthwise and trim away the tough core portions.

❧ In a large saucepan over medium heat, warm the olive oil. Add the garlic and cook, stirring, for 1 minute; do not brown. Add the fennel quarters and the fennel seeds. Season to taste with salt and pepper. Cook uncovered, stirring occasionally, until the fennel begins to soften, about 5 minutes.

❧ Reduce the heat to medium-low, add the water and lemon peel, cover and cook until the fennel is tender, 20–25 minutes.

❧ Using a slotted spoon, transfer the fennel to a serving platter and keep warm. Raise the heat to high and cook until only ¾ cup (6 fl oz/180 ml) liquid remains, about 5 minutes. Discard the lemon peel. Add the lemon juice, then taste and adjust the seasoning with salt and pepper.

❧ Drizzle the sauce over the fennel and garnish with lemon wedges. Sprinkle with the chopped fennel tops and garnish with the whole fennel fronds. Serve immediately.

## MIXED-GRAIN PILAF WITH CRANBERRIES AND PINE NUTS

SERVES 6

*Grains have been a symbol of the autumn harvest for centuries, although modern-day cooks have only recently begun to reintroduce themselves to some of the now lesser-known ancient varieties. A wide array of hearty grains—amaranth, quinoa, millet, barley, cornmeal and bulgur—is available in health-food stores. Here, several are combined in an appealing fall pilaf.*

½ cup (2½ oz/75 g) pine nuts
1 tablespoon canola or vegetable oil
¾ cup (5 oz/155 g) basmati rice
¼ cup (2 oz/60 g) amaranth
¼ cup (1 oz/30 g) quinoa
¼ cup (2 oz/60 g) millet
½ cup (2 oz/60 g) dried cranberries
¾ teaspoon salt
freshly ground pepper
2 cups (16 fl oz/500 ml) chicken stock
1 cup (8 fl oz/250 ml) water

In a frying pan over medium heat, toast the pine nuts, stirring constantly, until lightly golden, 2–3 minutes. Remove from the heat and set aside.

❧ In a saucepan over medium heat, warm the oil. Add the rice, amaranth, quinoa and millet and stir until the grains are coated with the oil and hot, 1–2 minutes. Raise the heat to high and add the cranberries, salt, pepper to taste, stock and water. Bring to a boil, reduce the heat to low, cover and simmer until the grains are tender and the liquid is absorbed, about 25 minutes.

❧ Add the pine nuts and fluff with a fork to mix. Taste and adjust the seasonings. Transfer to a warmed serving dish and serve immediately.

## SWEET POTATO OVEN FRIES

SERVES 6

*The skin color of sweet potatoes ranges from tan to orange-brown to dark red to purple, while the flesh varies from the creamy white of a popular Japanese variety to the deep orange of more common members of the clan.*

2½ lb (1.25 kg) sweet potatoes, well
    scrubbed
3 tablespoons olive oil
salt and freshly ground pepper
1 teaspoon chopped fresh sage
1 clove garlic, minced

Position a rack in the upper part of an oven and preheat to 450°F (230°C).
❧ Trim off the ends from the sweet potatoes. Cut in half lengthwise and place, cut sides down, on a work surface. Using a sharp knife, cut each half lengthwise into wedges ½ inch (12 mm) wide. Place the wedges in a large bowl, drizzle with 2 tablespoons of the olive oil and toss to coat evenly. Season well with salt and pepper. Place the wedges in a single layer on a large baking sheet, allowing ample space on all sides to ensure even cooking. Bake until golden and tender when pierced with a knife, about 50 minutes.
❧ Remove the baking sheet from the oven and, using a spatula, pile the sweet potatoes in the center of the pan, carefully loosening any that may have stuck to the baking sheet. In a small bowl or cup, combine the remaining 1 tablespoon olive oil, the sage and garlic. Pour over the hot sweet potatoes, toss well to coat and serve immediately.

## ROASTED SQUASH PURÉE WITH GINGER

SERVES 6

*A bowl of creamy squash purée is one of the comfort foods of the autumn table. Although squash is often boiled, roasting brings out its sweetness. Acorn, Hubbard, turban squash or pumpkin can be used in place of the butternut squash.*

1 butternut squash, 2½–3 lb
   (1.25–1.5 kg)
2 tablespoons unsalted butter, at room
   temperature
½ cup (4 fl oz/125 ml) milk
1½ teaspoons peeled and grated
   fresh ginger
salt and freshly ground pepper

Preheat an oven to 400°F (200°C). Lightly oil a baking sheet.

❧ Cut the squash in half through the stem end and place, cut sides down, on the prepared baking sheet. Bake until easily pierced with a knife, 45–50 minutes. Remove from the oven and set aside until cool enough to handle. Using a spoon, scoop out the seeds and fibers and discard. Spoon the flesh into a bowl and keep warm.

❧ In a small saucepan over medium heat, combine the butter and milk and heat until the butter melts and the milk is hot, about 1 minute. Remove from the heat.

❧ Using a potato masher, mash the squash until smooth. Alternatively, process the squash in a food processor fitted with the metal blade, pulsing several times until smooth, about 1 minute. Stir in the milk mixture and ginger and season to taste with salt and pepper.

❧ Transfer to a heavy saucepan and place over low heat. Reheat gently, stirring to prevent scorching. Spoon into a warmed serving bowl and serve immediately.

*Season of mists and mellow fruitfulness, Close bosom-friend of the maturing sun.*
   —*John Keats*

# *Autumn Desserts*
∾

There is a secret element that enlivens virtually all of the autumn desserts that follow. It isn't the season's tree fruits that are featured again and again in such tempting recipes as Baked Apples with Calvados Custard Sauce (page 200), Upside-Down Pear Gingerbread (page 197), Old-Fashioned Apple Pie (page 206) and Poached Quince Tart (page 195). Nor does the presence of the nut harvest betray that secret, although those indispensable items lend appealing crunch to Caramelized Nut Tart and Fig and Walnut Tartlets (pages 204–205).

The hidden ingredient behind so many of these dishes is, in fact, a pantryful of sweet spices, which lend their character not only to those desserts already mentioned, but also even more distinctively to the Warm Caramelized Pears with Clove Zabaglione on this page and a Spiced Pumpkin Pie (page 203). Cinnamon, nutmeg, allspice and cloves contribute intriguing taste and aroma and impart a warming glow that is welcome on the season's chilly evenings.

## WARM CARAMELIZED PEARS WITH CLOVE ZABAGLIONE

SERVES 6

*Zabaglione is one of Italy's great desserts. The ethereal foamy custard sauce is usually made with egg yolks, sugar and Marsala. In this recipe, the addition of golden raisins and spices gives it a festive flavor.*

FOR THE PEARS:
½ teaspoon ground cloves
¼ teaspoon ground allspice
¼ teaspoon ground cinnamon
⅛ teaspoon freshly grated nutmeg
½ cup (4 fl oz/125 ml) sweet Marsala
3 tablespoons honey
1½ tablespoons unsalted butter
2 lemon zest strips, each 3 inches (7.5 cm) long and ½ inch (12 mm) wide
6 Bosc or French Butter pears, peeled, halved with stems intact and cored

FOR THE ZABAGLIONE:
⅓ cup (2 oz/60 g) golden raisins (sultanas)
¾ cup (6 fl oz/180 ml) sweet Marsala
4 egg yolks
¼ cup (2 oz/60 g) sugar
2 tablespoons water

Preheat an oven to 350°F (180°C).
❧ To prepare the pears, in a small bowl, stir together the cloves, allspice, cinnamon and nutmeg. In a small saucepan over medium heat, combine the Marsala, honey, butter, lemon zest and half of the mixed spices and heat just until the butter melts. Remove from the heat. (Reserve the remaining spices for adding to the zabaglione.) Place the pears in a baking dish, hollow side down, and pour the Marsala mixture over them.

❧ Bake the pears, basting occasionally with the liquid in the dish and turning them over halfway through cooking, until easily pierced with a knife, 30–40 minutes. Remove from the oven and keep warm.
❧ Meanwhile, prepare for the zabaglione: Place the raisins and half of the Marsala in a small saucepan over high heat. Bring to a boil and immediately remove from the heat. Let stand until cool, about 30 minutes.
❧ About 15 minutes before serving, bring a saucepan half full of water to a gentle simmer. Using a whisk or hand-held electric mixer, beat together the egg yolks, sugar and water in a large heatproof bowl. Whisk in the remaining Marsala and set the bowl over the pan of barely simmering water. Do not allow the water to touch the bowl. Whisk constantly until the mixture is thick, frothy, begins to hold soft peaks and no liquid remains at the bottom of the bowl, about 10 minutes. Drain the raisins and discard the Marsala. Fold the raisins and the reserved spices into the zabaglione.
❧ To serve, place 2 pear halves in each individual bowl. Spoon the zabaglione onto the pears, distributing it evenly. Serve immediately.

# POACHED QUINCE TART

MAKES ONE 9-INCH (23-CM) TART; SERVES 8

*Thin slices of quince, nearly opaque
and pearlike in their raw state, take on
a delightful rosy hue when cooked.*

2½ cups (20 fl oz/625 ml) dry red wine
    such as Barolo, Cabernet Sauvignon
    or Côtes-du-Rhône
¼ cup (2 oz/60 g) sugar
8 whole cloves
3 lemon zest strips, each about
    2 inches (5 cm) long and ½ inch
    (12 mm) wide
2 cinnamon sticks
2½ lb (1.25 kg) quinces, peeled, halved,
    cored and cut into thin slices

FOR THE PASTRY:
⅔ cup (5 oz/155 g) unsalted butter, at
    room temperature
¾ cup (6 oz/185 g) sugar
3 egg yolks
1½ cups (7½ oz/235 g) all-purpose
    (plain) flour, or as needed
⅔ cup (4 oz/125 g) polenta
½ teaspoon salt

1 cup (8 fl oz/250 ml) heavy cream

In a large saucepan over medium-high heat, combine the wine, sugar, cloves, lemon zest and cinnamon sticks. Bring to a boil and boil until reduced to 2 cups (16 fl oz/500 ml), about 15 minutes. Add the quince slices, reduce the heat to medium-low and cook uncovered, gently pushing the slices under the liquid from time to time, until tender, 1–1½ hours.

❧ Remove from the heat and strain through a fine-mesh sieve into a bowl; discard the cloves and lemon zest and reserve the liquid. Place the quince slices on paper towels and let cool. Return the liquid to the pan and boil over high heat until only ½ cup (4 fl oz/125 ml) thick syrup remains.

❧ To make the pastry, in a food processor fitted with the metal blade, combine the butter and sugar and process until light in color, 2–3 minutes. With the processor on, add the egg yolks one at a time. Sift together the 1½ cups (7½ oz/235 g) flour, polenta and salt directly over the creamed mixture and process until the mixture comes together to form a dough, about 1 minute. Add additional flour, 1 tablespoon at a time, if the dough is sticky. Wrap the dough in plastic wrap and refrigerate for 30 minutes.

❧ Preheat an oven to 375°F (190°C). Cut the dough in half and return half to the refrigerator. Using your fingers, press the other half of the dough evenly over the bottom and sides of a tart pan 9 inches (23 cm) in diameter with a removable bottom. Place the drained quince slices in the tart shell. On a lightly floured work surface, roll out the remaining dough ¼ inch (6 mm) thick. Using a heart-shaped cookie cutter 2½ inches (6 cm) across at its widest point, cut out as many hearts as possible. Place the hearts on top of the quince slices, starting near the rim and with the widest part of each heart facing toward the edge. Overlap the hearts slightly and cover the top completely. Bake until golden brown, about 40 minutes. Transfer to a rack and let cool.

❧ In a bowl, whisk the cream until soft peaks form. Fold in 1 tablespoon of the reduced poaching liquid; reserve the remaining liquid for another use. Serve the tart with the cream on the side.

*They dined on mince,
and slices of quince,
Which they ate with
a runcible spoon;
And hand in hand,
on the edge of the sand,
They danced by the light
of the moon.
—Edward Lear*

# RUM RAISIN ICE CREAM WITH CIDER SAUCE

MAKES ABOUT 1½ QT (1.5 L); SERVES 6–8

**FOR THE ICE CREAM:**

½ cup (3 oz/90 g) dark raisins

½ cup (4 fl oz/125 ml) dark rum

8 egg yolks

¾ cup (6 oz/185 g) firmly packed
   light brown sugar

1¾ cups (14 fl oz/440 ml) milk

1¾ cups (14 fl oz/440 ml) heavy
   (double) cream

½ teaspoon vanilla extract (essence)

**FOR THE SAUCE:**

3 cups (24 fl oz/750 ml) apple cider

2 tablespoons dark brown sugar

2 teaspoons cornstarch (cornflour)

1 cinnamon stick

¼ teaspoon freshly grated nutmeg

½ cup (3 oz/90 g) golden raisins
   (sultanas)

1 tablespoon unsalted butter

To make the ice cream, in a saucepan over medium heat, combine the raisins and rum and heat until bubbling around the edges, about 2 minutes. Remove from the heat, transfer to a bowl and let cool, 30–40 minutes. In the same saucepan off the heat, stir together the egg yolks and sugar.

~ In another saucepan, combine the milk and cream. Place over medium heat until bubbles form around the edges of the pan, about 5 minutes. Remove from the heat and slowly add to the yolk-sugar mixture, whisking constantly. Place over medium heat and cook, stirring constantly with a wooden spoon, just until the mixture begins to thicken and coats the back of a spoon, 2–3 minutes. Immediately remove from

the heat and strain through a fine-mesh sieve into a bowl. Add the vanilla. Strain the raisins over a small bowl and add ¼ cup (2 fl oz/60 ml) of the rum to the custard base; reserve any remaining rum for the sauce. Set the raisins aside. Whisk the ice cream base for 1 minute to cool, then cover and chill well, about 2 hours.

~ Meanwhile, make the sauce: In a small bowl, whisk together ½ cup (4 fl oz/125 ml) of the cider, the brown sugar and cornstarch. Pour into a saucepan and add the remaining 2½ cups (20 fl oz/625 ml) cider, the cinnamon stick, nutmeg and golden raisins and

mix well. Bring to a boil over high heat. Reduce the heat to medium-high and simmer, uncovered, until only 1½ cups (12 fl oz/375 ml) remain, 10–15 minutes. Remove from the heat and discard the cinnamon stick. Stir in the butter and the reserved rum. Set aside.

~ Transfer the ice cream base to an ice cream maker and freeze according to the manufacturer's directions. Add the reserved raisins during the final few minutes of churning.

~ To serve, reheat the cider sauce. Scoop the ice cream into bowls and drizzle with the sauce.

## UPSIDE-DOWN PEAR GINGERBREAD

SERVES 9

*Boscs are firm pears particularly well suited to baking, broiling or poaching. Serve the gingerbread with whipped cream or vanilla ice cream, if desired.*

¾ cup (6 oz/185 g) unsalted butter, at
    room temperature
1 cup (7 oz/220 g) firmly packed
    brown sugar
3 Bosc pears, peeled, cored and thinly
    sliced
1 egg
¼ cup (3 oz/90 g) dark molasses
1½ cups (7½ oz/235 g) all-purpose
    (plain) flour
2 teaspoons ground ginger
1½ teaspoons ground cinnamon
½ teaspoon baking soda (bicarbonate
    of soda)
¼ teaspoon freshly grated nutmeg
¼ teaspoon ground cloves
pinch of salt
⅓ cup (3 fl oz/80 ml) boiling water

Place a 9-inch (23-cm) square cake pan over medium heat, add ¼ cup (2 oz/60 g) of the butter and allow to melt. Add ½ cup (3½ oz/110 g) of the brown sugar and stir just until the sugar melts. Add the pear slices and cook, stirring occasionally, until the pears just begin to soften, about 5 minutes. Arrange the pears in an even layer over the bottom of the pan and remove from the heat.

❧ Preheat an oven to 350°F (180°C).

❧ In a bowl, using an electric mixer set on high speed, beat together the remaining ½ cup (4 oz/125 g) butter and ½ cup (3½ oz/110 g) brown sugar until light, about 3 minutes. Add the egg and molasses and beat until well mixed, about 1 minute. Sift together the flour, ginger, cinnamon, baking soda, nutmeg, cloves and salt into another bowl. Dividing the flour mixture into 2 batches, and using a rubber spatula, fold the flour mixture into the butter-sugar mixture alternately with the water, beginning and ending with the flour. Do not overmix.

❧ Spoon the batter over the pears. Bake until springy to the touch, 30–40 minutes. Remove from the oven and let cool on a rack for about 5 minutes. Carefully invert the cake onto a serving plate. Cut into squares and serve warm or at room temperature.

# CARAMEL POTS DE CRÈME

SERVES 6

*This smooth, creamy custard flavored with bittersweet caramel is the ultimate cold-weather comfort food. Garnish each serving with a dollop of whipped cream and toasted walnuts or pecans.*

1 cup (8 oz/250 g) sugar
⅓ cup (3 fl oz/80 ml) plus ¼ cup (2 fl oz/60 ml) water
1½ cups (12 fl oz/375 ml) heavy (double) cream
1½ cups (12 fl oz/375 ml) milk
8 egg yolks
boiling water, as needed

Place the sugar and the ⅓ cup (3 fl oz/80 ml) water in a heavy saucepan over medium-high heat. Cover and bring to a boil. Uncover and cook until the sugar turns golden amber in color, 8–12 minutes. Be careful, as the caramel is very hot.

❧ Meanwhile, combine the cream and milk in a large saucepan over medium-high heat and warm until small bubbles appear along the edges of the pan. Remove from the heat.

❧ Preheat an oven to 325°F (165°C).

❧ When the caramel is ready, add the remaining ¼ cup (2 fl oz/60 ml) water and whisk vigorously until the bubbles subside. Pour the caramel into the hot cream mixture and whisk together until mixed. Let cool for about 10 minutes.

❧ In a bowl, whisk together the egg yolks. Slowly add the caramel mixture, stirring constantly until mixed. Strain through a fine-mesh sieve into a pitcher.

❧ Pour the custard into six ⅔-cup (5-fl oz/160-ml) ramekins. Place the ramekins in a baking pan. Pour boiling water into the pan to reach about 1 inch (2.5 cm) up the sides of the ramekins. Bake until the edges of the custards are set, 40–50 minutes. Remove the baking pan from the oven and transfer to a rack to cool for about 10 minutes.

❧ Remove the custards from the water bath and let cool. Refrigerate for several hours or overnight until well chilled. Serve chilled or at room temperature.

# MAPLE LEAF COOKIES

MAKES 2–2½ DOZEN

*These cookies are inspired by the changing colors of maple leaves in autumn. The dough can be made up to several days ahead, well wrapped and stored in the refrigerator until ready to bake.*

¾ cup (6 oz/185 g) sugar, plus sugar for dusting
1 cup (8 oz/250 g) unsalted butter, at room temperature
½ cup (5½ oz/170 g) pure maple syrup
1 teaspoon vanilla extract (essence)
1 egg yolk
3 cups (15 oz/470 g) all-purpose (plain) flour
¼ teaspoon salt

In a bowl, using an electric mixer set on high speed, beat together the ¾ cup (6 oz/185 g) sugar and the butter until light and fluffy, about 3 minutes. Add the maple syrup, vanilla and egg yolk and mix for 1 minute. Sift together the flour and salt directly onto the butter mixture, then beat on medium speed until combined, about 2 minutes. Shape the dough into a ball, wrap in plastic wrap and refrigerate overnight.

❧ The next day, preheat an oven to 350°F (180°C). Butter 2 baking sheets.

❧ Divide the dough into 2 equal portions. Working with 1 portion at a time, place the dough on a lightly floured work surface and, using a rolling pin, roll out ⅛ inch (3 mm) thick. Using a maple leaf–shaped cookie cutter 4 inches (10 cm) across at the widest part, cut out as many cookies as possible. As the cookies are cut, place them 1 inch (2.5 cm) apart on a prepared baking sheet. Then, using a small paring knife, mark each cutout in a pattern resembling the veins of a maple leaf. Gather up the scraps, reroll and cut out as many additional cookies as possible. Repeat with the second dough portion, placing them on the second prepared baking sheet. Dust each cookie with about ½ teaspoon sugar.

❧ Place the baking sheets on separate racks in the oven and bake the cookies until the edges are lightly golden, 10–12 minutes, switching the pans and rotating them 180 degrees halfway through baking. Remove from the oven and transfer to a rack to cool. Store in an airtight container at room temperature for up to 4 days.

## BAKED APPLES WITH CALVADOS CUSTARD SAUCE

SERVES 6

6 baking apples (see photo below)
½ cup (4 oz/120 g) firmly packed
   light brown sugar
4 tablespoons (2 oz/60 g) unsalted
   butter, at room temperature
½ cup (4 fl oz/125 ml) water
½ teaspoon ground cinnamon
½ teaspoon grated lemon zest
½ cup (2 oz/60 g) walnuts
⅓ cup (1 oz/30 g) dried apples,
   chopped

**FOR THE CUSTARD SAUCE:**

4 egg yolks
2 cups (16 fl oz/500 ml) milk
¼ cup (2 oz/60 g) granulated sugar
¼ teaspoon vanilla extract (essence)
2 tablespoons Calvados or other dry
   apple brandy

Preheat an oven to 375°F (190°C).
Peel the top one-fourth of each apple,
leaving the stem intact. Cut a slice
½ inch (12 mm) thick off the stem ends
and set aside. Core the apples, cutting
to within ½ inch (12 mm) of the base
but leaving the base intact.

❧ In a small pan over medium-high
heat, combine ¼ cup (2 oz/60 g)
of the brown sugar, 2 tablespoons of the
butter, the water, ¼ teaspoon of the
cinnamon and the lemon zest. Bring
to a boil, stirring to dissolve the sugar.
Remove the syrup from the heat and
set aside.

❧ Spread the walnuts on a baking
sheet and toast until lightly golden and
fragrant, 5–7 minutes. Let cool, chop
coarsely and place in a bowl. Add the
dried apples and the remaining ¼ cup
(2 oz/60 g) brown sugar, ¼ teaspoon
cinnamon and the remaining 2 tablespoons butter. Stir to mix well. Fill
the apples with the mixture, dividing
it evenly. Replace the stem ends.

❧ Arrange the apples in a 2-qt (2-l)
baking dish and pour the syrup over
them. Cover and bake until nearly
tender, about 30 minutes. Uncover,
baste with the pan juices and bake until

easily pierced, about 15 minutes longer.

❧ Meanwhile, make the sauce: In a
bowl, whisk the egg yolks until blended.
In a saucepan over medium-high heat,
combine the milk and granulated sugar
and heat, stirring until the sugar dissolves. When small bubbles appear along
the edges of the pan, slowly whisk the
milk mixture into the egg yolks. Return
the pan to medium heat and cook,
stirring constantly, just until the mixture
thickens and coats the back of a spoon,
3–4 minutes. Immediately remove from
the heat and strain through a fine-mesh
sieve into a bowl. Stir in the vanilla and
brandy. Cover and refrigerate.

❧ Remove the apples from the oven,
spoon some of the pan juices over
them and slip under a preheated broiler
(griller). Broil (grill) until lightly
golden, about 1 minute. To serve, spoon
the sauce onto individual plates and
place an apple in the center.

*The orchard seemed full of sun,*
*like a cup,*
*and we could smell the ripe*
*apples on the trees.*
*— Willa Cather*

*Many good baking apples are available this season. Try Rome Beauty, Golden*
*Delicious, Jonagold (all pictured here) or McIntosh for this dessert.*

# SPICED PUMPKIN PIE

MAKES ONE 9-INCH (23-CM) PIE; SERVES 6–8

**FOR THE PASTRY:**

1½ cups (7½ oz/235 g) all-purpose
   (plain) flour

½ teaspoon salt

1 tablespoon sugar

½ cup (4 oz/125 g) unsalted butter,
   chilled, cut into pieces

3 tablespoons vegetable shortening,
   chilled, cut into pieces

3 tablespoons ice water

**FOR THE FILLING:**

1 small pumpkin, 2½ lb (1.25 kg)

¼ cup (3 oz/90 g) maple syrup

¼ cup (2 oz/60 g) firmly packed
   light brown sugar

1½ teaspoons ground cinnamon

1 teaspoon ground ginger

½ teaspoon ground nutmeg

¼ teaspoon ground cloves

3 eggs, beaten

¾ cup (6 fl oz/180 ml) half-and-half
   (half cream)

1 cup (8 fl oz/250 ml) heavy (double)
   cream

2 tablespoons confectioners' (icing)
   sugar

½ teaspoon vanilla extract (essence)

To make the pastry, in a large bowl, mix together the flour, salt and sugar. Make a well in the center, add the butter and shortening and, using your fingertips, rub them into the flour mixture until small, flat pieces form. Sprinkle on the water and gently mix with a fork. Gather the dough into a rough ball; do not overwork. Wrap in plastic wrap and refrigerate for 2 hours.

❧ Preheat an oven to 350°F (180°C). Lightly oil a baking sheet.

❧ To make the filling, cut the pumpkin in half through the stem end and place, cut side down, on a baking sheet. Bake until easily pierced with a knife, about 1 hour. Let cool and, using a spoon, scoop out the seeds and fibers and discard. Spoon the flesh into a food processor fitted with the metal blade. Purée until smooth. Measure out 1½ cups (12 oz/375 g); set aside. Reserve the rest for another use. Raise the oven temperature to 375°F (190°C).

❧ On a well-floured work surface, roll out the dough into a 12-inch (30-cm) round. Transfer the dough to a 9-inch (23-cm) pie pan and gently press into the bottom and sides of the pan. Trim the edges, leaving a 1½-inch (12-mm) overhang, then fold under the overhang to make an even edge and crimp to form an attractive rim. Prick the bottom and sides of the pastry with a fork. Place in the freezer for 10 minutes.

❧ Line the pastry with aluminum foil and fill with pie weights. Bake for 15 minutes. Remove the weights and foil and continue to bake until lightly golden, 10–15 minutes. Transfer to a rack and let cool.

❧ In a bowl, whisk together the pumpkin purée, maple syrup, brown sugar, cinnamon, ginger, nutmeg, cloves, eggs and half-and-half until well mixed. Pour into the prebaked pie shell. Bake until a skewer inserted into the center comes out clean, 45–55 minutes. Transfer to the rack and let cool for at least 30 minutes before serving.

❧ In a chilled bowl, whisk the cream until soft peaks form. Sift the confectioners' sugar directly on top, add the vanilla and fold in. Serve the pie with the cream on the side.

*Oh, shine on, shine on,*
*harvest moon*
*Up in the sky.*
*—Jack Norworth*

# FIG AND WALNUT TARTLETS

SERVES 8

**FOR THE SHORT-CRUST PASTRY:**

1 cup (5 oz/155 g) all-purpose (plain)
    flour
1 tablespoon granulated sugar
pinch of salt
½ cup (4 fl oz/125 g) butter, out of
    the refrigerator for 15 minutes,
    cut into pieces
1–3 teaspoons water

**FOR THE FILLING:**

1 cup (4 oz/125 g) walnuts
⅓ cup (1½ oz/45 g) confectioners'
    (icing) sugar
2 tablespoons all-purpose (plain) flour
1½ tablespoons unsalted butter
1 egg
1 tablespoon brandy
1 teaspoon grated orange zest
9 fresh figs such as Mission or Kadota

1 cup (8 fl oz/250 ml) heavy (double)
    cream
1½ tablespoons confectioners' (icing)
    sugar, plus sugar for dusting
1 teaspoon vanilla extract (essence)
orange zest strips and walnut halves
    for garnish, optional

Preheat an oven to 375°F (190°C).

❧ To make the pastry, in a food processor fitted with the metal blade, combine the flour, 1 tablespoon sugar and the salt. Pulse just to mix. Add the butter and pulse until the mixture resembles coarse meal. With the motor running, add just enough water for the mixture to come together into a rough mass. Gather the dough into a ball and flatten into a disk 6 inches (15 cm) in diameter. Wrap in plastic wrap and refrigerate for 30 minutes.

❧ To make the filling, spread the walnuts on a baking sheet and toast until lightly golden and fragrant, 5–7 minutes. Let cool. In the food processor fitted with the metal blade, process the walnuts and half of the confectioners' sugar until finely ground, 30–60 seconds. Sift together the remaining confectioners' sugar and flour directly onto the nuts and pulse several times to mix. Add the butter, egg, brandy and orange zest and pulse until blended. Transfer to a bowl. Finely chop 4 of the figs and add to the bowl. Stir gently until well mixed.

❧ Divide the dough into 8 equal portions. Gently press each portion into an individual tart pan 3 inches (7.5 cm) in diameter, building up the sides slightly. Place the lined pans in the freezer for 15 minutes.

❧ Raise the oven temperature to 400°F (200°C). Place the tart pans on a baking sheet and bake until golden, about 15 minutes.

❧ Meanwhile, cut the remaining 5 figs into slices about ¼ inch (6 mm) thick. When the tart shells are ready, remove from the oven and pour the batter into them, dividing it evenly. Top each tart with an equal amount of the sliced figs and return them to the oven. Bake until set and the tops are golden, about 35 minutes.

❧ While the tarts are baking, in a bowl, beat the cream until soft peaks form. Sift the 1½ tablespoons confectioners' sugar directly on top and add the vanilla. Fold in just until mixed.

❧ Remove the tartlets from the oven and, if desired, garnish with orange zest strips and walnut halves. Dust with confectioners' sugar and serve immediately with the cream on the side.

## CARAMELIZED NUT TART

SERVES 8

1 9-inch short-crust tart shell (recipe on page 62), baked until lightly golden then cooled

### FOR THE FILLING:

½ teaspoon baking soda (bicarbonate of soda)

¼ cup (1¼ oz/37 g) hazelnuts (filberts)

¼ cup (1 oz/30 g) sliced (flaked) almonds

¼ cup (1 oz/30 g) chopped walnuts

¼ cup (1 oz/30 g) chopped pecans

¾ cup (6 fl oz/180 ml) heavy (double) cream

¾ cup (6 oz/185 g) sugar

½ teaspoon vanilla extract (essence)

To make the filling, fill a small saucepan half full of water, add the baking soda and bring to a boil. Add the hazelnuts and boil for 30 seconds. Drain, immediately place in a kitchen towel and rub to remove the skins. Chop the hazelnuts coarsely. Spread the hazelnuts, almonds, walnuts and pecans on a baking sheet and bake until the almonds are lightly golden, 3–5 minutes. Remove from the oven and set aside. Position a rack in the upper part of the oven and raise the temperature to 400°F (200°C).

❧ In a saucepan over medium-high heat, combine the cream, sugar and vanilla extract. Bring to a boil and boil until slightly thickened, about 3 minutes. Remove from the heat and stir in all the nuts. Let stand for 15 minutes.

❧ Pour the filling into the prebaked tart shell and place on a baking sheet. Bake until the top is a combination of creamy white and russet-caramel in color and is dotted all over with small holes, 30–35 minutes. Let cool on a rack for 15 minutes, remove the pan sides and slide the tart onto a serving plate. Serve at room temperature.

*For an elegant presentation, cut out leaves from the dough scraps and place them on top of the pie pastry after brushing it with the egg wash. Then brush the leaves with the wash and bake.*

*The grim frost is at hand,
when the apples will fall thick,
almost thunderous,
on the hardened earth.
—D. H. Lawrence*

## OLD-FASHIONED APPLE PIE

MAKES ONE 9-INCH (23-CM) PIE; SERVES 8

*Laying a slice of Cheddar cheese atop a wedge of warm apple pie is an American tradition. Today a scoop of vanilla ice cream is generally preferred.*

**FOR THE PASTRY:**

2½ cups (12½ oz/390 g) all-purpose (plain) flour
1 teaspoon salt
2 tablespoons sugar
10 tablespoons (5 oz/155 g) unsalted butter, chilled, cut into pieces
10 tablespoons (5 oz/155 g) vegetable shortening, chilled, cut into pieces
7 tablespoons (3½ fl oz/105 ml) ice water
1 teaspoon distilled white vinegar

**FOR THE FILLING:**

2½ lb (1.25 kg) baking apples, peeled, quartered, cored and cut lengthwise into slices ½ inch (12 mm) thick
½ cup (4 oz/125 g) sugar, or as needed
½ teaspoon ground cinnamon
¼ teaspoon ground nutmeg
1 tablespoon fresh lemon juice
2 tablespoons unsalted butter, cut into pieces

1 egg yolk
1 tablespoon heavy (double) cream

To make the pastry, in a large bowl, mix together the flour, salt and sugar. Make a well in the center, add the butter and shortening and, using your fingertips, rub them into the flour mixture until small, flat pieces form. Combine the water and vinegar and, using a fork, gently mix just enough of the liquid into the flour mixture for it to come together in a rough ball; do not over-work. Discard the remaining liquid. Divide the dough in half and wrap each half in plastic wrap. Refrigerate for 2 hours.

To make the filling, in a bowl, toss together the apples, sugar (adding more to taste if the apples are tart), cinnamon, nutmeg and lemon juice.

Preheat an oven to 400°F (200°C).

On a lightly floured work surface, roll out half of the dough (leave the other half refrigerated) into a round 12 inches (30 cm) in diameter and about ⅛ inch (3 mm) thick. Fold the dough in half and then into quarters and transfer it to a 9-inch (23-cm) pie pan. Unfold and gently press into the bottom and sides of the pan. Trim the edges even with the rim. Roll out the remaining dough into a 10-inch (25-cm) round about ⅛ inch (3 mm) thick.

Turn the apples into the pastry-lined pan, mounding them slightly in the center. Dot evenly with the butter. Brush the edges of the dough with water. Fold the dough round into quarters and unfold over the apples. Press together the top and bottom crusts to seal, then trim the edges flush with the pan rim and crimp to form an attractive edge. In a small bowl, beat together the egg yolk and cream and brush over the pastry. Make a few slits near the center of the pie to allow steam to escape.

Bake for 25 minutes. Reduce the heat to 350°F (180°C) and continue to bake until the apples are tender (insert a knife blade through a slit) and the top is golden brown, 15–20 minutes. Transfer to a rack and let cool for at least 20 minutes before serving.

# Winter

⌒

# Winter Openers
ဢ

Winter brings forth a bounty from the sea to open meals in gala style. Icy waters are ideal, in fact, for nurturing shellfish to plump, sweet perfection, ready to offer in the form of Steamed Mussels with Garlic and Herbs and Shrimp Cigars (both on page 217) or Oysters on the Half Shell (page 213). Although fresh fin fish are not as abundant now, their fragrant preserved forms also provide classic appetizers, such as the Buckwheat Blinis with Smoked Salmon and Caviar on this page and Smoked Trout in Endive Spears (page 214).

How fortunate it is, too, that warmer winter climates also yield a harvest of citrus fruits whose juices complement fresh and smoked seafood. Note the lemon wedges and twists that garnish so many of the plates on the pages that follow, ready to add their own bracingly zesty spritz of flavor.

## BUCKWHEAT BLINIS WITH SMOKED SALMON AND CAVIAR

SERVES 6

*Blinis, yeasted miniature buckwheat pancakes, are perfect vehicles for eating smoked salmon and caviar. They originated in Russia, where they were traditionally served with sour cream and salt herring.*

**FOR THE BLINIS:**

1 cup (3½ oz/105 g) buckwheat flour
1 cup (5 oz/155 g) all-purpose (plain) flour
¼ teaspoon salt
1 package (2½ teaspoons) active dry yeast
3 tablespoons plus ¾ cup (6 fl oz/ 180 ml) lukewarm water (110°F/43°C)
2 tablespoons sugar
1¾ cups (14 fl oz/430 ml) milk
3 eggs, beaten
¼ cup (2 oz/60 g) unsalted butter, melted
vegetable oil

**FOR THE TOPPING:**

6 oz (185 g) thinly sliced smoked salmon
1 cup (8 fl oz/250 ml) sour cream

To make the blinis, sift together the buckwheat flour, all-purpose flour and salt into a bowl. In a small bowl, combine the yeast, the 3 tablespoons lukewarm water, 1 tablespoon of the sugar and ¼ cup (2 oz/60 g) of the flour mixture; stir to mix well. Cover with plastic wrap and let stand in a warm place (75°F/24°C) until bubbly, about 30 minutes.

☙ In a large bowl, whisk together 1 cup (8 fl oz/250 ml) of the milk, the remaining ¾ cup (6 fl oz/180 ml) water, the eggs, butter and the remaining 1 tablespoon sugar. Stir in the yeast mixture and enough of the remaining flour mixture to make a batter the consistency of sour cream. Cover the bowl with plastic wrap and let the dough rise in a warm place until the mixture is frothy and doubled in volume, about 30 minutes.

☙ In a small saucepan, warm the remaining ¾ cup (6 fl oz/180 ml) milk until bubbles form around the edges of the pan. Pour the milk into the batter. Mix well.

☙ Place a large frying pan over medium heat and add about 1 teaspoon vegetable oil. Tilt the pan to coat the bottom with the oil. When the oil is hot, using a tablespoon, drop the batter onto the pan; do not crowd the pan. Using the back of the spoon, spread each spoonful of batter to make a round 2½–3 inches (6–7.5 cm) in diameter. Cook until bubbles appear on the surface and then break, about 10 seconds. Turn and cook on the second sides until lightly golden, 10–15 seconds longer. Transfer to a warmed plate and keep warm while you cook the remaining batter. You should have 32–36 blinis in all.

☙ To serve, place the blinis on a warmed serving plate. Top each blini with a piece of the smoked salmon, a small spoonful of sour cream, a tiny mound of caviar and a tiny sprig of dill.

## OYSTERS ON THE HALF SHELL WITH MIGNONETTE SAUCE

SERVES 6

*Folk wisdom holds that oysters may only be eaten safely during months with the letter r in their names. Although modern methods and standards for their cultivation now make them safe to eat year-round, the shellfish will be at their best in winter when the coastal waters from which they are harvested are at their coldest.*

**FOR THE MIGNONETTE SAUCE:**
½ cup (4 fl oz/125 ml) dry red wine
    such as Cabernet Sauvignon,
    Zinfandel or Pinot Noir
3–4 tablespoons red wine vinegar
4 shallots, minced
⅛ teaspoon red pepper flakes
freshly cracked black pepper

crushed or shaved ice
36 oysters in the shell
lemon wedges
flat-leaf (Italian) parsley sprigs

To make the mignonette sauce, in a small bowl, stir together the wine, 3 tablespoons vinegar, shallots, red pepper flakes and black pepper to taste. Taste and add more vinegar if needed.
❧ Place the bowl of mignonette sauce on a platter and surround it with a bed of ice. Discard any oysters that do not close tightly to the touch. Scrub each oyster thoroughly with a stiff-bristled brush, rinsing it well under cold running water. Holding each oyster flat-side up in a kitchen towel and using an oyster knife, slip the tip of the knife into the shell near the hinge and pry upward to open. Run the knife blade along the inside of the top shell to sever the muscle that joins the shells, then lift off the top shell. Run the knife underneath the oyster to free it from the rounded, bottom shell, being careful not to spill the liquor. Nest the oysters in their shells on the ice.
❧ Garnish the platter with lemon wedges and parsley sprigs and serve immediately.

## BLOOD ORANGE MIMOSA

SERVES 6

*Winter's blood oranges bring refreshing taste and vibrant color to this sparkling aperitif. Serve it alongside oysters or other shellfish or enjoy it alone. Don't use your best Champagne or sparkling wine; its nuances will be lost to the bold flavor of the juice.*

1 fifth (24 fl oz/750 ml) Champagne
    or sparkling wine (see note)
about 1½ cups (12 fl oz/375 ml) fresh
    blood orange juice
6 thin blood orange slices, each slit to
    the center

Fill Champagne flutes halfway with Champagne or sparkling wine. Pour in enough blood orange juice to fill the glasses. Garnish the rim of each glass with a blood orange slice and serve immediately.

*. . . from a grove beyond the wall came an erotic waft of early orange blossom.*
—*Giuseppe di Lampedusa*

## SMOKED TROUT IN ENDIVE SPEARS

SERVES 6

¼ cup (2 fl oz/60 ml) mayonnaise
6 green (spring) onions, thinly sliced
2 small cloves garlic, minced
1½ teaspoons fresh lemon juice
⅛ teaspoon cayenne pepper
½ teaspoon sweet paprika
salt and freshly ground pepper
1½ cups (7½ oz/235 g) flaked smoked
　trout fillet
4 heads Belgian endive (chicory/
　witlof)
lemon wedges

In a small bowl, combine the mayonnaise, green onions, garlic, lemon juice, cayenne, paprika and salt and pepper to taste. Mix well. Add the trout and stir to combine.

❧ Cut off the base from each endive and separate the heads into individual spears. Use only the larger endive spears; reserve the smaller ones for another use.

❧ Using the broad end of each spear, scoop up a heaping teaspoonful of the trout mixture, then spread it along the spears with a knife. Arrange on a platter and garnish with lemon wedges. Serve immediately.

## TWO-WAY SALMON TOASTS

SERVES 6

1 teaspoon olive oil
½ lb (250 g) fresh salmon fillet, about
　¾ inch (2 cm) thick, skin and any
　errant bones removed
salt and freshly ground pepper
6 oz (185 g) smoked salmon, coarsely
　chopped
3–4 teaspoons fresh lemon juice
3 tablespoons mayonnaise
3 tablespoons chopped fresh dill
2 tablespoons well-drained capers,
　chopped
½ baguette, cut on the diagonal into
　thin slices and lightly toasted
2 tablespoons snipped fresh chives
thin lemon slices, optional

In a nonstick frying pan over medium heat, warm the olive oil. Add the fresh salmon and cook on the first side for 3 minutes. Turn, season to taste with salt and pepper and continue to cook until the salmon is opaque throughout, 3–4 minutes longer. Remove from the heat and let cool.

❧ Chop the cooked salmon coarsely and place it in a large bowl. Add the smoked salmon, 3 teaspoons lemon juice, mayonnaise, dill and capers. Taste and add more lemon juice if needed.

❧ To serve, spread the salmon on the toasts, dividing it evenly. Garnish with the chives and lemon slices, if desired. Serve immediately.

## STEAMED MUSSELS WITH GARLIC AND HERBS

SERVES 6

3 lb (1.5 kg) mussels, debearded and
   well scrubbed
2 tablespoons extra-virgin olive oil
1 small red (Spanish) onion, chopped
4 cloves garlic, minced
3 cups (24 fl oz/750 ml) dry red wine
   such as Cabernet Sauvignon,
   Zinfandel or Pinot Noir
2 tablespoons coarsely chopped fresh
   flat-leaf (Italian) parsley, plus parsley
   sprigs for garnish
1 teaspoon chopped fresh thyme
½ teaspoon chopped fresh winter
   savory, optional
3 bay leaves
salt and freshly ground pepper

Discard any mussels that do not close
to the touch. In a large frying pan over
medium-low heat, warm the olive oil.
Add the onion and sauté until soft,
about 10 minutes. Add the garlic and
cook, stirring constantly, for 1 minute.
Pour in the red wine and add the
mussels, chopped parsley, thyme, savory
(if using) and bay leaves. Cover and
simmer until the mussels open, 3–5
minutes. Check the mussels periodically; as they open, transfer them to a
serving bowl and cover to keep warm.
Discard any that have not opened.

❧ When all of the mussels have been
removed from the pan, uncover and
reduce the cooking liquid over high
heat by one-fourth, 2–4 minutes.
Discard the bay leaves. Season to taste
with salt and pepper.

❧ Pour the reduced pan sauce over
the mussels and garnish with parsley
sprigs. Serve immediately.

## SPICED SHRIMP CIGARS

MAKES 18 ROLLS; SERVES 6

*These crispy rolls can be prepared up to
a day in advance: Simply shape, arrange
in a single layer on a baking sheet and
refrigerate. Bake before serving.*

2 tablespoons olive oil
½ lb (250 g) medium shrimp (prawns),
   peeled and deveined
salt and freshly ground pepper
¾ cup (4½ oz/140 g) peeled, seeded
   and chopped tomatoes (fresh or
   canned)
¼ cup (1½ oz/45 g) finely chopped
   yellow onion
2 cloves garlic, minced
3 tablespoons chopped fresh flat-leaf
   (Italian) parsley
¼ cup (⅓ oz/10 g) chopped fresh
   cilantro (fresh coriander)
1¼ teaspoons ground cumin
½ teaspoon sweet paprika
¼ teaspoon cayenne pepper
pinch of saffron threads
about ¼ cup (½ oz/15 g) fresh bread
   crumbs
9 sheets (about ½ lb/250 g) filo dough
2 tablespoons unsalted butter
2 tablespoons extra-virgin olive oil
lemon wedges

In a frying pan over medium heat,
warm the olive oil. Add the shrimp and
cook, stirring occasionally, until they
begin to turn pink, about 2 minutes.
Season to taste with salt and pepper.
Remove the pan from the heat and
transfer the shrimp to a cutting board;
chop coarsely and set aside.

❧ Return the pan to medium-low
heat. Add the tomatoes, onion, garlic,
parsley, cilantro, cumin, paprika, cayenne
and saffron and stir to mix well. Simmer
slowly, stirring occasionally, until the
moisture has evaporated, 5–10 minutes.

Remove the pan from the heat and add
the shrimp and enough bread crumbs
to make a fairly dry mixture. Mix well
and season to taste with salt and pepper.

❧ Preheat an oven to 400°F (200°C).
Lightly butter a baking sheet.

❧ Place the filo sheets in a neat stack
on a cutting board and cut the stack
crosswise into quarters, forming strips
about 4 inches (10 cm) wide. Cover
with a dampened kitchen towel until
ready to use.

❧ In a small pan over medium heat,
melt the butter with the extra-virgin
olive oil. Remove from the heat. Brush
1 filo strip very lightly with the butter
mixture and place a second strip on
top. Brush the second strip lightly with
the butter mixture. Place a heaping
teaspoonful of filling along a short end.
Fold in the sides, then roll up to form
a cigar shape. Place on the prepared
baking sheet and brush lightly with the
butter mixture. Repeat with remaining
filo and filling.

❧ Place the filo cigars on the prepared
baking sheet. Bake until golden, about
15 minutes. Transfer to a platter and
garnish with lemon wedges. Serve
immediately.

# Winter Soups & Stews

The hardy vegetables of winter seem tailor-made for long, slow simmering in soups and stews. Roots, which grow sweet in the cold ground, add robust flavor and body to such recipes as Parsnip and Carrot Soup (page 225) and Beef Stew with Turnips (page 226). Tubers, too, provide rich sustenance, whether in the form of the red potatoes in Chicken Pot Pie (page 229) or their more exotic cousins featured in Jerusalem Artichoke Soup with Hazelnut-Orange Butter (page 222). Various members of the onion family underscore the flavors of all these dishes, as well as starring in Three-Onion Soup (page 221).

The winter pantry also holds a wealth of dried beans and peas in prime condition from the last autumn's harvest, ready for adding to soups and stews. In dishes like Split Pea Soup (page 225) and Vegetarian Black Bean Chili (page 221), these staples bring back memories of spring and summer in the prime of winter.

## WILD MUSHROOM SOUP WITH BLUE CHEESE TOASTS

SERVES 6

*A warm bowl of this elegant soup is a welcome treat in the cold depths of winter. The fresh wild mushrooms preferred for this recipe are porcini, hedgehogs, chanterelles or shiitakes; if unavailable, substitute fresh button mushrooms.*

### FOR THE SOUP:
2½ tablespoons unsalted butter
1 yellow onion, chopped
1 lb (500 g) fresh button mushrooms, brushed clean and coarsely chopped
1 oz (30 g) dried porcini mushrooms
6 cups (48 fl oz/1.5 l) chicken stock
4 cups (32 fl oz/1 l) water
½ lb (250 g) fresh wild mushrooms (see note), brushed clean and thinly sliced
salt and freshly ground pepper
½ cup (4 fl oz/125 ml) heavy (double) cream
1 tablespoon fresh lemon juice

### FOR THE BLUE CHEESE TOASTS:
2 oz (60 g) blue cheese such as Roquefort, Stilton or Gorgonzola, at room temperature
1½ teaspoons unsalted butter, at room temperature
salt and freshly ground pepper
6 baguette slices, lightly toasted
2 tablespoons finely snipped fresh chives

To make the soup, in a large soup pot over medium-high heat, melt 1½ tablespoons of the butter. Add the onion and cook, stirring occasionally, until soft, about 10 minutes. Raise the heat

to high, add the button mushrooms, dried porcini mushrooms, stock and water and bring to a boil. Reduce the heat to medium-low and simmer, uncovered, until the mushrooms are tender, about 30 minutes. Remove from the heat and let cool for about 15 minutes.

Meanwhile, in a frying pan over medium-high heat, melt the remaining 1 tablespoon butter. Add the sliced wild mushrooms and sauté, stirring occasionally, until the mushrooms are soft and the mushroom liquid has evaporated, 6–8 minutes. Season to taste with salt and pepper. Transfer to a dish. Set aside.

Using a blender and working in batches, purée the soup until smooth, 3–4 minutes for each batch. Strain through a fine-mesh sieve into a clean soup pot. Add the cream and sautéed wild mushrooms and stir to combine. Stir in the lemon juice and season to taste with salt and pepper. Place over medium heat and reheat to serving temperature.

To make the toasts, in a small bowl, mash together the blue cheese and butter. Season to taste with salt and pepper. Spread the cheese onto the toasted baguette slices and place on an ungreased baking sheet. Broil (grill) until the cheese is bubbling around the edges, 30–60 seconds. Remove from the broiler (griller) and sprinkle with the chives.

To serve, ladle the soup into warmed bowls and float a blue cheese toast in the center of each bowl. Serve at once.

## THREE-ONION SOUP

SERVES 6

*Yellow onions, leeks and garlic are the three onion family members combined in this full-flavored soup. For a heartier rendition, toast slices of country-style bread on both sides until golden and rub them on one side with whole garlic cloves. Place a slice of bread in the bottom of each soup bowl and ladle the hot soup over the bread.*

3 tablespoons extra-virgin olive oil
4 large yellow onions, diced
4 leeks, including 1 inch (2.5 cm) of
  the tender greens, carefully rinsed
  and diced
3 oz (90 g) pancetta, finely diced
5 cloves garlic, minced
6 cups (48 fl oz/1.5 l) chicken stock
1¼ cups (10 fl oz/310 ml) fruity red
  wine such as Chianti or Zinfandel
2 tablespoons balsamic vinegar
1 tablespoon red wine vinegar
salt and freshly ground pepper
¾ cup (3 oz/90 g) freshly grated
  Parmesan cheese

In a soup pot over medium heat, warm the olive oil. Add the onions, leeks and pancetta and sauté, stirring occasionally, until the onions and leeks are soft, about 10 minutes. Add the garlic and sauté, stirring, for 1 minute. Add the stock and simmer, uncovered, over medium-low heat, until the vegetables are very soft, about 30 minutes.

❧ Just before serving, stir in the red wine, balsamic vinegar and red wine vinegar. Season to taste with salt and pepper. Place over low heat and reheat to serving temperature.

❧ To serve, ladle the soup into warmed bowls. Sprinkle the Parmesan cheese equally over each serving and serve immediately.

## VEGETARIAN BLACK BEAN CHILI

SERVES 6

*Dried beans are an age-old pantry staple of this time of year and nearly any variety will work well in this recipe; some good choices include navy beans, cannellini beans and red beans. If you like, garnish with sour cream and chopped fresh cilantro (fresh coriander).*

2¼ cups (1 lb/500 g) dried black beans
3 tablespoons olive oil
3 yellow onions, chopped
2 fresh serrano or jalapeño chili
  peppers, seeded and minced
5 large cloves garlic, minced
6 tablespoons (1 oz/30 g) chili powder
3 tablespoons ground cumin
¼ teaspoon cayenne pepper
1 teaspoon dried oregano
2 cans (28 oz/875 g each) crushed
  tomatoes
salt and freshly ground pepper
1 cup (4 oz/125 g) coarsely grated
  Monterey Jack cheese

Pick over the beans and discard any damaged beans or impurities. Rinse the beans. Place in a bowl and add water to cover generously. Let soak for about 3 hours. Drain the beans and set aside.

❧ In a large, heavy saucepan over low heat, warm the olive oil. Add the onions and chili peppers and sauté, stirring occasionally, until the onions are soft, about 10 minutes. Add the garlic, chili powder, cumin, cayenne and oregano and sauté, stirring, for 2 minutes longer. Add the beans, tomatoes and water to cover by 3 inches (7.5 cm). Bring to a boil over high heat. Reduce the heat to low and simmer, uncovered, until the beans are very tender and have begun to fall apart, 2½–3 hours. Add water if the beans begin to dry out but are not yet cooked.

❧ Season to taste with salt and pepper. Ladle into warmed bowls, sprinkle with the cheese and serve at once.

## JERUSALEM ARTICHOKE SOUP WITH HAZELNUT-ORANGE BUTTER

SERVES 6

### FOR THE SOUP:

3 tablespoons unsalted butter
3 celery stalks with leaves, diced
3 large yellow onions, diced
2½ teaspoons ground coriander
3 lb (1.5 kg) Jerusalem artichokes, unpeeled, cut into 1-inch (2.5-cm) pieces
2 orange zest strips, each 3 inches (7.5 cm) long and ¾ inch (2 cm) wide
9 cups (2¼ qt/2.25 l) chicken stock

### FOR THE HAZELNUT-ORANGE BUTTER:

¼ cup (1¼ oz/37 g) hazelnuts (filberts)
1 teaspoon grated orange zest
2 tablespoons unsalted butter, at room temperature
salt and freshly ground pepper

3 tablespoons fresh orange juice
salt and freshly ground pepper

To make the soup, in a large soup pot over medium heat, melt the butter. Add the celery and onions and sauté, stirring occasionally, until the vegetables are soft, about 10 minutes. Add the coriander and sauté, stirring, for 1 minute longer. Add the Jerusalem artichokes, orange zest and chicken stock and bring to a boil over high heat. Reduce the heat to medium-low and simmer, uncovered, until the Jerusalem artichokes are soft, about 30 minutes.

✸ Meanwhile, make the butter: Preheat an oven to 350°F (180°C). Spread the hazelnuts on a baking sheet and toast in the oven until lightly browned and fragrant, 5–7 minutes. Remove from the oven and, while the nuts are still warm, place in a kitchen towel and rub to remove the skins. Do not worry if bits of skin remain. Let cool, then finely chop the nuts and place in a small bowl with the orange zest and butter. Using a fork, mash together well. Season to taste with salt and pepper. Cover and chill for 15 minutes. Using a teaspoon, divide the butter into 6 equal portions, forming each into a ball. Flatten each ball slightly and place them on a plate. Cover and refrigerate until needed.

✸ When the Jerusalem artichokes are soft, remove from the heat and let cool slightly. Remove the orange zest and discard. Using a blender and working in batches, purée the soup on high speed until smooth, 3–4 minutes for each batch. Strain the purée through a fine-mesh sieve into a clean saucepan. Add the orange juice and mix well. Season to taste with salt and pepper.

✸ To serve, place the soup over medium heat and reheat to serving temperature. Ladle the soup into warmed bowls and place a piece of the hazelnut-orange butter in the center of each serving. Serve at once.

## CRAB BISQUE

SERVES 6

2 Dungeness crabs, 1–1½ lb (500–750 g) each, cooked
2 tablespoons unsalted butter
1 small yellow onion, chopped
1 carrot, peeled and coarsely chopped
1 celery stalk, coarsely chopped
1½ cups (9 oz/280 g) chopped tomatoes (fresh or canned)
1½ cups (12 fl oz/375 ml) dry white wine such as Sauvignon Blanc
1 tablespoon chopped fresh tarragon, optional
¼ cup (1¼ oz/37 g) all-purpose (plain) flour

3 cups (24 fl oz/750 ml) bottled clam juice
3 cups (24 fl oz/750 ml) water
1 cup (8 fl oz/250 ml) heavy (double) cream
1 tablespoon Cognac or other good-quality brandy
pinch of cayenne pepper
salt and freshly ground pepper

Clean and crack the crabs, except the claws, according to the directions on page 299. Set aside all the meat in a bowl. Crack the large claws and carefully remove the meat from each claw in a single piece. Slice the meat and set aside for garnish. Using kitchen shears, cut the shells into small pieces; set aside.

✸ In a saucepan over low heat, melt the butter. Add the onion, carrot and celery and sauté, stirring occasionally, until the vegetables are soft, about 15 minutes. Add the crab shells, tomatoes, wine and tarragon. Sprinkle the flour over the top and stir to mix well. Bring to a boil, reduce the heat to low, cover and simmer for 20 minutes. Remove from the heat and let cool slightly.

✸ In a bowl, combine the clam juice and water. Combine one-third of the clam juice mixture and one-third of the shell mixture in a blender. Pulse briefly to break up the shells. Place a fine-mesh sieve lined with cheesecloth (muslin) over a bowl. Pour the contents of the blender through the sieve. Repeat with the remaining clam juice and shell mixtures in 2 batches. Transfer to a clean soup pot.

✸ Place the pot over low heat and bring to a gentle simmer. Stir in the cream, brandy and cayenne and season to taste with salt and pepper. Add the reserved crab meat and heat through. Ladle into warmed bowls and garnish with the claw meat. Serve immediately.

## SPLIT PEA SOUP

SERVES 6

*Dried peas and beans have long been menu standards of the winter months. Richly flavored split peas paired with smoked ham hocks is a classic cold-weather combination. Top with buttery croutons before serving, if you like.*

2 smoked ham hocks (about ¾ lb/375 g each)
1½ cups (10½ oz/330 g) yellow or orange split peas
2 tablespoons unsalted butter
1 yellow onion, coarsely chopped
1 carrot, peeled and coarsely chopped
8 cups (64 fl oz/2 l) chicken stock, vegetable stock or water, plus extra as needed
salt and freshly ground pepper
coarsely chopped fresh flat-leaf (Italian) parsley

Bring a large saucepan three-fourths full of water to a boil. Add the ham hocks and simmer for 1 minute. Drain and set aside.

❧ Pick over the split peas and discard any damaged peas or impurities. Rinse the peas and drain.

❧ In a soup pot over medium heat, melt the butter. Add the onion and carrot and sauté, stirring occasionally, until the vegetables are soft, about 10 minutes. Add the ham hocks, split peas and stock or water. Bring to a boil, reduce the heat to low and simmer until the peas are soft, 50–60 minutes.

❧ Remove from the heat. Remove the ham hocks and let stand until cool enough to handle. Let the soup cool slightly.

❧ Using a blender and working in batches, purée the soup on high speed until smooth, about 2 minutes for each batch. Return the purée to a clean soup pot and thin with more stock or water, if needed. Place over medium heat and reheat to serving temperature. Season to taste with salt and pepper.

❧ While the soup is heating, remove the meat from the ham hocks and discard the skin and bones. Cut the meat into small pieces and add to the soup. Stir to heat through.

❧ To serve, ladle the soup into warmed bowls and garnish with parsley. Serve immediately.

## PARSNIP AND CARROT SOUP

SERVES 6

*Introduced to the United States from Europe in the early seventeenth century, the parsnip is a creamy white root vegetable similar in shape and sweetness to the carrot. The wintertime chill turns the parsnip's natural starch to sugar, giving it its distinctive sweetness.*

1½ tablespoons unsalted butter
1 yellow onion, chopped
1¼ lb (625 g) small parsnips, peeled and coarsely chopped
1 lb (500 g) carrots, peeled and coarsely chopped
6 cups (48 fl oz/1.5 l) chicken stock
4 cups (32 fl oz/1 l) water
salt and freshly ground pepper

**FOR THE YOGURT GARNISH:**
⅓ cup (3 oz/90 g) plain yogurt
about 2 tablespoons milk
salt and freshly ground pepper

1½ tablespoons chopped fresh flat-leaf (Italian) parsley

In a large soup pot over medium heat, melt the butter. Add the onion and sauté, stirring occasionally, until soft, about 10 minutes. Raise the heat to high, add the parsnips, carrots, stock and water and bring to a boil. Reduce the heat to medium-low and simmer, uncovered, until the vegetables are tender, about 30 minutes.

❧ Using a blender and working in batches, purée the soup on high speed until smooth, 3–4 minutes for each batch. Strain through a fine-mesh sieve into a clean soup pot. Place over low heat and reheat to serving temperature. Season to taste with salt and pepper.

❧ While the soup is heating, make the yogurt garnish: In a small bowl, whisk together the yogurt and enough milk to make a barely fluid paste. Season to taste with salt and pepper.

❧ To serve, ladle the soup into warmed bowls and drizzle with the yogurt. Sprinkle with the parsley and serve hot.

# BEEF STEW WITH TURNIPS

SERVES 6

*Turnips have a delicately sweet flavor when young, but as they mature they lose their sweetness and become woody. Therefore, it is best to buy them when they are at their peak, between November and February. The greens, which are edible, should be bright green and garden fresh. If unavailable, substitute Swiss chard (silverbeet), dandelion greens, beet greens or kale.*

¼ cup (2 fl oz/60 ml) olive oil

2 yellow onions, finely chopped

2 oz (60 g) bacon or pancetta, finely diced

3 lb (1.5 kg) beef stew meat such as chuck roast or sirloin tip, cut into 1–1½-inch (2½–4-cm) cubes

¼ cup (1½ oz/45 g) all-purpose (plain) flour

4 cloves garlic, minced

6 fresh parsley stems

2 fresh thyme sprigs

2 bay leaves

1½ cups (12 fl oz/375 ml) dry red wine such as Cabernet Sauvignon or Côtes-du-Rhône

3 cups (24 fl oz/750 ml) beef or veal stock

1 tablespoon tomato paste

4 turnips or 15 baby turnips, peeled and larger ones cut into wedges

1 bunch (about 10 oz/315 g) turnip greens, stems removed and leaves cut crosswise into strips

salt and freshly ground pepper

In a large, heavy pot over medium heat, warm the olive oil. Add the onions and bacon or pancetta. Sauté, stirring occasionally, until the onions are soft, about 10 minutes. Using a slotted spoon, transfer the onions and bacon or pancetta to a plate and set aside.

❧ Working in batches, add the beef to the pot in a single layer; do not crowd the pot. Cook uncovered, turning occasionally, until golden brown on all sides, 7–10 minutes. When all the meat is browned, return it to the pot, sprinkle with the flour and cook, stirring, until the meat is evenly coated, about 1 minute. Return the onions and bacon or pancetta to the pot and add the garlic. Using kitchen string, tie the parsley stems, thyme sprigs and bay leaves into a bundle and add to the pot as well.

❧ Raise the heat to high, pour in the wine and bring to a boil, stirring to scrape up any browned bits from the pot bottom. Reduce the heat to medium and simmer, stirring occasionally, until the liquid is reduced by one-fourth, 3–5 minutes. Add the stock and tomato paste and stir well. Bring to a boil over high heat, then reduce the heat to low, cover and simmer until the meat is tender when pierced with a knife, 1½–2 hours.

❧ Remove the herb bundle and discard. Add the turnips, cover and cook until tender when pierced with a fork, about 15 minutes. Add the turnip greens, cover and cook until wilted, about 2 minutes. Season to taste with salt and pepper.

❧ To serve, ladle the stew into warmed bowls and serve at once.

# CHICKEN POT PIE

SERVES 6

### FOR THE PIE FILLING:

1 chicken, 3½ lb (1.75 kg), cut into
    8 pieces and skinned
1 teaspoon chopped fresh thyme
2 bay leaves
7 cups (56 fl oz/1.75 l) chicken stock
    or water
½ lb (250 g) pearl onions
¼ cup (2 oz/60 g) unsalted butter
⅓ cup (1½ oz/45 g) all-purpose (plain)
    flour
3 carrots, peeled and cut into 1-inch
    (2.5-cm) pieces
2 celery stalks, cut into 1-inch (2.5-cm)
    pieces
¾ lb (375 g) red potatoes, unpeeled,
    quartered lengthwise
1 cup (5 oz/155 g) green peas
¾ lb (375 g) fresh button mushrooms,
    halved
salt and freshly ground pepper

### FOR THE BISCUITS:

2½ cups (12½ oz/390 g) all-purpose
    (plain) flour sifted with ¾ teaspoon
    salt and 1 tablespoon baking powder
½ cup (4 oz/125 g) unsalted butter,
    cut into pieces, at room temperature
¾ cup (6 fl oz/180 ml) buttermilk, at
    room temperature
5 green (spring) onions, sliced

To make the filling, in a soup pot over
high heat, combine the chicken, thyme,
bay leaves and stock or water. Bring
to a boil, reduce the heat to low and
simmer, uncovered, until the chicken
is tender, about 45 minutes.

❧ Meanwhile, peel the pearl onions:
Bring a saucepan half full of water to
a boil. Add the onions and boil for 2
minutes. Drain, rinse with cold water,
and drain again. Trim off the root ends,

then cut a shallow X into each trimmed
end. Slip off the skins. Set aside.

❧ Remove the soup pot from the
heat. Using a slotted spoon, remove the
chicken and set aside until cool enough
to handle. Discard the bay leaves. Remove the meat from the bones and cut
into 1-inch (2.5-cm) pieces. Using
a large spoon, skim the fat from the top
of the broth. Reserve the broth (about
5 cups/40 fl oz/1.25 l) and chicken
separately.

❧ In a saucepan over low heat, melt
the butter. Add the flour and stir for
1 minute. Whisk in the reserved broth,
bring to a boil over medium-high
heat and boil until thickened, about 2
minutes. Reduce the heat to medium-
low and add the carrots, celery, pearl
onions and potatoes. Cook until the
vegetables are tender, about 25 minutes.
Add the chicken, peas and mushrooms
and cook until the mushrooms are
tender, about 5 minutes. Season with
salt and pepper. Transfer to a 3½-qt
(3.5-l) round baking dish 7–8 inches
(18–20 cm) in diameter.

❧ Preheat an oven to 425°F (220°C).
To make the biscuits, place the sifted
mixture in a bowl. Using your fingers,
rub in the butter until the mixture
resembles coarse meal. Using a fork,
mix in the buttermilk and green onions
and form into a ball. Transfer to a
floured work surface and roll out into
a round ½ inch (12 mm) thick. Fold in
half and roll it out again. Repeat this
step a third time. Using a round biscuit
cutter 2 inches (5 cm) in diameter, cut
out 12 biscuits.

❧ Place the biscuits, evenly spaced and
touching slightly, on the chicken mixture. Bake until the biscuits are golden
and the stew is bubbling, 25–35 minutes. Spoon into warmed bowls and
serve immediately.

*Blow, blow, thou winter wind,*
*Thou art not so unkind*
*— William Shakespeare*

# Winter Main Courses

The favorite main dishes of winter often belie the celebratory nature of the season. Turkey with Chestnut Stuffing (page 241) and the Roast Goose with Apple, Pear and Cranberry Stuffing at right highlight wintertime's classic holiday birds with familiar ingredients from the seasonal pantry. Equally festive are dishes featuring the shellfish that is also at a seasonal peak, such as Cracked Crab with Horseradish Mayonnaise (page 234) and Lobster with Tangerine-Chive Butter (page 246).

After the holidays are over, however, we often find ourselves anticipating meals that bring us comfort and joy of a more casual sort. Some of the best seasonal main-course specialties oblige most heartily, from Choucroute Garnie rich with pork sausages to a golden brown Herb-Roasted Chicken (both on page 242).

## ROAST GOOSE WITH APPLE, PEAR AND CRANBERRY STUFFING

SERVES 6–8

**FOR THE GOOSE:**

1 goose, 9–10 lb (4.5–5 kg)
salt and freshly ground pepper
1 cup (4 oz/125 g) dried cranberries
¾ cup (6 fl oz/180 ml) port wine
1 cup (8 fl oz/250 ml) chicken stock
2 tablespoons unsalted butter
1 small red (Spanish) onion, diced
4 Granny Smith or pippin apples, peeled, halved, cored and cut into 1-inch (2.5-cm) pieces
3 Bosc pears, peeled, halved, cored and cut into 1-inch (2.5-cm) pieces
1 tablespoon chopped fresh sage
2 teaspoons chopped fresh thyme
½ teaspoon ground cinnamon
1 cup (4 oz/125 g) fine dried bread crumbs
boiling water, as needed

**FOR THE PAN GRAVY (OPTIONAL):**

1½ cups (12 fl oz/375 ml) chicken stock
1 teaspoon cornstarch (cornflour) blended with 2 tablespoons water

Rinse the goose under cold water, drain and pat dry with paper towels. Season the cavity and the outside skin of the bird with salt and pepper.

Ꙫ In a saucepan over low heat, combine the cranberries, port and stock. Bring to a simmer, cover and simmer gently until the cranberries are tender and about ¼ cup (2 fl oz/60 ml) liquid remains, about 10 minutes. Set aside.

Ꙫ Preheat an oven to 425°F (220°C). In a large frying pan over medium heat, melt the butter. Add the onion and cook, stirring occasionally, until soft, about 10 minutes. Add the apples and

pears, cover and cook, stirring occasionally, until the fruits are tender but retain their shape, 10–12 minutes. Transfer to a bowl. Add the cranberries and their liquid, sage, thyme, cinnamon and bread crumbs and stir together. Season to taste with salt and pepper.

Ꙫ Prick the skin around the thighs, back and lower breast of the goose. Stuff loosely with the stuffing, then truss as directed on page 298. Place, breast side up, on an oiled rack in a roasting pan. Roast for 15 minutes. Reduce the heat to 350°F (180°C) and continue to roast, basting with 3 tablespoons boiling water every 20 minutes, until the juices run a pale yellow when the thickest part of the thigh is pierced or an instant-read thermometer inserted into the thickest part of the thigh away from the bone registers 180°F (82°C), about 2½ hours longer. Transfer the goose to a serving platter. Cover loosely with aluminum foil and let stand for 15 minutes before carving.

Ꙫ Meanwhile, make the pan gravy, if using: Pour off the fat from the roasting pan and place the pan over high heat. Pour in the stock and deglaze the pan by stirring to dislodge any browned bits from the pan bottom. Boil until reduced by half, 2–3 minutes. Whisk in the cornstarch mixture and boil until thickened slightly, about 1 minute longer. Strain into a warmed sauceboat.

Ꙫ Snip the trussing string. Spoon the stuffing into a warmed serving bowl. Carve the goose at the table. Serve with the gravy, if using.

## BUTTERNUT SQUASH AND BACON RISOTTO

SERVES 6

*Butternut squash, a camel-colored, pear-shaped winter squash, is harvested in the fall but will keep well for several months in a cool, dry place. Other winter squash varieties—Hubbard, acorn, turban—can be substituted.*

⅓ cup (1½ oz/45 g) hazelnuts (filberts)
    or pecans
1 butternut squash, 2–3 lb (1–1.5 kg)
4½ tablespoons olive oil
salt and freshly ground pepper
4½ cups (36 fl oz/1.1 l) chicken stock
4½ cups (36 fl oz/1.1 l) water
3 slices bacon, finely diced
1 yellow onion, finely chopped
1½ teaspoons chopped fresh thyme
1½ teaspoons chopped fresh sage
¾ teaspoon chopped fresh rosemary
1¾ cups (12½ oz/390 g) Arborio rice
1 cup (4 oz/125 g) freshly grated
    Parmesan cheese

Preheat an oven to 375°F (190°C).

❧ Spread the nuts on a baking sheet and toast until lightly browned and fragrant, 5–7 minutes. Remove from the oven and let cool. Chop coarsely and set aside.

❧ Peel the squash and cut lengthwise into 8 wedges. Scoop out the seeds and discard, then cut crosswise into thin slices. In a large frying pan over medium heat, warm 1½ tablespoons of the olive oil. Add the squash, cover and cook, turning occasionally, until almost tender, 7–10 minutes. Season to taste with salt and pepper and set aside.

Meanwhile, in a saucepan, combine the stock and water and bring to a gentle simmer over medium heat.

❧ In a large saucepan over medium heat, warm the remaining 3 tablespoons olive oil. Add the bacon and onion and sauté until the onion is soft, about 10 minutes. Add the thyme, sage, rosemary and rice and cook, stirring constantly, until the rice is translucent around the edges, 2–3 minutes. Add approximately ½ cup (4 fl oz/125 ml) of the simmering stock-water mixture and stir to scrape the rice from the bottom and sides of the pan. When the liquid has been almost completely absorbed, add another ½ cup (4 fl oz/ 125 ml) liquid, stirring continuously. Continue in this manner, stirring almost continuously and keeping the grains slightly moist at all times, until the rice is firm but tender and the kernels are no longer chalky at the center, 20–30 minutes. (If you run out of liquid before the rice is ready, add hot water.)

❧ When the risotto is done, stir in another ½ cup (4 fl oz/125 ml) liquid, the squash, the toasted nuts and half of the Parmesan. Season to taste with salt and pepper. Transfer to a warm serving dish and sprinkle with the remaining Parmesan. Serve at once.

*Come, ye thankful people, come,*
*Raise the song of harvest-home;*
*All is safely gathered in,*
*Ere the winter storms begin.*
        *—Henry Alford*

## CROWN ROAST OF PORK WITH BAKED APPLES

SERVES 8

*A crown roast is formed by joining two center racks of rib chops into a circle, their trimmed rib ends resembling the points of a crown. Although it isn't too difficult to form the roast yourself, most good butchers will do it for you. Winter baking apples such as McIntosh, Cortland or Granny Smith complement the meat's inherent sweetness, as do wines like Gewürztraminer or Riesling.*

1 crown roast of pork with 16 chops, 6 lb (3 kg)
salt and freshly ground pepper
8 apples (see note)
½ cup (4 fl oz/125 ml) late-harvest white wine or French Sauternes
¼ cup (3 oz/90 g) honey
3 tablespoons unsalted butter
½ teaspoon finely grated lemon zest
½ teaspoon ground cinnamon
¼ teaspoon ground cloves

Preheat an oven to 400°F (200°C).

❧ Place a rack in a shallow roasting pan and set the crown roast on it. Season to taste with salt and pepper. Roast uncovered for 30 minutes. Reduce the heat to 325°F (165°C) and continue to roast, basting frequently with the pan juices, until an instant-read thermometer inserted into the center of the loin away from the bone registers 150°F (66°C), or until the meat is pale pink when cut in the thickest part, about 1 hour and 15 minutes longer; check the pork periodically and cover the rib bone ends with foil if they begin to burn before the meat is done.

❧ While the pork is roasting, peel the top third of each apple and then core the apples. In a small saucepan over high heat, combine the wine, honey, butter, lemon zest, cinnamon and cloves and bring to a boil. Remove from the heat and set aside.

❧ About 15 minutes before the pork is done, place the apples in a 2-qt (2-l) baking dish and pour the honey mixture evenly over them. Cover with aluminum foil and place in the oven with the pork. Cook the apples until tender when pierced with a knife, 20–25 minutes, checking periodically during baking to prevent drying. When the pork is done, remove it from the oven and cover loosely with aluminum foil. Let stand for 10 minutes before carving.

❧ Place the roast on a warmed platter and arrange the baked apples alongside. Drizzle the juices from the baking dish over the apples and the pork. At the table, cut the meat between the rib bones and serve with the apples.

## CRACKED CRAB WITH HORSERADISH MAYONNAISE

SERVES 6

*Cracked crab makes a simple, yet elegant main course for the holidays. Blue or stone crabs can be used if Dungeness are unavailable; adjust the cooking time accordingly. If time is short, purchase freshly cooked crabs and ask your fishmonger to do the cleaning and cracking.*

**FOR THE HORSERADISH MAYONNAISE:**
1 egg yolk
1 teaspoon whole-grain mustard
½ cup (4 fl oz/125 ml) olive oil
½ cup (4 fl oz/125 ml) vegetable, corn or safflower oil
2 cloves garlic, minced

1½ tablespoons fresh lemon juice, or as needed
3 tablespoons prepared horseradish
salt and freshly ground pepper
2 tablespoons warm water

**FOR THE CRABS:**
4 qt (4 l) water
1 tablespoon salt
3 live Dungeness crabs, 2–2½ lb (1–1.25 kg) each

To make the horseradish mayonnaise, in a small bowl, whisk together the egg yolk, mustard and 1 tablespoon of the olive oil until an emulsion forms. Combine the remaining olive oil and vegetable oil in a cup with a spout. Drop by drop at first and whisking constantly, gradually add the oil mixture to the emulsion. Stir in the garlic, 1½ tablespoons lemon juice and the horseradish. Season to taste with salt and pepper and more lemon juice, if needed. Whisking constantly, add the warm water to thin the mayonnaise slightly. Cover and refrigerate until needed.

❧ To prepare the crabs, in a large pot, bring the water to a boil over high heat. Once it boils, add the salt and the crabs, immersing them completely. Boil until cooked and the shells are red, about 12 minutes. Using tongs, transfer the crabs to a plate and let cool slightly.

❧ Clean and crack the crabs as directed on page 299, leaving the meat intact. If the crabs cool during the process, warm them on a steamer rack over boiling water for 5–7 minutes before serving.

❧ To serve, arrange the crabs on a platter and serve with small forks or lobster picks for extracting the meat. Offer the horseradish mayonnaise on the side.

## VEAL SCALLOPINI WITH ORANGE AND FENNEL

SERVES 6–8

*Fennel and orange form a delicious taste combination. For an elegant meal, accompany the veal with orange-scented rice and wilted kale.*

1¼ lb (625 g) thin veal scallops, cut from the sirloin
5 tablespoons (2½ fl oz/75 ml) extra-virgin olive oil
½ teaspoon finely grated orange zest
¼ cup (2 fl oz/60 ml) fresh orange juice
1½ tablespoons balsamic vinegar
salt and freshly ground pepper
2 large seedless oranges
2 fennel bulbs
¾ cup (4 oz/125 g) all-purpose (plain) flour
2 eggs
2 cups (8 oz/250 g) fine dried bread crumbs
2 tablespoons water
3 tablespoons unsalted butter
¼ cup (⅓ oz/10 g) loosely packed fresh flat-leaf (Italian) parsley leaves

Place each veal scallop between 2 pieces of waxed paper and pound with a flat meat pounder to a thickness of about ¼ inch (6 mm). Set aside.

In a small bowl, whisk together 2 tablespoons of the oil, the orange zest and juice, vinegar, and salt and pepper to taste to form a vinaigrette. Set aside.

Using a sharp knife, cut a thick slice off the top and bottom of each orange to reveal the flesh. Then, standing each orange upright on a cutting surface, cut off the peel and white membrane in thick, wide strips. Working with 1 orange at a time, hold the orange over a bowl and cut along either side of each segment to free it from the membrane, letting the segments drop into the bowl. Set aside.

Trim off any stems and bruised outer stalks from the fennel bulbs and discard. Cut the bulbs in half lengthwise, then cut crosswise into paper-thin slices. Set aside.

Place the flour, eggs and bread crumbs in 3 separate shallow bowls. Whisk the eggs lightly to blend them, then whisk in the water. Season the bread crumbs to taste with salt and pepper. Dredge both sides of each veal scallop with flour, shaking off the excess. Then, coat the veal scallops with the egg, letting the excess drip off. Finally, lightly coat both sides with bread crumbs.

In a large sauté pan over medium-high heat, melt 1½ tablespoons of the butter with 1½ tablespoons of the remaining olive oil. When hot, add half of the veal in a single layer. Sauté, turning occasionally, until golden brown on both sides, 3–4 minutes total. Repeat with the remaining butter, oil and veal.

To serve, divide evenly among warmed individual plates. In a bowl, toss together the fennel, parsley, orange segments and vinaigrette. Top each serving of veal with some of the salad and serve immediately.

*The bees are stirring — birds are on the wing — And winter slumbering in the open air, Wears on his smiling face a dream of Spring!*
*—Samuel Taylor Coleridge*

*If you can find blood oranges, they add an interesting spark of color to this dish. Their juice is a lovely shade of red and the fruit has a pleasant perfumy flavor.*

# HAM, POTATO AND CHEDDAR CHEESE GRATIN

SERVES 6–8

*The French term* gratin *means "crust," referring to the golden topping that develops when a dish such as this one is cooked in a large, shallow baking dish. The delectable results make a perfect buffet main course, surrounded with salads and assorted breads and rolls.*

2 cups (16 fl oz/500 ml) water
1 ham steak, 1½ lb (750 g) and ¼ inch (6 mm) thick, trimmed of all fat and cut into 1–1½-inch (2.5–4-cm) squares
3½ lb (1.75 kg) baking potatoes, peeled and cut into thin slices
3 cups (24 fl oz/750 ml) milk
¼ cup (2 oz/60 g) unsalted butter
6 tablespoons (2 oz/60 g) all-purpose (plain) flour
½ lb (250 g) extra-sharp Cheddar cheese, shredded
½ lb (250 g) smoked Cheddar cheese, shredded
2 tablespoons Dijon mustard
⅛ teaspoon cayenne pepper
salt and freshly ground black pepper

In a saucepan over high heat, bring the water to a boil. Add the ham and simmer for 30 seconds. Remove from the heat and drain well. Set aside.

❧ Oil a 9-by-13-inch (23-by-33-cm) baking dish. Distribute one-fourth of the potatoes evenly over the bottom of the prepared dish. Distribute one-third of the ham evenly over the potatoes.

Top with half of the remaining potatoes and then all of the remaining ham. Top with all the remaining potatoes, layering the slices attractively.

❧ Preheat an oven to 350°F (180°C).

❧ Pour the milk into a saucepan placed over medium heat and warm until small bubbles appear at the edges of the pan. Remove from the heat.

❧ In another saucepan over medium heat, melt the butter. Stir in the flour and cook, stirring constantly, for 2 minutes. (Do not brown.) Gradually stir in the hot milk and cook, stirring, until the mixture thickens, 4–5 minutes. Remove from the heat. Stir in the extra-sharp Cheddar cheese, smoked Cheddar cheese, mustard and cayenne pepper. Season to taste with salt and black pepper. Return the pan to low heat and stir just until the cheese melts, 1–2 minutes.

❧ Pour the cheese sauce evenly over the potatoes and ham. Bake, uncovered, until the potatoes can be easily pierced with a skewer and the top is golden brown, about 1 hour.

❧ To serve, spoon the gratin onto warmed individual plates and serve immediately.

*Small cheer and great welcome makes a merry feast.*
*— William Shakespeare*

# TURKEY WITH CHESTNUT STUFFING

SERVES 6

1 turkey, 10–12 lb (5–6 kg), with the
    giblets
2 teaspoons salt, plus salt to taste
3 large yellow onions
6 cups (48 fl oz/1.5 l) chicken stock
1 carrot, peeled and coarsely chopped
6 fresh parsley stems
¼ teaspoon dried thyme
1 bay leaf
1½ lb (750 g) fresh chestnuts
¾ cup (6 oz/185 g) unsalted butter
¼ lb (125 g) lean bacon, diced
4 celery stalks, finely diced
¼ cup (⅓ oz/10 g) chopped fresh
    parsley
1 tablespoon chopped fresh thyme
1 tablespoon chopped fresh sage
11 cups (22 oz/685 g) cubed
    (½-inch/12-mm) firm-textured
    sourdough bread, left at room
    temperature for 2–3 days
freshly ground pepper
1 tablespoon all-purpose (plain) flour
1 teaspoon cornstarch (cornflour)

Rinse the turkey and rub inside and out with the 2 teaspoons salt. Coarsely chop 1 onion and place in a saucepan. Finely dice the remaining 2 onions; set aside. Add the stock, carrot, parsley stems, dried thyme, bay leaf and giblets to the pan. Bring to a gentle simmer and cook, uncovered, for 1½ hours. Strain through a sieve. You should have about 5 cups (40 fl oz/1.25 l) stock.

❧ Meanwhile, make a cut across the flat side of each chestnut. Place the chestnuts in a saucepan, add water to cover, bring to a simmer and cook until easily pierced, 45–55 minutes. Remove from the heat. Peel away the hard shells and inner sheaths while the chestnuts are still hot. Chop the flesh coarsely and place in a large bowl.

❧ Preheat an oven to 400°F (200°C). In a frying pan over medium heat, melt ½ cup (4 oz/125 g) of the butter. Add the bacon, diced onions and celery and cook uncovered, stirring occasionally, until soft, about 12 minutes. Add to the chestnuts along with the chopped parsley, thyme and sage and the bread cubes. Toss and add enough stock (1–2 cups/8–16 fl oz/250–500 ml) for the mixture to form a ball when squeezed. Season with salt and pepper.

❧ Stuff the body and neck cavities loosely with the stuffing and truss as directed on page 298. Place, breast side up, on an oiled rack in a roasting pan. Melt the remaining ¼ cup (2 oz/60 g) butter and brush 1 tablespoon on the turkey. Soak a large, double-layer piece of cheesecloth (muslin) in the remaining butter.

❧ Roast for 45 minutes. Reduce the heat to 325°F (165°C). Drape the cheesecloth over the turkey and continue to roast, basting with pan drippings every 30 minutes, until the juices run clear when a thigh is pierced or an instant-read thermometer inserted into the thigh registers 180°F (82°C), 1½–2 hours longer. Transfer to a platter, cover loosely with foil and let stand for 20 minutes.

❧ Reserve 2 tablespoons drippings in the pan (discard the rest) and place over high heat. Whisk together the flour, cornstarch and ½ cup (4 fl oz/125 ml) stock, then whisk into the pan. Add the remaining stock and stir until thickened, 2–3 minutes. Strain through a sieve into a sauceboat. Remove the cheesecloth, carve the turkey and serve with the stuffing and gravy.

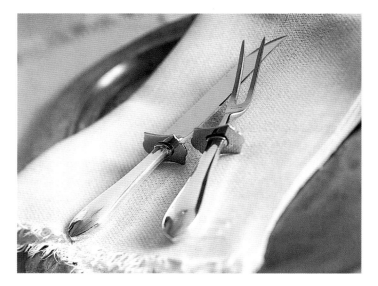

*Heating the platter before setting the turkey atop it will help keep the meat warm while the turkey is being carved. Metal platters, such as those of silver or pewter, retain heat especially well.*

## CHOUCROUTE GARNIE

SERVES 6

*Choucroute is French for "sauerkraut." This stick-to-your-ribs dish is made with much enthusiasm in the northeastern French region of Alsace. Serve with plenty of hot mustard for the sausage.*

3 lb (1.5 kg) store-bought sauerkraut, uncooked
2 tablespoons unsalted butter
2 yellow onions, minced
4 slices bacon, diced
2 bay leaves
4 whole cloves
20 juniper berries
2 cloves garlic, minced
2 cups (16 fl oz/500 ml) fruity white wine, preferably Riesling or Gewürztraminer
2 cups (16 fl oz/500 ml) chicken stock
8 pork sausages or 1 kielbasa sausage, about 2 lb (1 kg) total
2 lb (1 kg) red potatoes, unpeeled, cut into 1½-inch (4-cm) pieces
salt and freshly ground pepper

Place the sauerkraut in a large colander and rinse well with cold running water. Drain well and set aside.

❧ In a large, heavy pot over medium-low heat, melt the butter. Add the onions and bacon and sauté, stirring occasionally, until the onions are soft, about 10 minutes. Add the bay leaves, cloves, juniper berries, garlic, wine, stock and sauerkraut. Raise the heat to high and bring to a boil. Reduce the heat to low, cover and simmer gently until the sauerkraut is tender and the flavors have blended, 2–2½ hours.

❧ Prick the pork sausage or kielbasa all over with a fork and add to the pot along with the potatoes. Cover and continue to simmer until the potatoes

are tender, about 30 minutes longer. Season to taste with salt and pepper.

❧ To serve, remove the pork sausages or kielbasa from the pot and cut into slices. Return to the pot and mix well. Spoon the sauerkraut, sausages and potatoes onto a warmed platter and serve hot.

## HERB-ROASTED CHICKEN

SERVES 4

*Robust herbs such as sage, thyme, oregano and rosemary produce tough leaves that stand up to cooler temperatures. In mild climates, these herbs flourish in gardens throughout the colder months. Slipped under the skin of a whole roasting chicken, they add hearty flavor to one of the season's most venerable dishes.*

1 roasting chicken, 3½–4 lb (1.75–2 kg), giblets removed
salt to taste, plus ¼ teaspoon salt
freshly ground pepper to taste, plus ⅛ teaspoon ground pepper
1 tablespoon chopped fresh sage
1 teaspoon chopped fresh thyme

½ teaspoon chopped fresh oregano
½ teaspoon chopped fresh rosemary
4 thin lemon slices, seeds removed
2 tablespoons unsalted butter, melted

Preheat an oven to 375°F (190°C).

❧ Rinse the chicken under cold water, drain and pat dry with paper towels. Season inside and outside with salt and pepper.

❧ In a small bowl, mix together the sage, thyme, oregano, rosemary, ¼ teaspoon salt and ⅛ teaspoon pepper. Using your fingers, loosen the skin of the chicken that covers the breast by sliding your fingers between the skin and the flesh, being careful not to tear the skin. Slip half of the herbs inside the pocket defined by each breast half, distributing them evenly over the breast and thigh. Tuck the lemon slices inside the pockets between the skin and flesh, placing 2 slices on each side. Truss the chicken by tying the legs together with kitchen string. Brush the chicken with the melted butter.

❧ Place the chicken on its side on an oiled roasting rack in a roasting pan. Roast the chicken for 20 minutes. Turn the chicken onto its other side and roast for another 20 minutes. Turn the chicken breast side up and continue to roast until an instant-read thermometer inserted into the thickest part of the breast away from the bone registers 160°F (71°C) and in the thigh registers 170°F (77°C), or until the juices run clear when the thigh is pierced with a knife, 15–20 minutes longer.

❧ Remove the chicken from the oven and transfer to a platter. Cover loosely with aluminum foil and let stand for 10 minutes before carving.

❧ To serve, carve the chicken and serve immediately.

# CASSOULET

SERVES 8–10

*This abbreviated rendition of a classic peasant dish of southwestern France saves hours in the kitchen yet delivers authentic and satisfying flavors.*

2¼ cups (1 lb/500 g) dried Great
    Northern or flageolet beans
1 yellow onion pierced with 10 whole
    cloves
¾ lb (375 g) thickly sliced bacon,
    finely diced
2 lb (1 kg) boneless lamb cut from the
    leg, in one piece
2 lb (1 kg) pork loin, in one piece
salt to taste, plus 1 teaspoon salt
freshly ground pepper to taste, plus
    ½ teaspoon pepper
1 lb (500 g) Toulouse or other
    pork-and-garlic sausages
8 cloves garlic, minced
8 fresh parsley stems
1 teaspoon chopped fresh thyme
2 bay leaves
3 tablespoons tomato paste
1 teaspoon ground allspice
1½ cups (6 oz/185 g) fine dried
    bread crumbs

Pick over the beans and discard any damaged ones. Rinse, place in a bowl and add water to cover generously. Let soak for 3 hours. Drain and place in a saucepan with the onion and water to cover by 2 inches (5 cm). Bring to a boil, reduce the heat to low and simmer gently, uncovered, until almost tender, 40–50 minutes. Drain, discarding the onion and reserving the liquid.

❧ Preheat an oven to 350°F (180°C). In a large ovenproof stew pot over low heat, fry the bacon until it begins to turn golden, about 5 minutes. Using a slotted spoon, transfer to a plate. Reserve the drippings in the pot.

❧ Season the lamb and pork with salt and pepper and add to the stew pot. Place in the oven and roast, basting occasionally with the bacon drippings, until the meat is tender, about 1¼ hours. Remove from the oven, let cool and cut into 1-inch (2.5-cm) cubes. Set aside. Do not wash the pot.

❧ Meanwhile, prick the sausages with a fork. Place in a frying pan, add water to cover halfway and simmer gently, turning once, until almost cooked through, about 12 minutes total. Drain, let cool and slice on the diagonal.

❧ Place one-third of the drained beans in the reserved pot. Sprinkle with half of the bacon, lamb, pork, sausage, garlic and salt and pepper to taste. Using kitchen string, tie the parsley, thyme and bay leaves into a bundle. Add to the pot. Repeat the layers, using half of the remaining beans and all of the remaining garlic, meats and sausage. Season to taste with salt and pepper and top with the remaining beans.

❧ In a bowl, whisk together the tomato paste, allspice, the 1 teaspoon salt, the ½ teaspoon pepper and 2 cups (16 fl oz/500 ml) of the reserved bean liquid. Pour into the pot just to cover the beans. Bake, uncovered, for 1 hour; add more bean liquid, if necessary, to prevent the beans from drying out. Sprinkle with the bread crumbs and continue to bake until golden, about 1 hour longer.

❧ Discard the herb bundle and serve directly from the pot.

*There's a certain slant of light,*
*Winter afternoons —*
*—Emily Dickinson*

## PAPPARDELLE WITH RED WINE–STEWED DUCK

SERVES 6

*Use either a wild or pen-raised duck for this classic Tuscan preparation, which also works well with chicken or rabbit.*

1 tablespoon olive oil
1 duck, about 5 lb (2.5 kg), cut into
    8 pieces and skin and excess fat
    removed
1 large yellow onion, diced
1 large celery stalk, diced
1 large carrot, peeled and diced
3 oz (90 g) pancetta, finely diced
3 cups (18 oz/560 g) peeled, seeded and
    chopped tomatoes (fresh or canned)
2½ cups (20 fl oz/625 ml) dry red wine
    such as Chianti, Barolo or Cabernet
    Sauvignon
1 tablespoon chopped fresh rosemary
salt and freshly ground pepper
¾ lb (375 g) dried or fresh pappardelle
    noodles
½ cup (2 oz/60 g) freshly grated
    Parmesan cheese

In a large, heavy pot over medium–high heat, warm the olive oil. Add the duck

pieces and cook, turning as needed, until they begin to turn golden, about 10 minutes. Add the onion, celery, carrot and pancetta and continue to cook until the onion is soft, about 10 minutes longer. Add the tomatoes, 1½ cups (12 fl oz/375 ml) of the red wine and the rosemary and bring to a boil. Reduce the heat to low, cover and simmer for 1 hour. Add the remaining 1 cup (8 fl oz/250 ml) red wine, stir well and continue to simmer, un-covered, until the meat begins to fall off the bones and the sauce has thick-ened slightly, about 1¼ hours longer.

❧ Using tongs, transfer the duck pieces to a bowl and let stand until cool enough to handle. Remove the meat from the bones and tear into bite-size pieces; discard the bones. Return the meat to the sauce and bring to a boil over medium heat. Simmer until the sauce thickens a bit more, 5–10 minutes. Season to taste with salt and pepper.

❧ Meanwhile, bring a large pot three-fourths full of salted water to a rolling boil. Add the pappardelle, stir well and cook until al dente (firm but tender to the bite), 5–8 minutes. Drain the pappardelle and transfer to a large warmed serving bowl. Pour the sauce over the pasta and toss gently to coat evenly. Serve at once. Pass the Parmesan cheese at the table.

## LOBSTER WITH TANGERINE-CHIVE BUTTER

SERVES 6

FOR THE TANGERINE-CHIVE BUTTER:
¾ cup (6 oz/185 g) unsalted butter
½ teaspoon finely grated tangerine zest
3 tablespoons fresh tangerine juice
1 tablespoon Dijon mustard
¼ cup (⅓ oz/10 g) finely snipped fresh
    chives
salt and freshly ground pepper

FOR THE LOBSTERS:
4 qt (4 l) water
1 tablespoon salt
6 live lobsters, 1¼–1½ lb (625–750 g)
    each

To make the tangerine-chive butter, in a small saucepan, combine the butter, tangerine zest, tangerine juice, mustard and chives. Season to taste with salt and pepper. Place over medium heat and, as soon as the butter melts, remove from the heat. Let stand at room temperature for 1 hour.

❧ To prepare the lobsters, 10–15 min-utes before serving, bring the water to a boil in a large stockpot. Once it boils, add the salt and the lobsters, immersing them completely. Boil until dark red and fully cooked, about 10 minutes. Using tongs, transfer to a plate and let cool slightly.

❧ Reheat the butter until warm and divide among 6 small sauce bowls. Serve 1 lobster per person accompanied with a small bowl of the warm butter.

❧ To make eating the lobsters easier, crack the claws and cut down the underside of the tail with kitchen scissors, then serve the lobster with small forks or lobster picks for extract-ing the meat.

# *Winter Salads & Side Dishes*

୶

Want a quick survey of the range of produce available in winter? All you need to do is glance at the photograph of Pan-Roasted Winter Vegetables on page 253—a mix of Brussels sprouts, carrots, parsnips, yams and rutabagas—to see how generous nature can be even in the coldest months. That fact is further borne out by Wilted Kale with Lemon and Garlic and Purée of White Winter Vegetables (both on page 255).

The bright colors of winter salads, such as golden beets in Beet Salad with Stilton and Walnuts (page 252) or oranges and kumquats in Citrus Salad with Mint and Red Onions (page 251), also demonstrate how fresh produce can chase away the gloom. Other seasonal specialties can transform winter salads into satisfying main courses, as in the Romaine and Escarole Salad with Warm Duck Livers on this page and the Grilled Scallop, Pink Grapefruit and Frisée Salad (page 251).

## ROMAINE AND ESCAROLE SALAD WITH WARM DUCK LIVERS

SERVES 6

*The crucial step to preparing this delicious winter salad is to cook the livers so that they are still pink in the center. Overcooking them yields a leathery texture and strong flavor. This salad can also be made with chicken livers, for which the same cooking precautions apply.*

**FOR THE VINAIGRETTE:**
5 tablespoons (2½ fl oz/75 ml) extra-virgin olive oil
1 clove garlic, minced
1½ tablespoons whole-grain mustard
3 tablespoons red wine vinegar
salt and freshly ground pepper

**FOR THE SALAD:**
1 head escarole (Batavian endive), tough stems removed and leaves torn into large pieces
1 head romaine (cos) lettuce, tough stems removed and leaves cut crosswise into strips 1 inch (2.5 cm) wide

**FOR THE CROUTONS:**
¼ lb (125 g) country-style bread, crusts removed
3 tablespoons unsalted butter
2 cloves garlic, minced
salt and freshly ground pepper

**FOR THE LIVERS:**
¾ lb (375 g) duck livers
1 tablespoon unsalted butter

Preheat an oven to 400°F (200°C).

❧ To make the vinaigrette, in a small bowl, whisk together the olive oil, garlic, mustard, vinegar and salt and pepper to taste. Set aside.

❧ Place the escarole and romaine lettuce in a large bowl.

❧ To make the croutons, tear the bread into ½-inch (12-mm) pieces or cut into 1-inch (2.5-cm) cubes and spread on a baking sheet. Combine the butter and garlic in a small saucepan and place over medium heat. When the butter has melted, pour it evenly over the bread, season to taste with salt and pepper and toss well. Bake, stirring once or twice, until golden and crisp, 10–15 minutes. Remove from the oven and let cool. (Store in an airtight container at room temperature if not using immediately. The croutons will remain fresh for up to 4 days.)

❧ To prepare the livers, trim away any membranes. In a large frying pan over medium heat, melt the butter. Add the livers in a single layer and cook, turning occasionally, until slightly firm to the touch but still pink inside, 2–3 minutes. Season to taste with salt and pepper.

❧ Remove the livers from the heat and immediately transfer to the bowl containing the escarole and romaine lettuce. Drizzle with the vinaigrette and toss gently. Place the salad on a large platter. Sprinkle the croutons over the top and serve at once.

## CITRUS SALAD WITH MINT AND RED ONIONS

SERVES 6

*Citrus fruits are at their best during the winter months when they grow in profusion in tropical and temperate climates. Use any sweet citrus fruits for this recipe, such as oranges, blood oranges, tangerines, tangelos, mandarin oranges, grapefruits, pomelos and even kumquats.*

3 large, seedless oranges
2 blood oranges
1 Ruby grapefruit or other pink grapefruit
¼ small red (Spanish) onion, very thinly sliced
3 tablespoons fresh orange juice
1 tablespoon red wine vinegar
3 tablespoons extra-virgin olive oil
salt and freshly ground pepper
2 tablespoons coarsely chopped fresh mint
6 kumquats, thinly sliced and seeds discarded
seeds from ¼ pomegranate

Holding 1 orange over a small bowl, finely grate enough zest to measure 1 teaspoon. Using a sharp knife, cut a thick slice off the tops and bottoms of the oranges, blood oranges and grapefruit to reveal the flesh. Working with 1 fruit at a time, place it upright on a cutting surface and cut off the peel and white membrane in wide strips. Cut the oranges and grapefruit crosswise into slices ¼ inch (6 mm) thick. Cut the grapefruit slices into quarters. Using the tip of the knife, remove any seeds and discard. Arrange the orange and grapefruit slices on a serving platter, overlapping the various colors. Separate the onion slices and scatter over the top.

❧ Add the orange juice, vinegar and olive oil to the bowl containing the orange zest. Season to taste with salt and pepper and whisk to form a vinaigrette. Drizzle the vinaigrette evenly over the citrus and onion. Sprinkle with the mint, kumquat slices and pomegranate seeds. Serve immediately.

## GRILLED SCALLOP, PINK GRAPEFRUIT AND FRISÉE SALAD

SERVES 6

*Large sea scallops are at their best from mid-autumn to early spring, making this salad of citrus and greens an ideal light entrée for a winter meal. You could, if you wish, substitute smaller bay scallops, which reach their peak in late autumn. Buy scallops that look plump and moist and have a fresh, clean scent of the sea.*

1 large pink grapefruit
1 tablespoon balsamic vinegar
2 tablespoons fresh grapefruit juice
¼ cup (2 fl oz/60 ml) extra-virgin olive oil
salt and freshly ground pepper
1 lb (500 g) sea scallops, cut in half horizontally
1 tablespoon olive oil
1 head frisée, tough stems removed, torn into small pieces

Holding the grapefruit over a small bowl, finely grate enough zest to measure 1 teaspoon. Using a sharp knife, cut a thick slice off the top and bottom of the grapefruit to reveal the flesh. Then, standing the grapefruit upright on a cutting surface, cut off the peel and white membrane in thick, wide strips. Cut the grapefruit crosswise

into slices ¼ inch (6 mm) thick. Using the tip of the knife, remove any seeds and discard. Cut each slice into quarters and place in a large bowl. Set aside.

❧ To the bowl containing the grapefruit zest, add the balsamic vinegar, grapefruit juice and the extra-virgin olive oil. Season to taste with salt and pepper and whisk to form a vinaigrette.

❧ Preheat a ridged cast-iron grill pan or frying pan over medium heat. Brush the scallops with the olive oil. When the pan is hot, add the scallops in a single layer. Cook until seared on one side, about 1 minute. Turn over the scallops, season to taste with salt and pepper and continue to cook until seared on the second side and just firm to the touch, about 1 minute longer. Remove from the pan.

❧ Add the scallops and the frisée to the bowl containing the grapefruit. Drizzle with the vinaigrette, season to taste with salt and pepper and toss well.

❧ Transfer the salad to a platter or individual plates and serve at once.

## BEET SALAD WITH STILTON AND WALNUTS

SERVES 6

*Blessed with the lovely color of deep garnet or golden orange, beets are firm, round, hardy root vegetables. It is best to bake them rather than boil them, as baking intensifies their sweetness.*

⅓ cup (1½ oz/45 g) walnut halves
2 lb (1 kg) red or yellow beets
2 tablespoons olive oil
salt and freshly ground pepper
3½ tablespoons extra-virgin olive oil
2½ tablespoons red wine vinegar
1½ cups (2 oz/60 g) loosely packed
   watercress, tough stems removed
3 oz (90 g) Stilton cheese, crumbled

Preheat an oven to 375°F (190°C). Spread the walnut halves on a baking sheet and toast until lightly browned and fragrant, 5–7 minutes. Remove from the oven and let cool. Leave the oven set at 375°F (190°C).

❧ Rinse each beet with cold water and trim away all but ½ inch (12 mm) of the stem. Put the beets in a shallow baking dish and drizzle with the olive oil. Roll the beets to coat them with the oil and season to taste with salt and pepper. Cover with aluminum foil.

❧ Bake until the beets are tender when pierced with a knife, 50–60 minutes. Remove from the oven and set aside until cool enough to handle. Slip off the skins and cut each beet into thin wedges. Place in a bowl.

❧ Meanwhile, in a small bowl, whisk together the extra-virgin olive oil, vinegar and salt and pepper to taste to form a vinaigrette. Drizzle three-fourths of the vinaigrette over the beets, toss well and let cool completely.

❧ Place the watercress in a serving bowl, drizzle with the remaining vinaigrette and toss to coat. Add the beets and toss again to coat. Season to taste with salt and pepper. Distribute the crumbled Stilton and the walnuts evenly over the top and serve.

## PAN-ROASTED WINTER VEGETABLES

SERVES 6

*This mélange of fresh vegetables combines members of the cabbage family—rutabagas and Brussels sprouts—with such roots and tubers as carrots, parsnips and yams or sweet potatoes. Although most roots and tubers are harvested in the autumn months, their long storage capability makes them favorite winter ingredients as well.*

½ lb (250 g) rutabagas (swedes), peeled
   and cut into pieces
½ lb (250 g) carrots, peeled and cut
   into pieces
½ lb (250 g) parsnips, peeled and cut
   into pieces
½ lb (250 g) Brussels sprouts, trimmed

½ lb (250 g) yams or sweet potatoes,
   peeled and cut into pieces
1 tablespoon unsalted butter
1 tablespoon extra-virgin olive oil
2 teaspoons chopped fresh thyme
2 teaspoons chopped fresh sage
⅛ teaspoon freshly grated nutmeg
salt and freshly ground pepper
½ cup (4 fl oz/125 ml) Marsala wine

Preheat an oven to 450°F (230°C).

❧ Bring a large pot three-fourths full of salted water to a boil. Add the rutabagas, carrots and parsnips and simmer until the vegetables give slightly when pierced with a fork, about 4 minutes. Drain well.

❧ Place the rutabagas, carrots, parsnips, Brussels sprouts, and yams or sweet potatoes in a large roasting pan. In a small saucepan over low heat, melt the butter. Add the olive oil, thyme, sage and nutmeg and stir to mix well. Drizzle the butter mixture over the vegetables and toss to coat evenly. Season to taste with salt and pepper. Pour the Marsala into the bottom of the roasting pan. Cover tightly with aluminum foil.

❧ Bake for 40 minutes. Remove the foil, toss the vegetables and continue to bake, uncovered, until the Marsala evaporates and the vegetables can be easily pierced with a knife, 20–30 minutes.

❧ Place the roasted vegetables on a warmed platter and serve at once.

# PURÉE OF WHITE WINTER VEGETABLES

SERVES 6

*Common potatoes and turnips combine with the lesser-known celery root in this delicious purée. Celery root has an earthy flavor not unlike a cross between stalk celery and parsley. It is often eaten raw in salads or cooked in soups and stews.*

4 baking potatoes, peeled and coarsely chopped
2 turnips, peeled and coarsely chopped
1 large yellow onion, peeled and quartered
1 celery root (celeriac), 1½ lb (750 g), peeled and coarsely chopped
10 cloves garlic
2 tablespoons unsalted butter
2 tablespoons heavy (double) cream
3 tablespoons white wine vinegar
salt and freshly ground pepper

Place the potatoes, turnips, onion, celery root and garlic in a saucepan. Add water to cover and bring to a boil. Reduce the heat to low and simmer, uncovered, until the vegetables are completely tender when pierced with a knife, 20–25 minutes. Drain well, pressing the vegetables with the back of a spoon to drain off all the liquid.

❧ In a small saucepan over medium heat, melt the butter. Stir in the cream and remove from the heat. Place the drained vegetables in a food processor fitted with the metal blade and pulse several times until puréed.

❧ Transfer the mixture to a clean saucepan. Stir in the butter-cream mixture and the vinegar. Place over medium heat and reheat to serving temperature. Season to taste with salt and pepper. Spoon the purée into a serving dish and serve hot.

# WILTED KALE WITH LEMON AND GARLIC

SERVES 6

*The robust flavor of kale offers the perfect canvas for pairing with other, equally intense flavors. Garnish with lemon zest, if desired.*

2 tablespoons extra-virgin olive oil
2 tablespoons fresh lemon juice
2 cloves garlic, minced
salt and freshly ground pepper
2 teaspoons olive oil
2 bunches kale, about 2 lb (1 kg) total weight, stems removed and carefully rinsed

In a small bowl, whisk together the extra-virgin olive oil, lemon juice, garlic and salt and pepper to taste to form a vinaigrette. Set aside.

❧ In a large frying pan over medium heat, warm the olive oil. Cut the kale crosswise into 1-inch (2.5-cm) strips and add to the pan. Cover and cook, stirring occasionally, until the kale wilts, 5–7 minutes. Uncover, drizzle the vinaigrette over the kale and toss well. Season to taste with salt and pepper.

❧ Place on a warmed platter. Serve immediately.

## WINTER HERB AND LEMON SPAETZLE

SERVES 6

*Spaetzle are tiny dumplings that origin-ated in Germany and Austria. Served simply with melted butter, they are among that region's cherished comfort foods. Most spaetzle are formed by hand, although inexpensive spaetzle makers—typically a colanderlike tool for releasing the batter—can be found in cookware shops.*

2 cups (10 oz/315 g) all-purpose (plain) flour
3 tablespoons chopped fresh chives
2 tablespoons chopped fresh sage
2 tablespoons chopped fresh flat-leaf (Italian) parsley
1 tablespoon chopped fresh thyme
2 teaspoons chopped fresh winter savory, optional
1 teaspoon finely grated lemon zest
5 eggs
⅔ cup (5 fl oz/160 ml) milk
¾ teaspoon salt
⅛ teaspoon freshly ground pepper
1 tablespoon unsalted butter, melted

Butter a large ceramic baking dish and set aside.

🌢 Place the flour, all the herbs and the lemon zest in a bowl. In another bowl, whisk together the eggs until blended. Gradually whisk the eggs into the flour mixture. Stir in the milk, salt and pepper. Let stand for 30 minutes.

🌢 Preheat an oven to 275°F (135°C).

🌢 Bring a large pot three-fourths full of water to a boil. Working in batches, pour some of the batter into a large colander and, using the back of a large spoon, push strips of batter into the water. Alternatively, force the batter through the holes of a spaetzle maker into the water. As soon as the dumplings float to the surface, after 1–2 minutes, they are cooked. Using a slotted spoon, transfer them to the prepared baking dish and place them in the oven to dry the excess moisture. As each batch of dumplings is cooked, add it to the baking dish, gently tossing the freshly cooked dumplings with those already in the dish.

🌢 To serve, drizzle with the melted butter and toss gently to coat. Serve hot.

## BROCCOLI RABE WITH PANCETTA AND OLIVES

SERVES 6

*Buy broccoli rabe, also known as rapini, rape and cima di broccoli, when it is young and tender.*

4 tablespoons (2 fl oz/60 ml) olive oil
½ cup (2 oz/60 g) coarsely ground dried bread crumbs
salt and freshly ground pepper
¼ lb (125 g) pancetta, finely diced
3 bunches young, tender broccoli rabe, tough stems removed (about 2½ lb/ 1.25 kg trimmed)
3 tablespoons fresh lemon juice
3 cloves garlic, minced
½ cup (2½ oz/75 g) Kalamata olives, pitted and thinly sliced

In a large frying pan over medium heat, warm 2 tablespoons of the olive oil. Add the bread crumbs and toss con-stantly until lightly golden, 1–3 minutes. Season to taste with salt and pepper. Transfer to a small bowl and set aside.

🌢 Pour the remaining 2 tablespoons olive oil into the frying pan and place over medium heat. Add the pancetta and cook, stirring often, until lightly golden and almost crisp, 3–4 minutes. Add the broccoli rabe and cook, stirring often, until it wilts completely but is still bright green, 6–8 minutes.

🌢 Raise the heat to high and add the lemon juice, garlic and olives. Continue to cook, stirring, for 1 minute. Season to taste with salt and pepper.

🌢 Transfer to a warmed platter and sprinkle with the reserved bread crumbs. Serve immediately.

# Winter Desserts
⁂

The desserts on the following pages reflect a range of styles, from the delightfully simple Best Gingersnaps (page 265) to the more festive flambéed Persimmon Pudding (page 262). The latter recipe, along with Cranberry Upside-Down Cake (page 273) and Cinnamon-Poached Quinces with Nutmeg Cream (page 270), illustrates that winter fruits are ideal for cooking, resulting in recipes that deliver an extra note of comfort to winter-time menus.

The seasonal dessert pantry is further expanded by the wealth of dried fruits that fill the shelves around the holidays. Dried apricots, for example, add contrasts of taste, color and texture to the Polenta Custard with Port-Stewed Winter Fruits on this page. And both Wintertime Bread Pudding (page 266) and a classic Tuscan Panforte (page 269) rely on the intense flavor, chewy consistency and jewellike tones that these winter reliables can provide.

# POLENTA CUSTARD WITH PORT-STEWED WINTER FRUITS

SERVES 6

*Spiced pears and apricots top creamy custard in this hearty cold-weather dessert.*

**FOR THE STEWED FRUITS:**

3 cups (24 fl oz/750 ml) port wine

3 tablespoons honey

10 whole cloves

3 pears, preferably Bosc, peeled, halved and cored

1⅛ cups (7 oz/220 g) large dried apricots

**FOR THE POLENTA CUSTARD:**

¼ cup (2 fl oz/60 ml) grappa or other brandy

¼ cup (1½ oz/45 g) golden raisins (sultanas)

2¼ cups (18 fl oz/560 ml) milk

⅛ teaspoon salt

¾ cup (4 oz/125 g) Italian polenta

1 cup (8 oz/250 g) ricotta cheese

½ cup (4 oz/125 g) sugar

¼ teaspoon ground cinnamon

3 eggs, lightly beaten

**FOR THE TOPPING:**

⅓ cup (3 fl oz/80 ml) crème fraîche blended with 2 tablespoons milk

confectioners' (icing) sugar

To make the stewed fruits, in a saucepan over high heat, combine the port, honey and cloves. Bring to a boil, then reduce the heat to medium-low so that the port simmers. Add the pear halves and cook gently until tender and slightly translucent but not mushy, 20–30 minutes. Using a slotted spoon, transfer the pears to a cutting board. Discard the cloves. Add the apricots to the simmering port and cook gently until soft, about 10 minutes. Meanwhile, cut the pear halves lengthwise into wedges. When the apricots are done, remove the pan from the heat and add the pear wedges. Set aside.

To make the polenta custard, in a saucepan over medium heat, warm the brandy until hot. Remove from the heat, add the raisins and let stand for 30 minutes. In a large saucepan over high heat, combine the milk and salt. Bring to a boil, reduce the heat to medium and slowly whisk in the polenta. Continue to whisk for 2–3 minutes. Change to a wooden spoon and continue to simmer, stirring periodically, until the polenta is almost thick enough to hold the spoon upright, 15–20 minutes.

Preheat an oven to 375°F (190°C). Generously butter six ½-cup (4-fl oz/125-ml) ramekins.

In a large bowl, mix together the ricotta and sugar. Add the cooked polenta and stir well. Drain the raisins and add them with the cinnamon to the polenta. Stir in the eggs. Distribute evenly among the prepared ramekins. Place the ramekins, spaced well apart, on a baking sheet. Bake until set and a knife inserted into the center of a custard comes out clean, 20–22 minutes.

Just before the custards are done, gently reheat the fruits. Divide them and their liquid among 6 individual plates. Loosen the edges of the custards with a knife and invert them over the fruits. Drizzle with the crème fraîche mixture. Dust the tops with confectioners' sugar and serve.

# CHOCOLATE HAZELNUT TORTE

MAKES ONE 9-INCH (23-CM) TORTE; SERVES 10

*Paired with a glass of Champagne or cup of hot coffee, this dense cake is a lovely conclusion to any holiday meal.*

### FOR THE TORTE:

½ cup (2½ oz/75 g) hazelnuts (filberts), plus 12 hazelnuts for garnish

6 oz (185 g) bittersweet chocolate, finely chopped

½ cup (4 oz/125 g) unsalted butter, at room temperature

⅔ cup (5 oz/155 g) plus 2 tablespoons sugar

5 eggs, separated

¼ cup (1½ oz/45 g) all-purpose (plain) flour

¼ cup (¾ oz/20 g) unsweetened cocoa

⅛ teaspoon cream of tartar

### FOR THE GLAZE:

9 oz (280 g) bittersweet chocolate, finely chopped

¾ cup (6 oz/185 g) unsalted butter, at room temperature, cut into small pieces

1½ tablespoons light corn syrup

Preheat an oven to 375°F (190°C). Lightly butter and flour a 9-inch (23-cm) round springform cake pan.

❧ To make the torte, spread the ½ cup (2½ oz/75 g) nuts on a baking sheet and toast in the oven until lightly browned and fragrant, 5–7 minutes. While the nuts are still warm, place them in a kitchen towel and rub with the towel to remove the skins. Do not worry if bits of skin remain. Set aside.

❧ Place the chocolate and butter in a large heatproof bowl set over (not touching) gently simmering water in a pan. Stir often until the chocolate melts, then remove from the heat.

❧ In a food processor fitted with the metal blade or in a blender, combine the skinned nuts with the ⅔ cup (5 oz/155 g) sugar. Pulse until finely ground. Add to the chocolate mixture and stir until blended. Let cool; then, one at a time, add the egg yolks, beating well after each addition. In a bowl, sift together the flour and cocoa. Stir into the chocolate mixture.

❧ In another bowl, using an electric mixer, beat the egg whites and cream of tartar until soft peaks form. Add the 2 tablespoons sugar and beat until stiff peaks form. Using a spatula, fold one-fourth of the whites into the chocolate mixture to lighten it. Fold in the remaining whites just until no white streaks remain. Pour into the prepared pan.

❧ Bake until a skewer inserted into the center comes out almost clean, 35–40 minutes. Let cool in the pan on a rack.

❧ To make the glaze, combine the chocolate, butter and corn syrup in a heatproof bowl set over (not touching) gently simmering water in a pan. Stir often until the chocolate melts, then remove from the heat. Stir until smooth. Let cool, stirring occasionally, for 15 minutes; it will thicken slightly.

❧ Invert the torte onto the rack set over a baking sheet and lift off the pan. Pour on the glaze, tilting the torte to coat the top and sides completely. When the glaze stops dripping, place the 12 hazelnuts around the top of the cake. Transfer to a serving plate and serve.

*The setting sun,*
*and music at the close,*
*As the last of sweets,*
*is sweetest last,*
*Writ in remembrance*
*more than things long past.*
*— William Shakespeare*

## PERSIMMON PUDDING

SERVES 8

*Two of the most common persimmon varieties are the Hachiya and the Fuyu, both available from October to February. For this recipe you will want the larger Hachiya fruits, and will need to let them ripen until completely soft.*

¾ cup (3 oz/90 g) coarsely chopped pecans
2 ripe Hachiya persimmons (see note)
1¾ cups (9 oz/280 g) all-purpose (plain) flour
2 teaspoons baking powder
½ teaspoon baking soda (bicarbonate of soda)
1 teaspoon ground cinnamon
½ teaspoon ground ginger
¼ teaspoon freshly grated nutmeg
1¼ cups (9 oz/280 g) firmly packed dark brown sugar
2 eggs
1 cup (8 fl oz/250 ml) milk
¾ cup (4½ oz/140 g) golden raisins (sultanas)
boiling water, as needed
⅓ cup (3 fl oz/80 ml) brandy
vanilla ice cream

Preheat an oven to 375°F (190°C). Generously butter a 2-qt (2-l) steamed pudding mold and its cover.

*To ensure success with flamed puddings, make sure the pudding is warm and liberally sprinkled with extra brandy before pouring the flaming brandy from the pan over the top.*

*How great a matter a little fire kindleth.*
—*Book of James*

🐦 Spread the pecans on a baking sheet and toast until lightly browned and fragrant, 5–7 minutes. Remove from the oven and let cool. Reduce the oven temperature to 350°F (180°C).

🐦 Cut off the top from each persimmon, then cut in half. Scrape the pulp from the skin into a food processor fitted with the metal blade or into a blender. Purée until smooth; you should have 1 cup (8 fl oz/250 ml) purée.

🐦 Sift together the flour, baking powder, baking soda, cinnamon, ginger and nutmeg into a large bowl. In another bowl, combine the persimmon pulp, brown sugar, eggs and milk; whisk until blended. Gradually stir the persimmon mixture into the flour mixture until fully combined. Let the batter stand until thickened to the consistency of thin sour cream, about 20 minutes.

🐦 Stir the pecans and raisins into the batter. Pour into the prepared mold; cover with well-buttered waxed paper, overlapping the rim slightly, and then the cover. Place the mold in a larger baking pan in the oven. Pour boiling water into the baking pan to reach one-third up the sides of the mold. Bake until set and a skewer inserted into the center comes out clean, 2½–3 hours; check periodically and add water as needed to maintain its original level. Remove the mold from the baking pan and let stand, covered, for 10 minutes.

🐦 To serve, remove the cover, invert the pudding onto a serving plate and lift off the mold. In a small saucepan, warm the brandy over medium heat just until it begins to bubble around the edges. Immediately remove from the heat and ignite with a match. Pour the flaming brandy over the warm pudding. When the flames die, serve the pudding at once with ice cream.

## THE BEST GINGERSNAPS

MAKES ABOUT 2½ DOZEN COOKIES

*Double or triple this recipe around the holidays and have several rolls of the icebox cookies on hand in the freezer to bake on the spur of the moment. They are irresistible served with espresso, tea or hot spiced cider, or packed into tins for gift giving.*

1½ cups (7½ oz/235 g) all-purpose (plain) flour
1¼ teaspoons baking soda (bicarbonate of soda)
1½ teaspoons ground cinnamon
½ teaspoon ground ginger
¼ teaspoon ground cloves
¼ teaspoon freshly grated nutmeg
⅛ teaspoon salt
½ cup (4 oz/125 g) unsalted butter, at room temperature
⅔ cup (5 oz/155 g) sugar, plus about 5 tablespoons (2½ oz/75 g) sugar for dusting tops
½ teaspoon vanilla extract (essence)
1 egg yolk
¼ cup (3 oz/90 g) molasses

Sift together the flour, baking soda, cinnamon, ginger, cloves, nutmeg and salt into a bowl. In a large bowl, using an electric mixer set on high speed, cream together the butter and ⅔ cup (5 oz/155 g) sugar until light and fluffy, 1–2 minutes. Beat in the vanilla, egg yolk and molasses, mixing well. Add the flour mixture to the butter mixture in 3 batches, mixing on low speed until each addition is fully blended. Cover with plastic wrap and chill for 1 hour.

❧ Place the chilled dough on a piece of plastic wrap and shape it into a rough log about 1½ inches (4 cm) in diameter. Wrap the log in the plastic wrap and roll it back and forth until the surface of the log is smooth and even. Refrigerate the roll for 2 hours or freeze for up to 2 months.

❧ Preheat an oven to 375°F (190°C). Lightly oil 3 baking sheets.

❧ Remove the roll from the refrigerator or freezer and unwrap it. Cut it into slices ⅛ inch (3 mm) thick and place them, 1 inch (2.5 cm) apart, on the baking sheets. Sprinkle the tops with ½ teaspoon sugar each.

❧ If using 1 oven, place 2 baking sheets at a time in the oven; refrigerate the remaining sheet until ready to bake. Bake the cookies until golden around the edges but still soft, 8–10 minutes for chewy cookies and 10–12 minutes for crisp cookies; switch the pans halfway through the baking time. Using a spatula, immediately transfer the cookies to racks to cool. Store in an airtight container at room temperature for up to 3 days.

## ALL-SPICED CIDER

MAKES ABOUT 5 CUPS (40 FL OZ/1.25 L); SERVES 6

*This drink is the perfect accompaniment to a holiday dessert buffet. For added flavor and panache, make a swizzle stick for each cup by spearing a piece of crystallized ginger with a cinnamon stick.*

4½ cups (36 fl oz/1.1 l) apple cider
1 tablespoon light brown sugar
3 tablespoons fresh lemon juice
30 allspice berries
12 whole cloves
3 cinnamon sticks
¼ teaspoon freshly grated nutmeg

In a saucepan, combine the cider, brown sugar, lemon juice, allspice berries, cloves, cinnamon sticks and nutmeg. Bring to a boil over high heat, reduce the heat to low and simmer for 5 minutes.

❧ Remove from the heat and strain through a fine-mesh sieve into a warmed pitcher. Pour into warmed mugs and serve hot; or let cool, cover and refrigerate for up to 1 week. Before serving, warm over medium heat.

## WINTERTIME BREAD PUDDING

SERVES 6

**FOR THE CRÈME ANGLAISE:**

2 cups (16 fl oz/500 ml) milk

¼ cup (2 oz/60 g) granulated sugar

4 egg yolks

½ teaspoon vanilla extract

2 tablespoons dark rum

**FOR THE PUDDING:**

½ cup (3 oz/90 g) dried apricots, halved

½ cup (2 oz/60 g) dried pitted cherries

1 cup (8 fl oz/250 ml) dark rum or brandy

6 tablespoons (3 oz/90 g) unsalted butter

3 Bosc pears, peeled, cored and thinly sliced lengthwise

10 slices coarse-textured white bread, crusts removed and halved on the diagonal

1 cup (8 fl oz/250 ml) milk

1 cup (8 fl oz/250 ml) heavy (double) cream

⅔ cup (5 oz/155 g) granulated sugar

½ teaspoon ground nutmeg

1 teaspoon vanilla extract

3 egg yolks, plus 3 whole eggs

boiling water, as needed

confectioners' (icing) sugar

To make the crème anglaise, place the milk in a saucepan over medium heat. When bubbles appear at the pan edges, stir in the sugar until dissolved. Remove from the heat. In a bowl, whisk the egg yolks until blended. Gradually whisk in about ½ cup (4 fl oz/125 ml) of the hot milk. Then whisk the yolk-milk mixture into the milk remaining in the saucepan. Return to medium heat and cook, stirring, until the sauce coats the back of a spoon. Strain through a fine-mesh sieve into a bowl. Stir in the vanilla and rum, cover and refrigerate.

To make the pudding, combine the apricots, cherries and liquor in a bowl; let stand for 1 hour. Drain and reserve the fruits and liquor separately.

Preheat an oven to 375°F (190°C). Butter a 2-qt (2-l) baking dish.

In a frying pan over medium-low heat, melt 2 tablespoons of the butter. Add the pears, cover and cook, turning once, until tender, 4–6 minutes total. Set aside.

Melt the remaining 4 tablespoons (2 oz/60 g) butter. Place the bread slices on a baking sheet and brush the tops with the melted butter. Place on the top rack of the oven and toast until the edges are golden, about 8 minutes. Remove from the oven and leave the oven set at 375°F (190°C).

Spread one-third of the apricots, cherries and pears on the bottom of the prepared baking dish. Top with half of the bread, toasted side up, in a single layer. Layer half of the remaining fruits over the bread and top with the remaining bread slices, toasted side up. Scatter on the remaining fruit.

In a saucepan over medium heat, combine the milk, cream, granulated sugar, nutmeg and vanilla. Heat, stirring, until hot, 2–3 minutes; set aside. In a bowl, whisk together the egg yolks, whole eggs and 2 tablespoons reserved liquor. Slowly whisk the milk mixture into the egg mixture. Pour over the bread and fruit.

Put the baking dish in a larger baking pan and add boiling water to the pan to reach halfway up the sides of the dish. Bake until a skewer inserted into the center comes out clean, 50–60 minutes. Let cool for 20 minutes, then dust with confectioners' sugar. Serve with the crème anglaise.

*I dreamed that, as I wandered by the way, Bare Winter suddenly was changed to Spring.*
—*Percy Bysshe Shelley*

## PANFORTE

*Panforte is a rich, intense and chewy Italian confection made from candied fruits, nuts and spices. In Tuscany, brightly wrapped packages of the dark, candylike cake are a telltale sign that Christmas is around the corner. If stored in an airtight container, the cake will keep at room temperature for at least a month. Serve in thin wedges with strong coffee.*

¾ cup (4 oz/125 g) almonds
½ cup (2½ oz/75 g) hazelnuts (filberts)
1¼ cups (7½ oz/235 g) mixed candied
    citrus peel, chopped
⅓ cup (2 oz/60 g) all-purpose (plain)
    flour
1 teaspoon ground cinnamon
½ teaspoon ground cloves
½ teaspoon ground coriander
½ teaspoon freshly grated nutmeg
½ teaspoon ground allspice
⅛ teaspoon ground white pepper
½ cup (6 oz/185 g) honey
¼ cup (2 oz/60 g) granulated sugar
confectioners' (icing) sugar

Preheat an oven to 375°F (190°C). Butter an 8-inch (20-cm) round cake pan and line the bottom with a piece of parchment paper cut to fit precisely.
❧ Spread the almonds and hazelnuts on a baking sheet, keeping them separate, and toast until lightly browned and fragrant, 5–7 minutes. Remove from the oven, place the almonds on a cutting board and place the hazelnuts on a kitchen towel. Rub the hazelnuts with the towel to remove the skins. Do not worry if bits of skin remain. Place the hazelnuts on the board with the almonds. Coarsely chop all the nuts and place in a large bowl. Reduce the oven temperature to 350°F (180°C).

❧ Add the candied peel, flour, cinnamon, cloves, coriander, nutmeg, allspice and pepper to the nuts and mix well.
❧ In a small saucepan over medium heat, combine the honey and granulated sugar and heat, stirring occasionally, until the sugar melts, about 3 minutes. Stir the honey mixture into the almond-fruit mixture, mixing well. Transfer the batter to the prepared pan and, when cool enough to handle, wet your hands and press the mixture evenly into the pan.
❧ Bake until golden brown, 30–35 minutes. Remove from the oven and invert onto a rack. Lift off the pan and let cool. When cool, peel off the parchment. Using a sifter or sieve, dust the top liberally with confectioners' sugar.

## HOT GINGER-BUTTERED RUM

*Nothing takes the chill off a cold winter's night like hot rum. Ginger-flavored brandy adds an extra touch of spice, although regular brandy will do in a pinch. Garnish each mug with a thin slice of lemon.*

⅓ cup (2½ oz/75 g) firmly packed
    brown sugar
4 cups (32 fl oz/1 l) water
¼ cup (2 oz/60 g) unsalted butter, cut
    into pieces
2 cinnamon sticks
6 whole cloves
¼ teaspoon freshly grated nutmeg
6 thin fresh ginger slices, each ¾ inch
    (2 cm) in diameter, peeled
¾ cup (6 fl oz/180 ml) dark rum
½ cup (4 fl oz/125 ml) ginger-flavored
    brandy
1 tablespoon fresh lemon juice

In a saucepan over medium heat, stir together the brown sugar, water, butter, cinnamon sticks, cloves, nutmeg and ginger slices. Bring to a boil, reduce the heat to low and simmer for 5 minutes.
❧ Remove from the heat and strain through a fine-mesh sieve into a warmed pitcher. Add the rum, brandy and lemon juice. Stir to mix.
❧ Pour into warmed mugs. Serve hot.

## CINNAMON-POACHED QUINCES WITH NUTMEG CREAM

SERVES 6

*Sweet spices contribute a heartwarming quality to this homestyle dessert featuring a time-honored fruit of early winter. If you wish, you can cook the quinces up to 1 week in advance, allowing them to cool in their poaching liquid before storing them in the refrigerator. Reheat the fruit in their liquid before serving.*

8 cups (64 fl oz/2 l) water
2 cups (1 lb/500 g) granulated sugar
5 cinnamon sticks
5 quinces, about 10 oz (315 g) each, peeled, halved, cored and cut into eighths
1 cup (8 fl oz/250 ml) heavy (double) cream
1 tablespoon confectioners' (icing) sugar
½ teaspoon freshly grated nutmeg

In a large saucepan over high heat, combine the water, granulated sugar and cinnamon sticks. Bring to a boil, stirring occasionally, and add the quinces. Reduce the heat to low and simmer, uncovered, until the quinces are tender and have turned a deep rose color, 2–2½ hours. Add water during cooking if necessary to keep the fruit covered with the poaching liquid. Do not stir the quinces while they are simmering; instead, move them about gently if necessary for even cooking.

❧ Before serving, in a large bowl, using a whisk or an electric mixer, beat the cream until soft peaks form. Stir in the confectioners' sugar and the nutmeg. Cover and refrigerate until serving.

❧ To serve, using a slotted spoon, transfer the warm quinces to a serving bowl. Serve the cream on the side.

## CITRUS COMPOTE WITH HONEY AND GOLDEN RAISINS

SERVES 6

*Excellent served on its own, this compote can also be warmed over low heat and spooned over ice cream or sorbet. For the best flavor and most juice, choose pink, red or white grapefruits that are relatively heavy for their size and springy to the touch. The compote can also be made with tangerines, tangelos or blood oranges in place of the oranges and grapefruits.*

2 cups (16 fl oz/500 ml) sweet dessert wine such as late-harvest Gewürztraminer, late-harvest Riesling, French Sauternes or Muscat de Beaumes-de-Venise

1 cup (8 fl oz/250 ml) fresh orange juice
2 tablespoons honey
½ vanilla bean
½ cup (3 oz/90 g) golden raisins (sultanas)
5 seedless oranges
2 grapefruits (see note)
3 kiwifruits

Pour the wine, orange juice and honey into a saucepan. Split the vanilla bean in half lengthwise and, using the tip of a knife, scrape the seeds into the pan. Then add the pod as well and bring to a boil. Reduce the heat to medium and simmer, uncovered, until about 1 cup (8 fl oz/250 ml) remains, about 15 minutes. Remove from the heat and stir in the raisins. Transfer to a bowl and set aside to cool.

❧ Using a sharp knife, cut a thick slice off the top and bottom of each orange to reveal the flesh. Then, standing each orange upright on a cutting surface, cut off the peel and white membrane in thick, wide strips. Working with 1 orange at a time, hold the orange over a bowl and cut along either side of each segment to free it from the membrane, letting the segments drop into the bowl. Repeat this same technique with the grapefruits, using the tip of a knife to remove any seeds.

❧ Peel the kiwifruits. Cut each into 8 wedges and add to the oranges and grapefruits. Add the cooled liquid and raisins, removing the vanilla pod, and stir together.

❧ To serve, spoon the fruit into individual bowls.

# CRANBERRY UPSIDE-DOWN CAKE

MAKES ONE 9-INCH (23-CM) CAKE; SERVES 8–10

*This festive holiday cake is inspired by a recipe from Lindsey Shere, former longtime pastry chef at Chez Panisse restaurant in Berkeley, California. Fresh cranberries are abundant this time of year, although frozen ones will also work fine.*

### FOR THE TOPPING:

¼ cup (2 oz/60 g) unsalted butter
¾ cup (6 oz/185 g) firmly packed
  brown sugar
¾ lb (375 g) cranberries

### FOR THE CAKE:

1½ cups (7½ oz/235 g) all-purpose
  (plain) flour
2 teaspoons baking powder
¼ teaspoon salt
½ cup (4 oz/125 g) unsalted butter
1 cup (8 oz/250 g) granulated sugar
2 eggs, separated
1 teaspoon vanilla extract (essence)
½ cup (4 fl oz/125 ml) milk
⅛ teaspoon cream of tartar

### FOR THE WHIPPED CREAM:

1 cup (8 fl oz/250 ml) heavy (double)
  cream
¼ teaspoon vanilla extract (essence)
1 tablespoon confectioners' (icing) sugar

To make the topping, butter a 9-inch (23-cm) round cake pan. Put the butter and brown sugar in the prepared pan and place the pan over medium heat. Heat, stirring occasionally, until the butter is melted and the sugar has dissolved. Scatter the cranberries over the butter-sugar mixture. Set aside.

❧ Preheat an oven to 350°F (180°C).

❧ To make the cake, in a bowl, mix together the flour, baking powder and salt. In another bowl, using an electric mixer set on medium-high speed, beat together the butter and granulated sugar until light and fluffy, 2–3 minutes. Add the egg yolks, one at a time, beating well after each addition. Add the vanilla and mix well. Using a rubber spatula, fold in the flour mixture in 3 batches, adding it alternately with the milk.

❧ In a bowl, using a whisk or an electric mixer, beat the egg whites until soft peaks form. Add the cream of tartar and continue to beat until stiff peaks form. Using the spatula, fold the whites into the batter.

❧ Spoon the batter over the cranberries in the cake pan, spreading it evenly. Bake until a skewer inserted into the center comes out clean, 55–60 minutes. Remove from the oven and let cool on a rack for 15 minutes. Run a knife around the edges of the pan to loosen the cake. Invert onto a serving plate, let stand for 5 minutes, then lift off the pan.

❧ To make the whipped cream, in a bowl, using a whisk or an electric mixer, whip the cream until soft peaks form. Stir in the vanilla and the confectioners' sugar.

❧ To serve, cut the cake into wedges and serve with the whipped cream.

*Nature is often hidden; sometimes overcome; seldom extinguished.*
—*Francis Bacon*

## CITRUS FRUITS

**1. YELLOW GRAPEFRUITS**   Available from early winter throughout most of the spring, grapefruits, reportedly so-named because the fruits bunch together on the tree in clusters reminiscent of grapes, are enjoyed for their bracingly tart-sweet flavor. Yellow grapefruits, also referred to as white, have pale yellow skins and whitish yellow flesh. A common variety is Marsh.

**2. PINK GRAPEFRUITS**   Pink-fleshed grapefruits, generally sweeter than yellow varieties, may be distinguished by an orange-red blush on their skins. Generally speaking, the darker the flesh, the sweeter the taste, with the Ruby variety grown in Texas among the sweetest of choices. Other popular varieties include the Rio Star, Ray, Henderson and Flame.

**3. MEYER LEMONS**   Juicy, roundish, sweet-tasting lemons, available in spring and into early summer. They are prized for their exceptionally sweet, aromatic flesh and juice and thin, soft edible peel. If unavailable, any regular lemon variety may be substituted in recipes, although they will not impart the same sweetness.

**4. EUREKA LEMONS**   Commonly available thick-skinned lemons. Used regularly for their juice and flavorful zest. Another common variety is the smoother-skinned Lisbon lemon.

**5. LIMES**   Entering their peak in late spring, limes are smaller than lemons, with thin green skins and pale yellowish green flesh. They also yield a more acidic juice than lemons.

**6. NAVEL ORANGES**   Variety of large orange descriptively named for the indentation in the skin at its stem end. A carryover from winter into early spring, navels have sweet, juicy flesh and are easily peeled and virtually seedless.

**7. VALENCIA ORANGES**   This small, smooth-skinned variety, available throughout the spring, is the most common sweet orange. Valencias yield excellent and abundant juice and are also good candidates for cutting up and eating.

**8. BLOOD ORANGES**   Available from midwinter throughout the spring, these sweet, aromatic, small-to medium-size oranges are distinguished by the reddish blush on their skins and their sweet, flavorful, deep red flesh and juice.

## BERRIES

**9. STRAWBERRIES**   Widely popular, these deep pink to red, heart-shaped berries may be found year-round, but are at their peak from early spring into early summer.

**10. FRAISES DES BOIS**   Also known as Alpine strawberries, this tapered, thumbnail-sized berry variety may still be found growing wild in wooded areas of Europe—hence the French name, meaning "woodland strawberries." Today, they are also cultivated commercially, to be appreciated for their mild, sweet, musky flavor. The tiny red berries have a flavor resembling a cross between strawberries and raspberries; white varieties carry a scent reminiscent of vanilla. Considered a delicacy, fraises des bois are often served simply adorned with a sprinkle of sugar or a splash of cream or cassis (red currant liqueur).

## TROPICAL FRUITS

**11. PINEAPPLES**   Pineapples were named by Spanish and Portuguese explorers who likened the prickly fruits, native to Paraguay, to a pinecone. Buy those that have fully ripened; immature fruits will be less sweet and will not ripen well indoors. Fruits grown in Hawaii, particularly the Cayenne variety, generally offer the best quality. Refrigerate the pineapple in a plastic bag, using it within a few days of purchase. To prepare a pineapple, twist or cut off its leaves and cut a thin slice off the base to stand the fruit upright. Using a large, sharp knife, carefully cut off the skin in thick vertical strips. With a paring knife, cut out any remaining woody "eyes" along the sides. Then cut up the fruit as directed in individual recipes, cutting away the tough core portions.

**12. COCONUTS**   Coconuts are sturdy fruits that keep well. The white meat and the milk that is made from the meat may be used fresh, but the coconut most commonly used in cooking today is the pre-packaged meat, sold dried, sweetened or plain, and grated, in fine shreds or in large shards. Look for the latter in health-food stores.

**13. BANANAS**   Available year-round from various tropical countries, bananas are routinely harvested when green. Best purchased when hints of green still linger at their ends, they ripen perfectly at home, stored at room temperature. In addition to commonly available dessert or Cavendish bananas, seek out the small, sweet variety known as the Ladyfinger.

**14. PAPAYAS**   Smooth-textured, sweet and eminently digestible due to the enzyme papain that its flesh contains, this pear-shaped native of the Caribbean is available year-round, but is at a peak of quality and plenitude in spring. Papayas range in size from about 6 inches (15 cm) long to three times that size and can weigh in at over 20 pounds (10 kg). Small varieties have pale yellow to deep orange skin and flesh when ripe; large varieties usually maintain a dark green skin but reveal a flesh that is bright orange. Buy those that are only partially ripe, their skins roughly equal parts yellow and green; they will ripen at room temperature, away from sunlight, within about 5 days.

**15. PASSION FRUITS**   Cut in half, this wrinkly-skinned, egg-sized fruit reveals a yellowish orange, sweet, aromatic pulp full of edible black, crunchy seeds. Strained of the seeds, the pulp makes a wonderful sauce for sweet or savory dishes, as well as an exotic flavoring for desserts. The smooth, immature fruits will ripen at room temperature within 5 days; they can be stored in the refrigerator for several days, and the pulp can be frozen in an airtight container for up to several months.

**16. MANGOES**   Spring sees crops from Florida, the Caribbean and Mexico of this sweet, highly aromatic tropical fruit native to India. The yellow-orange flesh has a soft, juicy texture reminiscent of a very ripe peach. Harvested when still green, mangoes ripen easily at home when stored at room temperature; once ripe, they may be refrigerated for up to a week. To prepare a mango, score the slightly leathery skin lengthwise into quarters and peel it off, then cut off the flesh in two thick slices from either side of the large, flat pit; the remaining fruit should be trimmed from around the pit's edges.

# Spring Vegetables Glossary

## Cabbage Family

**1. Broccoli Rabe**   These slender, firm stalks with deep green leaves are topped with small florets. They are prized for their slightly bitter, nutlike taste when cooked.

**2. Swiss Chard**   The dark green leaves and crisp, white or red stems taste similar to, but milder than, spinach. Also known as chard or silverbeet.

**3. Kale**   Early spring vegetable with a spicy flavor and coarse texture. Ranges in color from blue-green to purple, yellow to white. Also known as curly kale.

## Leafy Vegetables

**4. Mâche**   French name for small, soft, delicate-tasting salad leaves; also known as lamb's lettuce or corn salad. Available in early spring.

**5. Belgian Endive**   Crisp, white, spear-shaped leaves edged with pale yellow-green or pinkish red and packed in cone-shaped heads. The slight bitterness, mildest in smaller heads, comes through both raw and cooked. Also known as chicory or witloof.

**6. Spinach**   Mildly astringent, dark green leaves. Reserve smaller, more tender specimens for salads and larger, thicker leaves for cooking.

**7. Dandelion Greens**   Cultivated variety of the wild plant. Young leaves are used in salads, while older, more bitter ones must be cooked.

**8. Arugula**   Young arugula (pictured here) has small, round leaves that become edged with notches as they mature. Its mild, peppery taste and tender texture are enjoyed raw or cooked. Also known as rocket.

**9. Watercress**   Principally eaten raw in salads or sandwiches, or cooked in soups. Early spring sees the smallest, sweetest sprigs of this spicy-sweet member of the mustard family.

**10. Sorrel**   Lemony, sword-shaped leaves are used in salads, soups and sauces. Perennial plant available throughout spring and summer.

**11. Lettuces**   Basket includes lettuces and other salad greens at peak in spring, including (clockwise, from top) long, crisp romaine (cos); slightly bitter frisée (chicory or curly endive); red-leaf lettuce; radicchio; oakleaf lettuce; and butter (Boston) lettuce.

## Peas and Beans

**12. Snow Peas**   Pea variety of flat, edible pods and tiny peas. Also called Chinese peas or mange-touts.

**13. Sugar Snap Peas**   A recent pea hybrid, these plump, edible pods are prized for their sweetness, crisp texture and bright color.

**14. Pea Shoots**   Tender, sweet shoots plucked from pea vines. Sold predominantly in Asian markets.

**15. Fava Beans**   This variety of flat, kidney-shaped bean grows in thick pods. When very small, they may be eaten raw, pod and all; more mature beans, in long, thick pods, require shelling and peeling (see page 296). Also known as broad beans or horse beans.

## Baby Vegetables

**16.** Tiny immature vegetables—baby carrots and summer squashes such as crookneck and zucchini (courgette)—are prized for their tenderness.

## Onion Family

**17. Green Garlic**   Harvested in late spring, immature specimens of the pungent bulb are mild, sweet and aromatic.

**18. Green Onions**   Mild variety of onion eaten when immature, green stalks and all. Also known as spring onions or scallions.

**19. Sweet Onions**   Sweet yellow onions such as Vidalia onions (from Georgia), Maui onions (from Hawaii) and Walla Walla onions (from Washington), appear in late spring.

**20. Baby Leeks**   This mild relative of the onion is harvested in spring and fall. Small, sweet baby leeks are often cooked and eaten whole.

## Shoots and Stalks

**21. Asparagus**   Tender springtime shoots in colors ranging from bright green to purplish green to ivory (the latter the result of being covered with earth to blanch them as they grow).

**22. Fennel**   The bulblike cluster of stalk bases of a plant related to the herb of the same name. Prized for its crispness and mild, sweet anise flavor.

**23. Rhubarb**   Tangy, reddish stalks resembling celery. Discard any leaves or roots, which are toxic. Served cooked, most often sweetened in desserts.

**24. Artichokes**   The first of this cultivated thistle's two annual crops of immature flowers comes in spring. Baby artichokes need just light trimming before eating whole; only the leaf bottoms and hearts of large artichokes are edible (see page 296).

## Mushrooms

**25. Button Mushrooms**   Descriptive name for common, cultivated mushrooms harvested when small, with their caps still tightly closed.

**26. Oyster Mushrooms**   Named for the similarity to the bivalve seen in their fan shape and gray color. Wild variety, now commonly cultivated.

**27. Morel Mushrooms**   Wild, honeycomb-capped mushrooms known for their rich, earthy taste.

**28. Shiitake Mushrooms**   Asian wild variety, now widely cultivated. Prized for their rich, meaty taste and texture.

## Roots and Tubers

**29. Radishes**   Crisp, cool and spicy, these roots of a type of mustard plant come in a range of shapes, sizes and colors, including red, white and purple.

**30. New Potatoes**   Small, immature potatoes harvested while their skins are still thin and their waxy flesh is sweet.

**31. Beets**   Small specimens of this sweet root vegetable are harvested in late spring. Colors range from red, gold, pink and candy striped to white.

**32. Ginger**   Rhizome, popular as a seasoning, with cream-colored paper-thin, edible skin and pink tips when young.

**33. Daikon**   Large, white, cylindrical Japanese radish used both raw and cooked.

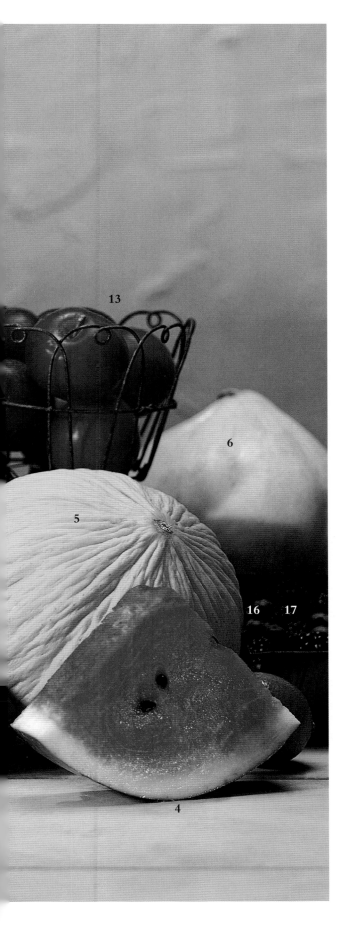

## MELONS

**1. HONEYDEW MELONS**  Although the most common honeydew melon has a pale yellow, waxy rind and pale green flesh, other types in a range of colors are now available. Orange honeydew has a flavor similar to cantaloupe, while the bright yellow honeydew has milky-colored flesh and a tropical, almost-pineapplelike taste. The green-and-orange Temptation variety combines the flavor of honeydew with a hint of cantaloupe. All have juicy, tender flesh—hence the dew part of their name. Most are also notable for their strong perfume that some people liken to honey.

**2. PERSIAN MELONS**  Resembling oversized cantaloupes with deep green or golden rinds covered in a tan weblike pattern, these melons have moist, fragrant, orange or salmon flesh and a mild, not overly sweet flavor similar to that of the cantaloupe.

**3. CANTALOUPES**  One of the oldest varieties of melon, named after the town of Cantalupa, Italy. Their familiar tan netlike rinds conceal firm, moist orange flesh with a fairly firm texture and a sweet and fragrant, slightly musky flavor.

**4. WATERMELONS**  Among the oldest known melons, distinguished by their large size and hard, deep green, mottled green or green-and-white rinds. Many varieties exist. Whether the flesh is rosy red, deep pink or bright yellow, and whether it has the familiar shiny dark brown or black seeds or is seedless, all share a characteristic crisp, slightly granular consistency coupled with a refreshingly high water content and appealing sweetness.

**5. CASABA MELONS**  Available from late summer to early autumn, these melons are distinguished by their deeply wrinkled, yellow to pale green rinds and moderately large spherical shape tapering to a point at the stem end. Prized for their pale green, highly sweet, juicy flesh reminiscent of honeydew.

**6. CRENSHAW MELONS**  Teardrop-shaped melons with thin, smooth yellow-orange rinds. Their flesh, ranging from orange to salmon-pink, is highly aromatic, juicy and sweet, with a notable hint of spice. Sometimes called Cranshaw melons.

## TREE FRUITS

**7. CHERRIES**  Sweet, juicy cherries enjoy a brief season in markets, harvested from the end of spring through midsummer. Most common are the ruby-red to almost purple-black Bing (pictured here) and Lambert varieties, followed by scarcer, more delicately flavored cherries with yellow flesh and skins blushed with red, such as the Royal Ann (also pictured) and Rainier varieties.

**8. MANGOES**  Crops from Florida, Mexico and the Caribbean, which begin producing in spring, continue to yield this tropical fruit, a native of India, into high summer. Soft and juicy as a peach, the yellow-orange flesh has a sweet, highly aromatic flavor. Harvested when still green, mangoes ripen easily at home when stored at room temperature; once ripe, they may be refrigerated for up to a week. To prepare a mango, score the slightly leathery skin lengthwise into quarters and peel it off, then cut off the flesh in two thick slices from either side of the large, flat pit. Trim the remaining fruit from around the pit's edges.

**9. NECTARINES**  Sometimes incorrectly referred to as a hybrid of the peach and the plum, nectarines are in fact a relative of the peach and are notable for their pleasantly smooth, fuzz-free skins and the sweet flesh whose juiciness inspired their name.

**10. PEACHES**  Hundreds of different peach types exist, grouped variously as cling peaches, including such familiar types as Maycrest and Springcrest, in which the fruits' pulp clings tightly to the pit; or freestone, including the Elberta and O'Henry varieties among others, from which the pit may be easily and neatly removed. Peaches also, depending upon variety, may have yellow-orange flesh or paler yellow "white" flesh.

**11. APRICOTS**  Although they originated in China, where they were cultivated more than 4,000 years ago, apricots derive their name from the Latin for "precocious," an indication that these fruits, which resemble small, yellow to deep orange peaches, arrive in markets on the threshold of summer.

**12. FIGS**  These small, pear-shaped fruits thrive worldwide in semidesert areas. Several varieties may be found in markets year-round, but summer sees an abundance of such types as the purple-black Black Mission fig (pictured in bucket), whose soft skin conceals intensely flavored, sweet pink flesh; the Calimyrna (pictured below center), a California hybrid of the Turkish Smyrna fig with green skin, white to pale pink flesh, and a sweet, nutlike taste; and the Kadota, a small, yellowish green fig with sweet purple-pink flesh.

**13. PLUMS**  More than 2,000 different plum hybrids are grown throughout the world, many of them developed within the past two centuries. Depending upon variety, they arrive in markets anywhere from late spring to the earliest days of autumn. Early summer plums, shown here, include the red-skinned Red Beauty and the purple-tinged Santa Rosa (in basket), and the blackish red Black Beauty (pictured below right).

## BERRIES

**14. BLACKBERRIES**  Available from the first days of summer almost to season's end, these glossy, plump, purple-black berries (pictured here in their unripened form) are enjoyed for their rich, almost winelike flavor and juiciness.

**15. RASPBERRIES**  Plump berries enjoyed for their juiciness and delicate, sweet flavor with just a hint of tartness. Most familiar are red raspberries, although pale gold, purple and almost-black varieties also exist. Grown in cooler climates and available throughout the summer, raspberries will be at their peak approaching midseason.

**16. BLUEBERRIES**  At their best from June through midsummer, these small, round, smooth-skinned berries abound in rich-tasting, sweet and flavorful juice. Rare wild blueberries are generally smaller in size and have a more intense flavor than the cultivated varieties.

**17. BOYSENBERRIES**  Stout, deep purple hybrid of the blackberry, red raspberry and loganberry. Grown in lesser quantities than those other berries from which they are derived, boysenberries may take some sleuthing in well-stocked groceries and farmers' markets.

# Summer Vegetables Glossary

## Vegetable Fruits

**1. Bell Peppers**   Bell-shaped peppers (capsicums) with crisp flesh and a flavor that becomes even sweeter as the summer sun ripens them to shades varying from yellow to orange to red. The flesh is at its most digestible when the pepper has been roasted and peeled. Roasted or raw, peppers should be stemmed, ribbed and seeded before use (see summer techniques, page 297).

**2. Poblano Chili Pepper**   Variety of milder chili pepper with rich, relatively spicy flavor. Poblano chilies resemble tapered, triangular bell peppers and range in color from dark green to brick.

**3. Pasilla Chili Pepper**   Slightly elongated chili pepper characterized by its moderately hot taste with a hint of berry. Ranges in color from dark green to almost black. Also known as chilaca.

**4. Jalapeño Chili Pepper**   Common variety of spicy chili. Sold in its immature dark green and, less often, ripened red forms.

**5. Serrano Chili Pepper**   Smaller, more slender and significantly hotter than the jalapeño variety. Available in both its green and red forms.

**6. Avocados**   This favorite summer vegetable is grown in temperate climates worldwide, making it available almost year-round. Of the several varieties available, the Hass (sometimes spelled Haas) pictured here is preferred for its rich flavor and especially smooth texture. It may be recognized by its dark green, pebbly textured skin, which turns almost black when the avocado is ripe. A second popular variety, the Fuerte, has smooth, dark green skin.

**7. Tomatoes**   A wide variety of tomatoes is available now. Look for the popular spherical beefsteak tomatoes and elongated plum tomatoes, also known as Romas; descriptively named little cherry tomatoes (far right), in both red and yellow; medium-sized, spherical orange or yellow tomatoes; and tiny, orange or yellow pear- or teardrop-shaped tomatoes. Also seek out rarer heirloom tomato varieties, which come in varied patterns of white, red and yellow.

**8. Cucumbers**   Cool, crisp, refreshing vegetable usually eaten raw or pickled. Most common varieties are little pickling cucumbers; plump, dark-green-skinned, nearly seedless English or hothouse cucumbers (pictured here); and long, slender Mediterranean or Middle Eastern cucumbers. Also look for rarer varieties such as the mild, spherical, yellow-skinned lemon cucumber (also pictured).

**9. Eggplants**   Of Asian origin, the eggplant (aubergine) migrated across the Middle East to Europe, reaching Italy by the 15th century. Its multitude of varieties include among them an ivory-skinned type resembling a goose egg, the source of its English name. The two most common types are the large, plump globe eggplant (pictured near right) and the long, slender Asian eggplant (pictured far right). The latter has fewer seeds and a finer flavor and texture.

## Summer Squash Family

**10. Zucchini**   Slender, cylindrical members of the squash family with soft, dark green skin and tender, pale green flesh. Smaller specimens have a finer flavor and texture and tiny edible seeds. Available in other varieties, including yellow zucchini and striped or spherical Italian types. Also known as courgettes.

**11. Pattypan Squashes**   Small, mild summer squash with pale green skin and a shape resembling a flattened, scallop-edged top. Also known as custard or cymling squash. Slightly larger and plumper varieties include the green or yellow scallopini squash.

**12. Yellow Crookneck Squashes**   Similar in size to zucchini, a golden-skinned summer squash with pale yellow flesh, a rounded base and a swanlike, slender neck.

**13. Zucchini Flowers**   Delicate blossoms of the vegetable, sold separately or sometimes still attached to baby zucchini in farmers' and specialty produce markets. Best used on the day of purchase.

## Leafy Vegetables

**14. Red Leaf Lettuce**   Mild lettuce with long, medium-green leaves fringed in reddish brown.

**15. Frisée**   Head of frilly leaves with a bitter edge of flavor at its mildest in the paler inner leaves. At its best in early summer.

## Onion Family

**16. Shallots**   Relative of the onion, with smaller bulbs thought by some to resemble in taste a cross between onion and garlic.

**17. Garlic**   Pungent bulb, harvested in early summer, whose individual cloves, whether whole, chopped, crushed or puréed, raw or cooked, season a wide variety of savory dishes.

## Beans and Seeds

**18. Cranberry Beans**   Variety of fresh shell beans, available from midsummer through fall, whose white pods and beans are streaked with cranberry red.

**19. Purple Beans**   Variety of wax beans, eaten whole like green beans, with deep purple pods that turn green when cooked.

**20. Wax Beans**   Also called yellow beans, these fresh, edible pods are distinguished by their waxlike sheen.

**21. Green Beans**   Refers to any of several different varieties of fresh beans eaten whole. The Blue Lakes pictured here and Kentucky Wonders are among those with the best flavor and texture.

**22. Haricots Verts**   French term for tender green beans harvested when immature, with very slender pods measuring no more than about 3 inches (7.5 cm) in length.

**23. Corn**   Yellow and white varieties are the commonly available, with the former generally carrying a more intense corn flavor and the latter a sweeter taste. Look for yellow-white hybrids at farmers' markets.

## Roots and Tubers

**24. Yukon Gold Potatoes**   Medium-sized waxy-fleshed potatoes prized for their golden color and buttery flavor. Yellow Finn is a similar variety.

**25. Ginger**   Pungent, sweet-hot seasoning of Asian origin. Although it resembles a root, it is in fact the underground stem, or rhizome, of the tropical ginger plant.

## HERBS

**1. THYME**   An ancient herb of the eastern Mediterranean, with fragrant, clean-tasting small leaves that, whether fresh or dried, complement poultry, light meats, seafood or vegetables. Lemon thyme, which has a zesty citrus flavor, should be used with discretion, although it goes particularly well with seafood, poultry and even some fruit desserts.

**2. MARJORAM**   A close relative of oregano, but with a milder, yet still pungent flavor and heady aroma that is well suited to seasoning seafood, poultry, meats, egg dishes and vegetable fruits such as eggplant (aubergine) and tomatoes. Use in fresh form, if possible, to show off its delicate flavor.

**3. SAGE**   Strongly flavored, highly aromatic herb, used either fresh or dried, and generally with some discretion. Popular in the cuisines of Europe and the Middle East, it goes particularly well with fresh or cured pork, lamb, veal or poultry, and also appears in sauces and salads.

**4. ROSEMARY**   Mediterranean herb, used either fresh or dried. The needlelike leaves, sometimes decked in tiny blue flowers, have a highly aromatic flavor well suited to lamb, veal, pork, poultry, seafood and vegetables. Use sparingly, as the strong taste can overpower dishes. Summertime grilling, however, allows more extravagant additions of the herb; its woody branches can be thrown on hot coals to produce a fragrant smoke or stripped of their leaves and used as skewers that impart subtle flavor.

**5. CHIVES**   Slender shoots of a plant related to the onion, used fresh to impart a mild, almost sweet onion flavor. Although chives are available dried in the seasonings section of food stores, fresh chives possess the best flavor.

**6. OREGANO**   A hardy perennial form of marjoram, also sometimes known as wild marjoram. It has a more powerful, pungent flavor than its milder fresh cousin, especially when dried. Goes well with a wide range of savory dishes, particularly those featuring tomatoes and other vegetables.

**7. BASIL**   A spicy-sweet herb popular in Italian and French kitchens. Grows abundantly in summer and shares a special affinity with the season's vine-ripened tomatoes, whether eaten raw in salads or cooked in sauces. Also good with other vegetables, seafood, chicken and rice dishes.

**8. PARSLEY**   Popular fresh herb that originated in southern Europe and is still widely used there and in other Western cuisines to season and garnish a wide range of savory dishes. Available in two main types: the more common curly-leaf parsley, a popular garnish, and flat-leaf parsley, also known as Italian parsley, which has a more pronounced flavor and is preferred for use as a seasoning.

**9. MINT**   Fragrant herb with a sprightly, cooling flavor that is especially welcome in both savory and sweet warm-weather dishes ranging from lamb, poultry and vegetables to fruit and chocolate desserts. Mint grows so well in gardens that, unchecked, it can overrun other plants. Spearmint, the most common variety, has a strong flavor and is generally preferred for seasoning. Try milder peppermint as well, or such distinctively scented varieties as apple mint and orange mint.

**10. SUMMER SAVORY**   This green herb has a slightly peppery taste that highlights the flavors of beans, tomatoes, seafood and poultry.

**11. BAY LEAVES**   Pungent, spicy dried whole leaves of the bay laurel tree, which grows abundantly in the Mediterranean and in similar sunny climates such as that of California. Commonly used as a seasoning in simmered dishes, including soups and braises or stews of meat, poultry or seafood; in marinades for those same main ingredients; and in pickling mixtures. French bay leaves, sometimes found in specialty-food shops, possess a milder, sweeter flavor than those from California.

**12. DILL**   The fine, feathery fresh leaves thrive in full summer sunlight and yield a sweet, aromatic flavor that wonderfully complements pickling brines, vegetables, seafood (especially salmon), chicken, veal and pork.

**13. PURPLE BASIL**   Several varieties of the popular summer herb have reddish purple leaves, including dark opal basil and purple ruffle basil. Their flavors tend to be stronger and spicier than ordinary green basil, calling for more judicious use; the leaves also make a particularly attractive garnish.

**14. CILANTRO**   Botanically related to the carrot, this green, leafy herb resembles flat-leaf (Italian) parsley, but has a sharp, aromatic, notably astringent flavor. Used for seasoning a wide range of savory dishes in the kitchens of Latin America, the Middle East and Asia. Also commonly referred to as fresh coriander or Chinese parsley.

## FLOWERS AND SPICES

**15. NASTURTIUMS**   Members of the watercress family, these yellow to bright orange to orange-red blossoms have a distinctive peppery taste recalling that leafy vegetable. Green nasturtium leaves may also be eaten.

**16. PANSIES**   Delicate flowers that contribute a subtle perfume and colors ranging from orange to deep violet.

**17. ROSES**   The petals of this familiar flower lend their delicate perfume and wide rainbow of vibrant colors as both fresh and crystallized garnishes.

**18. BORAGE**   Bright blue, small, star-shaped blossoms of an herb with a mild cucumber flavor that grows wild throughout the Mediterranean and in similar climates.

**19. LAVENDER**   Sweetly fragrant purple flowers of a plant related to mint, adding bright color and heavy perfume to savory and sweet dishes. Dried lavender has a much more intense flavor than the fresh blossoms.

**20. VANILLA BEANS**   These dried aromatic pods of an orchid variety native to southern Mexico are one of the world's most popular sweet flavorings. Vanilla beans from Madagascar are generally considered best. To remove the tiny, flavorful seeds from a vanilla bean, split the bean in half lengthwise with a small, sharp knife. Then use the tip of the knife to scrape out the seeds within each half. The scraped-out pods may be buried in a jar filled with granulated sugar to make vanilla sugar.

# Autumn Fruits Glossary

## Pears

**1. Seckel**  Comparatively small variety with thick, russet-yellow skin, buttery yet firm flesh and spicy flavor. Available from late summer through mid-winter. Good for eating plain, poaching and preserving.

**2. French Butter**  Plump, yellow-green fruit with a smooth, rich, butterlike texture and a delicate flavor accented by a hint of lemony acidity. Available from midsummer to early autumn. Good for eating raw or cooking.

**3. Bartlett**  Medium-sized, bell-shaped, early autumn pears with pale green to golden, and sometimes red, skin. Creamy-textured, mild, sweet and juicy flesh has a sweet, distinctive fragrance. Available from early summer to early November. Equally good for eating, cooking and preserving. Also called Williams' pears.

**4. Bosc**  Medium-sized to large, slender, tapered pears with yellow, green and russet skins, buttery yet spicy flavor and firm, slightly grainy flesh. Available from late summer to early spring. Good for eating or for cooking by any method.

**5. Comice**  Large, round pears with short necks, red-tinged, speckled greenish yellow skins and soft, juicy, aromatic flesh. Usually enjoyed raw. Available from midsummer through late autumn.

**6. Anjou**  Large, plump pears with short necks and thin, often russet-yellow skins. Available from autumn to early winter. Medium-grained to coarse-textured and juicy, with a hint of spice. Popular for cooking when slightly underripe, or for eating raw when fully ripened. Also sold as d'Anjou.

## Apples

**7. Pippin**  Firm, crisp apples with green to yellow-green skin and a slightly tart, refreshing flavor. Well suited to eating raw on its own or using in fruit salads or baked desserts.

**8. Rome Beauty**  Bright red apples, sometimes striped with yellow, enjoyed for their juiciness and slightly tart flavor. Available throughout autumn and into late spring. The apple of choice for baking, in part because it holds its round shape so well; it may also be eaten raw.

**9. Red Delicious**  Big, sweet-tart, crisp and juicy apples with distinctive bright red skins. Best suited to eating raw on its own or in fruit salads.

**10. Granny Smith**  Native to Australia and notable for their bright green skins, these crisp, juicy apples are refreshingly tart. They are often enjoyed raw. They are also a good choice for cooking because they hold their shape well.

**11. McIntosh**  Slightly tart, juicy and tender apple, Canadian in origin, with distinctive red-and-green skin. Available from late summer to late spring, but at the height of their season in autumn. Excellent for eating or for use in applesauce and baked desserts.

## Other Tree Fruits

**12. Quinces**  Ancient fruits of central Asia that look like large, slightly lumpy apples or pears. Unpleasantly hard and rough-textured when raw, the fruits soften during cooking, acquiring a lovely pink cast in the process. High in pectin, quinces are frequently made into jams or jellies. They should be skinned and cored before cooking, and their raw flesh must be rubbed with lemon juice to prevent discoloration.

**13. Mission Figs**  California variety of a fruit mentioned often in the Bible. Prized for its soft, dark purple-black skin and sweet pink flesh, which may be enjoyed eaten raw, baked in desserts or preserved. Also called Black Mission.

**14. Pomegranates**  Sometimes known as Chinese apples, these large, spherical, heavy fruits are first distinguished by their skins, ranging in color from yellow-orange to red to deep purple. Beneath the skin, embedded in spongy white membranes, is an abundance of tightly packed seeds (according to Persian folklore, precisely 613), each enclosed in juicy ruby-red flesh. For easy peeling, the pomegranate's skin is scored with a sharp knife and the bitter white membrane surrounding the kernels is discarded (see technique, page 298). The seeds may be enjoyed on their own or used as an edible garnish for fruit desserts or salads. More often, however, their juice—which stains easily—is extracted for use as a flavoring, sometimes sweetened and boiled down to make a syrup. Commercial grenadine syrup is derived from pomegranate juice.

**15. Persimmons**  Native to Asia, these autumn fruits are enjoyed for their bright orange color, lustrous, smooth skins and the delectable tart-sweet character of their orange flesh. The tomato-shaped Fuyu persimmons (pictured here) are best enjoyed while still as crisp as an apple, although they eventually soften. More widely available heart-shaped Hachiya persimmons must be ripened to a point of complete, mushy softness; before that time, the fruit tastes unpleasantly astringent.

## Grapes

**16. Ruby**  Very sweet and juicy seedless grapes with distinctive purplish red, tender skins and a pleasantly firm, crisp texture. Flame Seedless and Ribier are similar varieties.

**17. Thompson Seedless**  Widely available California-grown variety of medium-sized, slightly elongated grapes with pale green skins and mild, sweet, refreshingly juicy flesh.

## WINTER SQUASHES

**1. ACORN SQUASHES**   Acorn-shaped medium-sized squashes, up to 8 inches (20 cm) long, with ribbed, dark green skin that turns orange with storage. The mild, sweet flavor and light, smooth texture of the orange flesh is best complemented by baking.

**2. TURBAN SQUASHES**   Squashes with flattened, circular, bumpy orange bases up to 15 inches (37.5 cm) in diameter crowned by distinctive, smaller turban-shaped orange tops with blue-green stripes. The flesh is bright orange and rich in flavor.

**3. BUTTERNUT SQUASH**   Cylindrical squashes up to 12 inches (30 cm) in length, with the flower end slightly enlarged to a bulblike shape. The flesh is bright orange, moist and fairly sweet.

**4. SPAGHETTI SQUASHES**   Until recently grown largely in home gardens as a novelty vegetable, this elongated, melon-shaped, yellow-skinned squash takes its name from the long, thin strands into which its flesh separates after cooking. It has a mild flavor and delicately crunchy texture. Now commercially grown in California and Florida.

**5. SUGAR PUMPKINS**   Smaller, globe-shaped relatives of the familiar pumpkin, with bright orange, ridged skin and deep orange, dense, sweet flesh.

**6. HUBBARD SQUASHES**   Large, irregularly shaped squashes with an often unattractive, greenish gray shell concealing rich orange flesh.

## MUSHROOMS

**7. PORCINI**   The common Italian term for *Boletus edulis* and also known by the French name *cèpes*. Porcini grow wild throughout North America and may be found from middle to late fall. Very plump, which explains their Italian name of "little pigs," these popular brown-capped, thick-stemmed mushrooms have a rich, meaty flavor with hints of hazelnut (filbert). They are best appreciated by grilling or baking, but may also be eaten raw and thinly sliced.

**8. SHIITAKES**   Rich and meaty, this Asian variety, once harvested in the wild, is now cultivated commercially. The caps are notable for their velvety dark brown color and their flat, floppy, circular shape. The stems, which are quite tough, must be trimmed away before cooking.

**9. BUTTON MUSHROOMS**   Immature variety of common cultivated mushrooms harvested soon after they have first emerged from the soil, when their caps are still small and tightly closed, resembling buttons. Good eaten raw, in salads, or lightly cooked to preserve their delicate texture and flavor. Select those with gills fully concealed. Also known as common white mushrooms.

**10. CHANTERELLES**   Distinguished by their pale gold color that is sometimes compared to that of scrambled eggs and by their 2–3-inch (5–7.5-cm) trumpetlike shapes, these woodland mushrooms are prized for fine flavor that can range from nutlike to meaty. Available throughout the autumn months, they are now also cultivated commercially in the Pacific Northwest. Before use, brush away any dirt with a mushroom brush or paper towel; do not rinse or the mushrooms will become soggy.

## ROOTS AND TUBERS

**11. SWEET POTATOES**   Not true potatoes, although resembling them in form, these tubers from a tropical American plant have light tan to deep red skins and pale yellow to orange flesh prized for its sweetness. The light-skinned variety is the most common. Sweet potatoes may be cooked in any of the ways common for regular potatoes; baking, however, tends to intensify their natural sweetness, so sweet potatoes are often cooked in the oven rather than boiled when intended for mashing.

**12. PARSNIPS**   Although similar in shape and texture to the carrot, this ivory-colored root, which first appears in abundance in markets around mid-autumn, is never eaten raw. Cooked, however, it has an appealingly sweet, rich, almost nutlike flavor. Although the Italians feed parsnips to the pigs they raise for their famed Parma hams, Americans have prized parsnips as a popular staple since early colonial days, when they were mistakenly believed to be poisonous if pulled before the first frost. Deep, cold storage does, however, sweeten their flavor, transforming the root's starch into sugar.

**13. RUTABAGAS**   Also known as swedes or Swedish turnips. Although these spherical, ivory-and-purple–skinned roots resemble large turnips, they are members of the cabbage family, with their own distinctively sweet, pale yellow-orange flesh. Rutabagas were introduced to America from Europe by Thomas Jefferson.

**14. ROSE FIR POTATOES**   Small to medium-sized waxy potatoes with thin, delicate, pale pink skins and creamy, flavorful flesh.

**15. RED POTATOES**   Various types of small to medium-sized potatoes with red skins and creamy flesh that, depending on the variety, may range in color from ivory to pale red. Generally good for boiling or roasting.

**16. YUKON GOLD POTATOES**   Small to medium-sized, waxy-fleshed potatoes, available in markets only in recent years. Prized for their golden color, rich, buttery flavor and creamy texture. Ideal for baking, panfrying, mashing and gratins.

**17. PURPLE POTATOES**   Small to medium-sized potatoes with tender purple skins and flavorful white or purple flesh; suitable for boiling or frying.

**18. YELLOW FINN POTATOES**   Similar in texture and flavor to the Yukon Gold (see above); well suited to roasting, frying, baking or mashing.

## CHICORY FAMILY

**1. ESCAROLE**  Also known as Batavian endive. Variety of chicory with broad, bright green, refreshingly bitter leaves.

**2. BELGIAN ENDIVE**  Crisp, white, spear-shaped leaves edged with pale yellow-green or pinkish red are tightly packed in small, cone-shaped heads. The slight but discerning bitterness, mildest in smaller heads, comes through both raw and cooked. Also known as chicory or witloof.

**3. FRISÉE**  Head of frilly leaves with a bitter edge of flavor that is at its mildest at the paler center.

## BULBS

**4. LEEKS**  Long, cylindrical members of the onion family with white root ends, dark green leaves and a delicate, sweet flavor that has earned them the nickname of "poor man's asparagus." All leeks are grown in sandy soil and require thorough washing with cold running water to remove any grit lodged between their multilayered leaves. Leeks enjoy a long season; look for them in markets from late summer to early spring.

**5. FENNEL**  Autumn sees the year's second crop of this plant related to the herb of the same name; the first comes in spring. Its bulbous cluster of stalk bases has a crisp, celerylike texture and a mild anise flavor.

**6. SHALLOTS**  These smaller relatives of the onion are thought by some to resemble in taste a cross between onion and garlic, making them a popular seasoning in their own right.

**7. PEARL ONIONS**  These immature onions of many varieties are picked in summer when small and dried for use in autumn. Flavor tends to be fairly pungent, but cooking or preserving brings out a rich sweetness. Pearl onions must be peeled before eating. A special technique removes the skin and keeps the layers intact during cooking (see technique, page 298).

## BRASSICAS

**8. NAPA CABBAGE**  Also known as Chinese cabbage or celery cabbage, the latter for the juicy crispiness of its long, mild, pale green to white leaves. Available in Asian markets and well-stocked food stores.

**9. RED CABBAGE**  At the peak of its almost 10-month-long season in autumn, this variety has crisp, tightly packed leaves ranging from dark purplish red to bright crimson.

**10. GREEN CABBAGE**  Firm cabbage with fairly smooth, pale green leaves tightly packed in a compact sphere.

**11. SAVOY CABBAGE**  Firm, round, fine-flavored variety of cabbage with dark green leaves marked by a lacy pattern of pale green veins.

**12. BROCCOLI**  Cabbage family member with green to purple-green, tightly clustered, unopened budding sprouts—known as florets—growing at the end of sturdy stalks. Both the florets and the stems, if the latter are thickly peeled, may be eaten. Although available year-round, broccoli is at its best during the autumn months.

**13. CAULIFLOWER**  Member of the cabbage family bred for its tightly clustered, ivory or sometimes purple, unopened budding heads. Both the heads, which may be separated into florets, and the more tender parts of the stems may be eaten.

**14. BRUSSELS SPROUTS**  A species of cabbage first selectively bred in Belgium in the 13th century to form bite-sized, perfect little balls clustered on a heavy stalk. Brussels sprouts are sometimes found in farmers' markets still on their stalk, although they are more commonly sold already detached.

## VEGETABLE FRUITS

**15. EGGPLANTS**  Of Asian origin, the eggplant (aubergine) migrated across the Middle East to Europe, reaching Italy by the 15th century. Its multitude of varieties include many different shapes and sizes, among them an ivory-skinned one resembling a goose egg, the source of its English name. The most common variety available to Western cooks, still abundantly available in autumn, is the large, plump globe eggplant (pictured here); long, slender Asian eggplants, which have fewer seeds and are considered finer in flavor and texture, may also be found during this season.

**16. RED BELL PEPPERS**  Crisp-fleshed, bell-shaped peppers (capsicums) have a mild flavor that grows ever sweeter as they mature in autumn from green to their fully ripened red state. Whether enjoyed raw or roasted, peppers should have their stems and white interior ribs cut or pulled out and their seeds removed before use.

## FRESH HERBS

**17. ROSEMARY**  Mediterranean herb, used either fresh or dried. The needlelike leaves, sometimes decked in tiny blue flowers, have a highly aromatic flavor well suited to lamb, veal, pork, poultry, seafood and vegetables. Use sparingly, as the strong taste can overpower dishes.

**18. PARSLEY**  A native of southern Europe, this widely popular fresh herb is available in two main types: the more common curly-leaf parsley, a popular garnish, and flat-leaf parsley (pictured here), also known as Italian parsley, which has a more pronounced flavor and is preferred for seasoning.

**19. THYME**  An ancient eastern Mediterranean herb prized for its fragrant, clean-tasting small leaves that complement poultry, light meats, seafood or vegetables. Also commonly available in a lemon-scented variety.

**20. SAGE**  Strong-flavored herb, used either fresh or dried in the cuisines of Europe and the Middle East. Well suited to fresh or cured pork, lamb, veal or poultry, as well as some sauces and salads.

**21. BAY LEAVES**  Pungent, spicy dried whole leaves of the bay laurel tree, which grows abundantly in the Mediterranean and in similar sunny climates such as that of California. Commonly used as a seasoning in simmered dishes, including soups and braises or stews of meat or seafood; in marinades for those same main ingredients; and in pickling mixtures. French bay leaves, sometimes found in specialty-food shops, possess a milder, sweeter flavor than those from California.

## APPLES

**1. GRANNY SMITH**  Native to Australia, these apples have bright green skins and crisp, juicy flesh with a refreshing tartness. Most often eaten raw, they also hold their shape well when cooked.

**2. MCINTOSH**  These slightly tart, juicy, tender apples, which originated in Canada, have distinctive red-and-green skins. Excellent for eating, baking and making applesauce.

**3. PIPPIN**  Fruits with firm, green to yellow-green skin and dense, slightly tart, refreshing flesh. Delicious raw or cooked.

## CITRUS FRUITS

**4. YELLOW GRAPEFRUITS**  At their peak in winter, the large citrus fruits—named for the grape-like bunches they form on the tree—are enjoyed for their bracingly tart-sweet flavor. Also called white grapefruits, the yellow variety have pale yellow skins and whitish yellow flesh.

**5. RUBY GRAPEFRUITS**  Often sweeter than yellow grapefruits, pink- or red-fleshed varieties have an orange-red blush on their skins and dark, sweet flesh.

**6. BLOOD ORANGES**  Available throughout the winter, these sweet, aromatic, small- to medium-sized oranges are distinguished by the reddish blush on their skin and their sweet, intensely flavorful, deep red flesh and juice.

**7. KUMQUATS**  Resembling elongated, miniature oranges, kumquats are usually eaten whole; the sweetness of their skins balances the tartness of their flesh.

**8. POMELOS**  Generally thought to be ancestors of the grapefruit, these largest citrus fruits have thick, bumpy skins and bittersweet, seedless flesh that ranges from yellow to pink to red. Also sometimes spelled pummelo.

**9. MANDARINS AND TANGERINES**  Two interchangeable terms for a wide variety of small- to medium-sized fruits with loose peels and mild, sweet flesh. At their peak in mid- to late December, they are a traditional holiday favorite. Among the more familiar types are sweet, seedless Satsumas, originally from Japan; Clementines, a flavorful, seedless North African cross between a mandarin and a Seville orange; and the Dancy, an aromatic American hybrid.

**10. LEMONS**  One of the most familiar citrus varieties, these year-round fruits have bright yellow skins, pale yellow flesh and a sharply acidic juice that sparks both savory and sweet dishes.

**11. TANGELOS**  A cross between a tangerine and a pomelo or grapefruit, these sweet-tart fruits resemble large oranges with knobs at their stem ends. Also known by the name Minneola.

**12. NAVEL ORANGES**  Available from early to midwinter, this orange variety gets its name from the indentation in the skin at its flower end. These large oranges have sweet, juicy flesh, are easily peeled and are virtually seedless.

## OTHER TREE FRUITS

**13. QUINCES**  Middle Eastern in origin and grown today primarily in the Mediterranean and South America, these ancient fruits resemble in shape large, slightly lumpy apples or pears. Unpleasantly hard and rough-textured when raw, the flesh softens when cooked and turns a lovely pink. High in pectin, quinces are frequently made into jams or jellies.

**14. POMEGRANATES**  The name pomegranate is derived from the French for "apples with seeds." Sometimes called Chinese apples, these large, spherical, heavy fruits have leathery skins that range from yellow-orange to red to deep purple. Inside, an abundance of tightly packed kernels, each encased in ruby-red flesh, is embedded in spongy white membranes. The kernels may be eaten on their own, their tart-sweet pulp sucked away, or used as an edible garnish. More often, however, pomegranate juice is extracted as a flavoring, sometimes sweetened and boiled down to make a syrup. Commercial grenadine syrup is made from pomegranate juice.

**15. KIWIFRUITS**  Kiwis, as they are sometimes called, have fuzzy brown skins that conceal a bright green, soft, juicy, sweet flesh with a flavor reminiscent of melon and berries. Asian in origin, they are also known as Chinese gooseberries.

**16. PERSIMMONS**  Native to Asia, persimmons are enjoyed for their bright orange color, their lustrous smooth skins and the delectable sweetness of their jellylike orange flesh. The heart-shaped Hachiya persimmons pictured here are the most widely available. They must be ripened to a point of mushy softness, or they will taste unpleasantly astringent. Fuyu persimmons, a more rounded variety, can be enjoyed while still as crisp as an apple, although they eventually soften.

**17. BOSC PEARS**  Medium-to-large, tapered pears with russeted yellow skins and firm, slightly grainy flesh with a buttery, spicy taste. Picked or purchased when unripe and still very hard, Bosc pears will ripen and soften slightly when left at room temperature. Good for eating raw or for cooking.

## BERRIES

**18. CRANBERRIES**  Round, tart, deep red berries, grown primarily in wet, sandy coastal lands—or bogs—in the northeastern United States. Available fresh from late autumn to the end of December and frozen year-round.

## DRIED FRUITS

**19. PRUNES**  Dried plums, prunes are prized for their rich flavor and dense, fairly moist flesh.

**20. GOLDEN RAISINS**  These dried, sweet seedless grapes are also known as sultanas.

**21. DRIED FIGS**  The two most common forms of dried figs are those made from the Black Mission variety, which has a dark, dense flesh and an intense flavor; and the golden Calimyrna variety, prized for its sweet, nutty taste.

**22. DRIED CHERRIES**  Kiln-dried cherries are generally made from pitted sour red cherries, with a little sugar added as a preservative.

**23. DRIED APRICOTS**  Pitted whole or halved apricots develop a sweet, slightly tangy taste and a slightly chewy texture when dried.

**24. DRIED CRANBERRIES**  Cranberries (see above) are generally lightly sugared and then kiln-dried, which intensifies their flavor and deep red color, while giving them a shape and texture similar to raisins.

# WINTER VEGETABLES GLOSSARY

## WINTER GREENS

**1. BULB FENNEL**   Available year-round, this bulbous cluster of stalk bases has a crisp texture resembling celery and a mild anise flavor. It may be eaten raw in salads or cooked on its own or with other ingredients, like fish or chicken, that are complemented by its sweetness.

**2. WATERCRESS**   Available year-round, this spicy-sweet, tender member of the mustard family may be enjoyed raw in salads, where it is particularly prized for its sharp, peppery taste; cooked with eggs, poultry or seafood; or puréed in a sauce or in soups.

**3. FRISÉE**   These thin, frilly leaves, which grow in loosely bunched heads, are most often eaten raw in salads. Like their cousins escarole (Batavian endive) and dandelions, they have an appealing bitterness that is at its mildest in the paler inner leaves.

**4. KALE**   At its peak of season throughout the cold months, this hardy member of the mustard family is cooked and enjoyed for its strong, spicy flavor. The leaves of this loose, long-leaved green come in different shapes and in colors ranging from blue-green and red (pictured near right) to purple, yellow or white. Many varieties are sold, but the leaves generally have serrated edges and a crinkly surface, leading the most commonly available type also to be known as curly kale (pictured far right).

**5. ESCAROLE**   Variety of chicory distinguished by its broad, bright green leaves, which grow in loose heads. Escarole has a refreshingly bitter edge, while being notably less bitter than other relatives of the chicory family. Generally eaten raw in salads. Also known as Batavian endive.

**6. LEEKS**   Available throughout winter, these long, cylindrical members of the onion family have white root ends, dark green leaves and a delicate, sweet flavor that has earned them the French nickname of "poor man's asparagus." The white parts are more tender and have a finer flavor, although the greens are often included in long-simmering dishes. Because leeks are grown in sandy soil, they require thorough washing with cold running water to remove any grit lodged between their multilayered leaves.

**7. BELGIAN ENDIVES**   Distinctive cone-shaped heads with crisp, white, spear-shaped leaves edged in pale yellow-green or pinkish red. They have a light, refreshing bitterness that is mildest in smaller heads and comes through whether enjoyed raw or cooked. Also known as chicory or witloof.

**8. BRUSSELS SPROUTS**   This species of cabbage was first selectively bred in Belgium in the 13th century to form the familiar small, bite-sized balls, which grow in rows on a heavy stalk. They are widely available from autumn almost to the end of winter. Brussels sprouts may sometimes be found in farmers' markets still attached to their stalk, although they are more commonly sold already separated from it.

## MUSHROOMS

**9. BUTTON MUSHROOMS**   Harvested soon after they emerge from the soil, when their caps are still small and tightly closed with almost no stem visible, these immature cultivated mushrooms are sometimes said to resemble buttons. They have a fine texture and mild flavor and are excellent eaten raw in salads or lightly and quickly cooked.

**10. HEDGEHOG MUSHROOMS**   Fancifully thought to resemble hedgehogs, these wild woodland mushrooms are distinguished by their orange caps, white stems and compact shapes. Eaten cooked, often in egg or rice dishes, they are enjoyed for their fine, slightly tangy flavor, pale color and succulent texture. Known in French as *pied de mouton,* "sheep's foot."

**11. CHANTERELLES**   These trumpet-shaped mushrooms, which average 2–3 inches (5–7.5 cm) in length, are generally pale gold. Some aficionados claim they give off a faint scent reminiscent of apricots. Their fine flavor and tender texture are best appreciated when only lightly cooked. Picked wild in woodlands, particularly where oak and beech trees grow, they are now also cultivated in the Pacific Northwest. Rare black chanterelles are also sometimes found.

**12. PORCINI**   Meaning "little pigs" in Italian, these plump mushrooms have brown caps and thick stems with a tender texture and a rich, earthy taste that hints of hazelnuts (filberts). Found in the wild throughout North America, they are also known by the French *cèpes,* by the Latin *Boletus edulis,* and in Britain by the descriptive "penny buns." The mushrooms taste best when grilled, sautéed or baked, although they may also be thinly sliced and eaten raw.

**13. SHIITAKES**   Originally from Asia but now widely cultivated in the United States and Europe, these rich mushrooms have a meaty taste and texture and are often cooked in dishes featuring red meat. The broad, fairly flat circular caps are dark, velvety brown. The stems are tough and must be trimmed away before cooking.

## CHILI PEPPERS

**14. JALAPEÑO CHILIES**   Among the dozens of commercially cultivated chilies, these moderately hot peppers are arguably the most common. Jalapeños generally measure 2–3 inches (5–7.5 cm) in length and about 1 inch (2.5 cm) wide. They are usually sold in their immature dark green state, although ripened red ones may also be found. When handling any hot chili peppers, take great care to avoid touching your eyes or any other sensitive areas because the chilies—particularly their seeds and pale interior membranes, or "veins"—contain volatile oils that can cause painful burning. Wash your hands well with warm, soapy water after handling chilies.

**15. SERRANO CHILIES**   These small, slender chilies are noticeably hotter than jalapeños and may be found in both their underripe green and ripened red forms. See the cautionary note in the previous entry regarding working with hot chilies.

## WINTER SQUASHES

**1. HUBBARD SQUASH** Although it has an unattractive, murky yellow or greenish gray shell, this large, irregularly shaped squash contains flavorful, rich orange flesh.

**2. ACORN SQUASH** The name derives from the acornlike shape of this medium-sized squash, which measures up to 8 inches (20 cm) in length and has a ribbed, dark green shell that turns orange with storage. The orange flesh has a mild, sweet flavor and light, smooth texture best complemented by baking.

**3. BUTTERNUT SQUASH** Cylindrical squash up to 12 inches (30 cm) long, its flower end slightly enlarged to a bulblike shape. Butternut squashes have bright orange, moist, fairly sweet flesh.

**4. TURBAN SQUASH** This winter squash variety is distinguished by the small, turban-shaped top—orange with blue-green stripes—that crowns a flattened, circular, bumpy orange base up to 15 inches (37.5 cm) in diameter. Its rich flesh is bright orange.

## HERBS

**5. MINT** Refreshing herb used to flavor a variety of dishes. Spearmint is the variety most commonly used in cooking.

**6. CHIVES** These long, thin, green shoots contribute a mild flavor reminiscent of the onion, to which they are related.

**7. SAGE** Fragrant herb used either fresh or dried in European and Middle Eastern cuisines. Complements fresh or cured pork, lamb, veal or poultry, and some sauces and salads.

**8. THYME** Eastern Mediterranean herb with fragrant, clean-tasting small leaves that marry well with poultry, light meats, seafood or vegetables.

**9. PARSLEY** Widely popular fresh herb native to southern Europe. Available in two main types: the more common curly-leaf parsley, traditionally used as a garnish; and flat-leaf parsley, also known as Italian parsley, with a more pronounced flavor that makes it preferable as a seasoning.

**10. ROSEMARY** Mediterranean herb with needle-like leaves, sometimes decked in tiny blue flowers. Highly aromatic, rosemary goes well with lamb, veal, pork, poultry, seafood and vegetables.

**11. BAY LEAVES** Pungent, spicy dried whole leaves of the bay laurel tree, used to season simmered dishes, including soups, braises and stews; marinades; and pickling mixtures. French bay leaves, sometimes found in specialty-food shops, are milder and sweeter than the bay leaves commonly grown in the United States.

## ROOTS AND TUBERS

**12. RUTABAGAS** These spherical, ivory-and-purple-skinned members of the cabbage family resemble large turnips. They have sweet, pale yellow-orange flesh and a firm texture. Also known as swedes or Swedish turnips.

**13. JERUSALEM ARTICHOKES** Although many people consider the taste of these tubers to resemble that of artichokes, they are not related. Jerusalem is most likely a corruption of the Italian *girasole,* for the sunflowers to which the plant is related. The small, knobby tubers have brown or purplish red skins that are most easily removed after cooking. They can also be eaten raw, unpeeled, in salads.

**14. CELERY ROOT** Also known as celeriac or celery knob. This hardy winter vegetable, a large, knobby root related to the plant that gives us the more familiar celery stalks, has a sweet, rich flavor reminiscent of its cousin. Celery root may be cooked, or shredded and eaten raw in salads.

**15. YAMS** Not the true, starchy yams of Africa, these are in fact a variety of sweet potato native to the Caribbean, with dark skins and deep orange flesh that becomes sweet when cooked.

**16. SWEET POTATOES** Although these tubers resemble potatoes in form, they come from a tropical American cousin of the morning glory and have light tan to deep red skins and pale yellow to orange flesh prized for its sweetness. The light-skinned variety is the most common. Sweet potatoes may be cooked in any of the ways used for regular potatoes; baking, however, intensifies their natural sweetness.

**17. RED POTATOES** Red-skinned potatoes of various types, ranging in size from small to medium, with creamy-tasting flesh that, depending upon the variety, may range from ivory-white to pale red. Generally good for boiling or baking.

**18. BAKING POTATOES** Distinguished by their large, elongated size and shape and their thick, brown skins, these potatoes have dry, mealy textures that make them the perfect choice for baking, mashing or deep-frying. Also known as russet or Idaho potatoes.

**19. BABY TURNIPS** Immature specimens of the turnip, a root vegetable of the cabbage family, which begin to appear in late winter and are prized for their sweetness and tenderness.

**20. PARSNIPS** These ivory roots, similar in shape and texture to carrots, are never eaten raw. When cooked, they have a sweet, rich, almost nutlike taste.

**21. BEETS** The earliest beets find their way into markets in late winter. Most common are red beets, although golden, pink, white, and even red-and-white varieties may be found.

## DRIED BEANS

**22. GREAT NORTHERN BEANS** Common variety of white, kidney-shaped bean smaller than Italian cannellini and larger than navy beans. Great Northerns may be substituted for either variety.

**23. BLACK BEANS** Robust, somewhat mealy beans distinguished by their relatively small size and black skins. Also called turtle beans.

**24. NAVY BEANS** Small, white, thin-skinned oval beans, similar to cannellini or Great Northerns. Also known as soldier or Boston beans.

**25. RED BEANS** Resembling small, dark kidney beans, with a similar texture but a slightly sweeter taste.

**26. CANNELLINI** Popular Italian variety of small, white, thin-skinned oval beans, similar to Great Northern or navy beans.

**27. FLAGEOLETS** Small, pale green beans harvested and dried before they mature. A specialty of Brittany in northern France, they are now also being grown in the United States.

# Spring Techniques

## Preparing Artichokes

Large artichokes must have their tough outer layers and prickly chokes removed before eating. Baby artichokes need only have their outer layers trimmed. Rub cut surfaces with lemon to prevent browning.

*Cut off the top half of a large or small artichoke. Strip off the tough outer leaves until you reach the pale inner ones. Trim off the stem end and peel away the tough, dark green outer layer.*

*To remove the choke of a large artichoke, cut in half length-wise. Using a small, sharp-edged metal spoon, scoop out the prickly choke fibers.*

## Preparing Asparagus

The woody stem ends of mature asparagus spears must be removed before cooking. When served whole, all but the pencil-thin spears also require peeling of the tough skin from about mid-spear to the base.

*Using a small, sharp knife, cut off the woody stem end of each asparagus spear. Alternatively, firmly grasp the end and snap it off; the stalk will break naturally at the proper point.*

*Using a vegetable peeler, strip away the tough outer skin of the asparagus spear, starting 1–2 inches (2.5–5 cm) below the base of the tip and cutting slightly thicker as you near the end.*

## Preparing Fava Beans

Fresh fava (broad) beans are doubly protected—first by their thick outer pods and then by the tough skin encasing each bean. Remove the beans from the pod, then from the skins before cooking.

*Using your thumbs, press down along the seam of the fava bean pod to split it open. Run a thumb or finger along the inside of the pod to pop out the individual beans.*

*Blanch the beans in boiling water for 20 seconds, then drain. Split open the translucent skin along the long edge of a bean and pop the bean free of its skin.*

## Rinsing Greens

All spring greens trap dirt in their leaves and must be rinsed clean. Spinach (shown here) needs particularly thorough washing because it is grown in sandy soil.

*Put the leaves in a sink or bowl filled with cold water. Swish the leaves well, then lift out and drain the water. Rinse the sink or bowl and repeat until no sand or grit remains in the bottom.*

## Segmenting Citrus Fruits

Citrus fruits may be segmented for attractive presentations. First, cut off the peel thickly to remove the outermost membrane of each segment.

*Hold the peeled fruit over a bowl. Using a small, sharp knife, carefully cut between the fruit and membrane on either side of a segment to free it, letting it drop into the bowl with the juices.*

## Zesting Citrus Fruits

A lively flavor source, zest—the bright outermost layer of citrus peel—is easily removed with a zester. Or use a vegetable peeler to strip off the zest, then mince it.

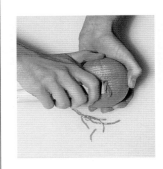

*Grasp the citrus fruit in one hand and the zester in the other. Draw the sharp edges of the zester's holes across the fruit's peel to cut away the brightly colored zest in thin shreds.*

# SUMMER TECHNIQUES

## PEELING TOMATOES

Although summer salad recipes often call for nothing more than coring and slicing tomatoes, cooked or more refined raw dishes often require peeling off the vegetables' shiny skins before use.

*Using a paring knife, cut out the core from the stem end of the tomato. At the opposite end, score an X in the skin. Bring a pot three-fourths full of water to a boil and fill a large bowl with ice water.*

*Immerse the tomatoes in the boiling water for 15–20 seconds. Using a slotted spoon, transfer them to the ice water. When cool, peel away the skins, using the knife and starting at the X.*

## SEEDING TOMATOES

Tomatoes contain watery pockets, or "sacs," of indigestible seeds that can dilute the consistency or mar the appearance of some dishes. The seeds are easily removed.

*Cut the tomato in half crosswise. Hold each half over a bowl or the sink and squeeze gently to force out the seed sacs. Or use a fingertip or a small spoon to scoop them out.*

## SEEDING & DERIBBING BELL PEPPERS

Before bell peppers (capsicums) are used, their flavorless, indigestible seeds and the core and white ribs to which they are attached should be removed.

*Using a sharp knife, cut the pepper in half through its stem end. With your fingers, pull out the stem and attached seed cluster. Pull out the white ribs and any remaining seeds.*

## ROASTING & PEELING BELL PEPPERS & CHILI PEPPERS

Roasting loosens the tough skins of bell and chili peppers so they can be easily peeled. It partially cooks their flesh, making them tender and intensifying their natural sweetness.

*Preheat a broiler (griller). Place halved and seeded peppers, cut sides down, on a baking sheet. Roast until blackened and blistered. Remove the peppers and drape with aluminum foil.*

*Leave the roasted peppers covered to steam and cool for about 10 minutes. Then, using your fingertips or, if necessary, a paring knife, peel away the blackened skins.*

## SEEDING FRESH VEGETABLES

Some vegetables, such as cucumber and chili pepper, require specialized seeding techniques. Note that chilies contain oils that can irritate your skin. Wash your hands well after handling them.

*To seed a cucumber, cut it in half lengthwise. Using a teaspoon, scoop out the seeds along the length of each half before cutting up the cucumber.*

*To seed a fresh chili, cut it in half through its stem end. Using the tip of the knife, cut out the stem, pale ribs and all attached seeds from each half; then scrape out any remaining seeds.*

## CUTTING FRESH HERBS

Cutting fresh herbs helps to release their flavors before adding them to recipes. Basil, owing to the size and shape of its leaves, is easily shredded if rolled and thinly sliced.

*Neatly stack about 6 good-sized fresh basil leaves and roll them tightly lengthwise to make a cigar shape. Using a paring knife, thinly slice the roll crosswise to make fine "chiffonade" threads.*

# Autumn Techniques

## Roasting a Turkey

A turkey is trussed before roasting to give it a compact shape that cooks more evenly and looks more attractive. Diligent basting during roasting yields moist results.

*Stuff the turkey, if desired. Tie the drumsticks together. Place the turkey, breast side up, on a rack in a roasting pan. Secure the wings against the bird by tucking their tips beneath the breast (left).*

*Roast the turkey at 400°F (200°C) for 45 minutes, then drape it with butter-soaked cheesecloth (muslin). Continue roasting at 325°F (165°C), basting every 30 minutes, until the turkey tests done.*

## Carving a Turkey

Before carving, let the turkey rest at room temperature for 20 minutes, tenting it with aluminum foil to keep it warm. Hot juices will settle back into the meat, yielding moister meat that cuts more smoothly.

*Place the turkey on a carving board. Pull back the leg to locate the thigh joint; cut through it with a sharp knife to remove the leg. Cut apart the thigh and drumstick. Carve the breasts into thin slices.*

## Preparing Winter Squash

The firm flesh of hard winter squashes becomes tender and sweet when cooked. It can then be easily scooped out or, for spaghetti squash, removed in long, thin strands.

*Cut the squash— here, acorn squash— in half. Bake, cut sides down, on a baking sheet. Let cool. With a spoon, scoop out the seeds and fiber, discarding them, and then spoon out the tender flesh.*

*Once a spaghetti squash has been cooked, let cool, then cut in half and scoop out and discard the seeds. Using a fork, gently scrape out the flesh, which will separate into spaghettilike strands.*

## Seeding Pomegranates

Using this technique, seeding pomegranates can be easy and free of any juicy mess. Simply score the skin with a sharp knife roughly, peel back the skin, and pull the seeds away in a bowl of water.

*Score the pomegranate skin into quarters. Submerge the fruit in a bowl of water and peel away the skin. Then pull the seeds from the membrane, letting them sink to the bottom of the bowl.*

## Peeling Pearl Onions

This simple technique not only removes the skins of pearl onions easily with minimal waste, but also helps keep the onions' layers from separating during cooking.

*Boil the onions in water for 2 minutes. Drain, rinse with cold water and drain again. Trim the root ends, then cut a shallow X on the trimmed end to prevent the layers from telescoping during cooking.*

*One at a time, grasp each trimmed onion between your thumb and fingertips. Squeeze gently but firmly to pop the onion from its outermost layer of skin.*

## Peeling Chestnuts

A specialty of colder months, fresh chestnuts have hard, dark brown outer shells and fuzzy inner coats that must be steamed until loose, then removed before the nuts can be eaten.

*Cut a shallow X on the flat side of each chestnut. Cook in simmering water until the nut meats are tender when pierced, 45–55 minutes. Drain, then peel away the hard shells and inner sheaths.*

## SEGMENTING CITRUS FRUITS

Recipes in which citrus fruits—here, Ruby grapefruit—are featured often call for segments, or sections, to be cut away from the pith and membranes.

*Using a sharp knife, cut a thick slice off the top and the bottom of each fruit, exposing the pulp. Hold the fruit upright and slice off the peel in thick strips, cutting around the contours of the fruit.*

*Hold the peeled fruit over a bowl. Using the knife, carefully cut between the fruit and membrane on either side of each segment to free it, letting it drop into the bowl with the juices. Discard any seeds.*

## TOASTING HAZELNUTS

Toasting nuts enriches their flavor and gives them a crunchier texture. In the case of hazelnuts (filberts), it also loosens their skins for removal. Roast all nuts in an oven preheated to 350°F (180°C).

*Spread the nuts in a baking pan and toast until fragrant and lightly browned, 5–7 minutes. Let cool. Place the nuts between 2 layers of a kitchen towel and then rub them with the towel to loosen the skins.*

## CLEANING WHOLE CRAB

Whether you cook a whole crab yourself or buy it already cooked from a seafood shop, these steps will help you extract all the meat. The job gets easier with practice.

*Twist off the legs and claws. Pry off the small, triangular shell flap (left) from the underside of the crab. Insert your thumbs in the crevice between the top shell and the body and pull them apart.*

*Remove and discard the feather-shaped gills (right) and any gray intestines, rinsing well. Cut the body in half. Use a lobster cracker to crack open the legs and claws. Remove all the meat.*

## SHUCKING OYSTERS

Buy fresh oysters alive, in the shell, from a good seafood merchant. To open an oyster shell, hold it in a kitchen towel, flat side up and hinge toward you. Pry open with the twist of a short, sturdy oyster knife.

*Push the knife into one side of the oyster's hinge and twist to open. Run the blade completely around the oyster to sever the muscle holding the shells together, then lift off the top shell.*

## MAKING GRAVY

Preparing gravy is one of the simplest ways to add flavor and finish to any roast poultry dish. Gravy can be made in many different ways, but most involve adding stock and deglazing congealed juices from the roasting pan, adding body with a thickening agent—here, cornstarch (cornflour)—then boiling until the gravy thickens to a saucelike consistency. For a more velvety texture, strain the gravy through a fine-mesh seive to remove any browned bits. Season to taste with salt and pepper and stir a few pats of unsalted butter into the gravy to finish the sauce, if you wish.

*Remove the roast from the pan and pour off the fat. Place the pan over high heat. Pour in a liquid—here, chicken stock—and deglaze the pan, stirring to remove any browned bits from the bottom.*

*Boil the liquid until reduced by about one-half. Meanwhile, dissolve cornstarch in a little water. Whisk the cornstarch mixture into the boiling liquid. Boil, stirring, until the gravy thickens.*

# INDEX